Darby,
You are what
friendship is all
about. Thank you
for your support, my friend!
Ron Bassman

"From his unique position as a man who has experienced psychiatry from both sides of the locked door, Ron Bassman offers the reader an unflinching and heart-rending description of his own incarceration as a young man, and sheds light on the sorry state of today's public mental health system. As his inner journey from passive mental patient to compassionate psychologist and activist demonstrates, the medical model of psychiatry does not support the growth and healing of those who experience extreme emotional distress. Rich, thoughtful, and beautifully written, *A Fight To Be* is one of those rare books that seamlessly weaves together the personal and the political to offer a new way out of an old dilemma."
Darby Penney, co-author of *The Lives They Left Behind: Suitcases from a State Hospital Attic*

"Dr. Bassman's emotional problems, his two forced incarcerations, the treatments forced upon him and the difficulties placed in his way to resuming a normal life might well have killed him or made him a life-long cripple. But he recovered, and his account of his life and his treatment is a moving and accurate description of what we do to make recovery IMPOSSIBLE, while we believe we are doing it to help. Every mental health professional, administrator, or concerned political leader ought to read and learn from this book."
Bert Karon, Ph.D., Professor of Psychology Michigan State University, coauthor of *Psychotherapy with Schizophrenia*

"Ron Bassman's story – his descent into a psychiatric abyss and his ultimate triumph to live a purpose-filled and self-directed life – should be required reading for anyone who has ever been diagnosed with a mental illness, those who love them and those professionals who have the power to label and diagnose. *A Fight to Be* deconstructs the myth that a label of schizophrenia means a diminished capacity to create a meaningful life for oneself. As you open the pages of this book, be prepared to learn that there is more to treatment than pills, that there is always meaning in madness – if you dare to look and listen – but most of all be prepared to find hope for recovery. A very personal and precious gift from an oh so gifted writer."
Laurie Ahern, Associate Director, Mental Disability Rights International

"An insightful and exciting glimpse into psychology's potential for those who have entered the mental health system. Ron Bassman is truly a pioneer whose courage and faith in himself will revolutionize treatment of an often overlooked segment of our society."
Pat DeLeon, Ph.D. J.D, 2000 President, American Psychological Association

"Ron Bassman has written a book about severe mental illnesses that works on so many levels and that speaks eloquently to so many kinds of people. Ron's compelling life story of his recovery from schizophrenia is always educational, typically challenging and thought provoking, and often times inspirational. Mental health professionals, educators and their students, the general public, and people with mental illnesses and their families will find *A Fight to Be* a unique and riveting read. You will be glad you read this beautifully written book."
William A. Anthony, Ph. D. Professor & Director Center for Psychiatric Rehabilitation, Boston University

"In this thoughtful and thought-provoking book, Ron Bassman tells the story of his journey from a diagnosis of hopeless and chronic schizophrenia to being a psychologist, activist, and father. Bassman indelibly chronicles his suffering in institutional settings and challenges mental health professionals to broaden their understanding of serious emotional conditions and explore possibilities of recovery beyond medication and day treatment programs. He provides hope to people who have been diagnosed with psychiatric disabilities and creates a framework for recovery that is both radical and realistic."
Susan Stefan, J.D., Attorney, Center for Public Representation and author of *Unequal Rights: Discrimination Against People with Mental Disabilities and the Americans with Disabilities Act*

"A Fight to Be is a compelling first-person account of schizophrenia, psychiatric treatment, and recovery. It makes us aware of our intolerance and lack of support for those who do not fit our definition of 'normal.' Dr. Ron Bassman advocates for positive alternatives that promote everyone's right to flourish. This book will be highly useful to those experiencing such alternative states of mind and their families, as well as mental health students and professionals."
Ronald F. Levant, Ed.D., 2005 President, American Psychological Association Dean & Professor of Psychology, University of Akron

"Dr. Bassman explodes the myth of 'progressive, incurable brain disorder' that is now the general view. We have trusted too long in the mechanical medical model that denies the strength and the spirit of ordinary human beings. I recommend this book to clinicians, family members, and the many people who have in some way been touched by mental illness."
Joanne Greenberg – author, *I Never Promised You A Rose Garden*

"Ron Bassman's remarkable *A Fight to Be* is among the very best writings by a psychiatric survivor I've ever read. This landmark work should be essential reading for anyone who has ever challenged, or even questioned, the ideology and practices of the 'mental health' system. Bassman offers a new, enlightened way of understanding people in crisis (in psychiatric terms, people undergoing 'psychotic episodes') and humane, practical, freely chosen alternatives to involuntary psychiatric interventions. After finishing this book, a caring person will be hard pressed not to conclude that what is needed for the psychiatrically oppressed is an Emancipation Proclamation."

Leonard Roy Frank, author of *History of Shock Treatment; Influencing Minds and the Random House Webster's Quotationary*

"This masterfully told story of a horrific yet beautiful journey of transformation gives voice to those who have traveled this ground; Ronald Bassman's personal metamorphosis and resilient spirit will inspire those struggling down a similar path, enlighten those unaware of the everyday atrocities perpetrated in the name of treatment, and finally will frighten— yet reward—those 'mental health' professionals who have the courage to face the harsh truth of abuse, oppression, and other violations inflicted on individuals for 'their own good'."

Barry Duncan, Ph.D. Co-Director Institute for the Study of Therapeutic Change, author of *What's Right With You: Debunking Dysfunction and Changing Your Life*

"Dr. Bassman's unique trifecta of vantage points a former mental patient, a clinical psychologist and an advocate extraordinaire offers the reader a most informative and breathtakingly comprehensive view of emotional distress and the way our society deals with it. After reading this book, no one will be able to reduce madness and recovery to the simplistic (and dangerous) notions of biological psychiatry and mechanistic treatment. A hero of the empowerment movement has given us a heroic account of survival and inspiration for generations to come."

Peter Stastny, M.D., Associate Professor of Psychiatry, Albert Einstein College of Medicine, co-editor, Alternatives Beyond Psychiatry, co-author, *The Lives They Left Behind: Suitcases from a State Hospital Attic*

Grateful acknowledgment for permission to reprint previously published
material:
>   Leonard Roy Frank for excerpts from The History of Shock Treatment
>   Ty Colbert for excerpts from Broken Brains or Wounded Healers
>   Yale University Press for excerpts from Stories of Sickness by Howard
>   Brody

A Fight to Be: A psychologist's experience from both sides of the locked
door.
Tantamount Press
Albany New York 12203

http://www.ronaldbassman.com

ISBN 978-0-9796266-0-9

Index and bibliographical references

Library of Congress Catalog No. 2007903765

Designed by Integrated Targeting Solutions
Cover designed by Ann Weinstock and Jesse Bassman
Edited by Dania Sheldon

1. Mental Illness 2. Psychology 3. Psychiatry
4. Philosophy 5. Recovery 6. Psychotherapy
7. Schizophrenia

First Edition 2007

A Fight to Be

*A Psychologist's Experience
from Both Sides of the Locked Door*

Ronald Bassman Ph.D.

Tantamount Press
Albany, New York

I dedicate this book to my mother, Mollie, my wife, Lindsey and my son Jesse. Their collective wisdom, love and support fill my heart and imbue my words with purpose.

CONTENTS

Part II

Integrating Knowledge Derived from Living and Working on Both Sides of the Locked Door

Introduction

Too brief and infrequent are the moments when thoughts and feelings are stilled and I am just present. Beneath the tall pines, standing in the backyard, I glance over at my son frolicking with our dog and at my wife reading in the sunlight – I breathe deeply and absorb all that I can before ego intervenes and intellectual pride demands answers. Why me? How did this pastoral scene insert itself into the fractured life story of a city boy who sought to find himself in madness? I look upwards at the sky and silently ask, what is guiding me? How was it possible for me to become who I am today? What have I learned from more than forty years spent studying the phenomena known as madness – my own and others?

Whether I am conducting a workshop for professionals, teaching a class of psychology students or speaking to a group of people like myself who have been diagnosed and treated for major mental illness, I am privileged to witness their intense search to find helpful information. Regardless of the venue or the makeup of the participants, the questions have become predictable.

How did you recover from schizophrenia?

Do you take medication now?

What was it like studying to become a psychologist?

How did you become psychotic?

What was the experience of schizophrenia like?

Are you afraid it will happen again?

What was the most helpful therapy?

What do you think would help me (or the people I work with)?

And the comments from the critics:

You must have been misdiagnosed.

Mental illness is a neurobiological disorder with no cure and can only be controlled with drugs.

What you are saying will discourage people from taking the medications they need.

Your example will only give false hope to the low-functioning people I work with.

My daughter cannot survive unless she is forced into inpatient hospital care.

Most listeners praise me for my courage in sharing such painful private experiences, but I believe that rather than being a matter of courage, it is something I must do. What I share has not become automatic or dull from repetition. My stomach continues to flutter, my hands tremble and my voice at times cracks, as much from my passionate belief in the value of what I am communicating, as from exploring the pain and meaning of my travels through madness, its treatment and my personal journey of transformation.

Not far from Manhattan, on the Jersey side of the Hudson River, there's a clearing among the trees and rocks where Alexander Hamilton fought his fatal duel with Aaron Burr. Years earlier I went there with friends to innocently laugh and enjoy our youthful self-centered exuberance. At night, gazing across the river at the New York skyline, where lights, shapes and imagination taunted reality's constraints, I first encountered that seductive charge of energy and power. Awakened to an emotional state in which excitement and possibility replaced the angst and ennui of extended adolescence, a door opened. The invitation to enter another reality, one that offered unlimited possibilities was irresistible.

After my release from the hospital, I returned to that spot frequently. Sitting on those once-familiar rocks and staring into the distance, I searched and waited for a feeling or memory to infuse my apathetic body with that mystical power the hospital staff had shocked out of me. There was no magic to be recaptured, no opening of the mind and the senses, just the dull pain of longing for what once was. Along with so many others hoping and praying at their public and private shrines, I joined what Albert Schweitzer called the "brotherhood of those that bear the mark of pain."

For two and a half years I faithfully went to my twice-a-week psychotherapy sessions. Without questioning their value, I obediently rode the bus from Irvington, New Jersey to the New York Port Authority Building, then two subway trains to the upper East Side of Manhattan. I hated those sessions. Each excruciating minute of awkward silence affirmed my inadequacy. I felt dull, numb and barely capable of short answers to simple questions. I blamed myself for my inability to think of anything to say. I floated in a dense foggy space with no anchors, cut off from past aspirations and not knowing what I believed or valued. No goals, but one all-consuming priority guided me – to stay out of the hospital.

Therapy was supposed to be my shield. Would I forever be this person they said was schizophrenic? Electroshock and insulin coma treatments had left huge holes in my memory. I plodded along and endured the emptiness by stubbornly holding onto the hope that I could find a way to change and become the person I once believed I had the potential to be. The return trip was my respite; nothing more would be expected of me until the next session. The people and places I passed elicited no interest or feeling and I was reassured by their lack of interest in me.

Twenty-three years old, the life I had been leading and the many opportunities I expected to be available were torn from me. Experts preached that it was necessary for me to accept a life sentence of schizophrenia. They warned that my choices were governed by the demands of mental illness and my freedom would be dependent upon my compliance with treatment recommendations. A hopeless and helpless mental patient, I had to surrender my power to those with credentialed authority.

Innocently, I had waded into the sea of madness hoping to find myself. Instead, psychiatry found me. They said I would drown if I did not take the lifeline they threw to me. I heard them shouting at me, but wondered why they were so excited about me playing in the waves. I told them I would just tread water until I learned to swim in the turbulence. They said no. I refused to leave the water. I was too young and naive to know that the doctors posed more of a danger than the sea. I was an inexperienced lightweight jutting out my jaw and challenging the mighty, government-sanctioned heavyweight champion. Knocking me out with forty shots of insulin, the doctors dragged my unconscious body to shore and left my spirit in the sea of madness. Psychiatry became my life-long nemesis.

Doctor, you act as if you are far superior to me. You talk down to me. You say I have a sick mind, a brain disease. You try to make me see the world the way you see it. I resist. I don't want to be like you. Yes, I do want to be what I am not. I must strive to be more than I am.

I did not know that my journey would be so painful. You made me suffer with the help you forced upon me. First you subjected me to humiliation and brain washing. This state you call schizophrenia has a vastly different meaning to me. Dangerous, yes, but for those of us who must battle the "disease" of feeling too much, of seeing what others do not see, and not meeting expectations that were never our own, it is ripe with opportunity to transform ourselves.

With so many of us out here, and our numbers increasing all the time, doesn't that make you question what you construe as normal? As the expert, you say you are the most qualified to help people like me. How healthy are you and how sick am I? You put me in the hospital and electrocuted my brain. You thought that by injecting me with insulin and forcing me into forty comas I would learn to accept your reality. You did not approve of the way I searched to find me. My quest to explore other possibilities was unacceptable to you. The unknown makes you uneasy. Control and predictability soothes you.

Doctor, is your ego immune to the searing, soul-searching questions that haunt me? I wonder who I am and what it means to be a human being. Do you? You act as if you have access to a special cache of wisdom, but I don't believe you are as self-assured as you pretend. My dog knows what it means to be a fully realized dog. She moves with natural grace, perfectly attuned to her wants and desires. The sight of food in her bowl inspires a frenzy of tail-wagging pleasure. Perhaps you mistook me for a dog and believed that your psychic and physical abuse would make my irrational mind heel to your commands. I did not respond to your rewards and punishments. If Pavlov had performed his classical conditioning experiments on cats instead of dogs, he would not have observed cats salivating at the sound of his bell. I cannot be a dog.

Every Christmas, *It's a Wonderful Life* returns to television to stir nostalgia in its loyal fans and attract a new generation of viewers. Director Frank Capra and actor Jimmy Stewart tapped into an archetypical need with their movie's defining theme: No one is born to have a life without meaning.

The right to strive to live one's life with meaning and purpose is not among the mutually agreed upon treatment goals available to the schizophrenic mental patient. The existential questions were considered to be too dangerous for me.

I was no longer eligible to struggle with the dilemma that Walt Whitman pondered:

> I cannot understand the mystery but
> I am always conscious of myself as two.
> Do I contradict myself?
> Very well then I contradict myself,
> I am large, I contain multitudes.[1]

Few of us with the diagnosis of schizophrenia are permitted the opportunity to live large. I wanted to dance again with expansive possibility. The experts said safety had to be the first priority. Frozen and vulnerable, I had to heal the wounds, feel the hurt, be angry and shed the dead skin so that I might reclaim me. When safety dictates all the rules, such a journey of reclamation cannot be conducted.

The strange and frightening world of mental illness resists reductionist explanations. It seems as if we automatically seek to distract ourselves from confronting our inevitable mortality. Like children, we crave simple explanations to soothe us after our nightmares. Medical anthropologist and cancer survivor Arthur Frank writes about how life changes when one's being is disrupted by illness. Our capacity to reconstruct our interrupted stories offers transformative opportunities. And when those who survive and thrive bear witness, their testimony helps others move through the experience of an illness-interrupted life.

I remain frustrated that mental health professionals have been slow to accept the value of experience-based knowledge and have not integrated that wisdom into the services they provide. Too many treatment practices remain tethered to physical interventions, and continue to constrict a person's chances for recovery and transformative growth. Intolerance and lack of support for emotional pain and instability leave psychiatric drugs as the primary treatment option. The resulting drug-induced stability may bypass the current pain, but too easily invites that person to take on the role of chronic mental patient. The precipitating crisis may be deflected, but the opportunity for personal growth and development is sacrificed. I was fortunate that in the late 1960s and early 1970s when I was being treated, psychiatric drugs had not yet reached the esteemed and heroic status they enjoy today. Unlike many individuals subjected to the prime emphasis of current practice – forcing people to continue taking their psychiatric drugs – I was allowed to follow through in my choice to stop taking drugs.

The treatments that are available for people in extreme emotional states are generally ineffective and often harmful. The search for biochemical solutions has become an obsession. New drugs, rather than decreasing emotional pain, have created more severe iatrogenic problems. According to the professional experts, the number of people with mental disorders is increasing. The types of psychiatric disorders in the American Psychiatric Association's best-selling publication, the *Diagnostic and Statistical Manual of Mental Disorders*, keep expanding. Ironically, long-term research from the World Health Organization has shown that people with schizophrenia who live in developing countries recover at a significantly higher rate than those in the United States.[2]

Manic-depressive disorder, renamed bipolar disorder and once considered rare, has become the new disease *du jour*. Recently, a nurse practitioner bragged to me of prescribing Prozac for a three-year-old she had diagnosed as bipolar. With a stunning lack of self-awareness, she was proud to tell me of confirming the validity of the Prozac prescription, much to the surprise of the conscientious pharmacist who called to see if a mistake had been made. I shudder to think of how this child will have to struggle with not only a label that was stuck on her at such an early age, but the unpredictable developmental effects of this psychiatric drug.

The practice of psychiatry is now the practice of drug prescription. Psychiatrists are so busy prescribing drugs that they have found it highly profitable to expand their practice by employing and signing off on the orders of physician assistants and nurse practitioners. Pharmaceutical companies have found that they can increase the demand for psychiatric drugs by advertising directly to the public. Taking very little time to understand their patients' needs and problems, health professionals are prescribing these powerful and often dangerous drugs to help their patients cope with the trials and tribulations of life.

In my psychotherapy practice, I get referrals from family physicians who routinely give depression screening tests. Patients arrive for their first psychotherapy sessions with prescriptions for a combination of anti-depressants and anti-anxiety drugs. To be sad has become an intolerable condition that requires a quick pill remedy. It is certainly legitimate for people who are in severe distress to seek a drug-based solution. What is unacceptable is the misleading promise that the psychiatric drug has been scientifically proven to work for your accurately diagnosed mental disease. Can we find real remedies by simply checking off a list of symptoms and behaviors so that a diagnosis can be identified and the appropriate drug prescribed?

Sometimes a psychiatric drug will effectively work on the immediate problem and sometimes not. Which drug will work on which person is a gamble, an educated guess at best, made after months or even years of painful guesswork – that is, painful for the patient. I am not opposed to using a substance to deal with pain. I am opposed to the subtle coercions, the misrepresentation and lack of full information presented to people who are vulnerable and seeking expert advice. A person in extreme psychic or physical pain will most likely choose to take the quickest, most effective substance for relief. Whether or not it provides temporary relief should not be the only factor that guides the decision. Just as it is dangerous to ignore the guidance that physical pain provides, to anesthetize ourselves from psychic and emotional pain deters us from finding better solutions. Unfortunately, the physical and emotional consequences of our reliance on drugs only emerge and demand attention later.

The psychiatrists did not do very well in predicting my future. Thirty-five years ago, after I was discharged from my second psychiatric hospitalization, I aimlessly walked the streets of New York City. Despair and loneliness were my constant companions. I needed people. I wanted to be around people, but how could I relate to others when my feelings were dominated by fear and embarrassment? Empty, nothing to say, nothing to contribute, only with anonymity's protection could I be around people and not be humiliated by my inadequacies. How well I remember believing that a bleak future with no friends was my destiny. Marriage and children would not be available to me. Dull and slow, devoid of spontaneity, I hardly had the energy to hate my life.

Now, no matter how down I might get, when I consider those bleak days and nights, my perspective is always jerked back and the picture becomes clear and bright. My good fortune and hard-fought recovery and success have never dimmed my insider's knowledge of what has been done, is being done, in the name of treatment – to and for but rarely with those lacking the power or voice to fight the abuses and keep their basic human rights. I survived and learned how to swim in the sea of my personal madness, and with that privilege came the obligation to tell my story and make my experiences available for others to use. I began to enjoy and value being me when I was able to move beyond survival into making it matter how I survived.

This narrative explores the evolution and development of my identity and concludes with an examination of more humane and effective ways of dealing with the extraordinary emotional states labeled as mental illnesses. There have to be more creative options than supportive outpatient clinic visits and, when that is not enough inpatient hospital treatment. We need a variety of services tailored to meet the specific needs of an individual within a specific context at a specific time and developmental stage of life. All of us have the capacity for excruciating emotional pain; perhaps it is the blessing and curse attached to the expansive forms of consciousness that are unique to human beings. We can do much better in supporting each other.

For the unheard voices of those who have been lost in the labyrinth of the mental health system, for the families, lovers and friends who seek understanding and guidance, for the mental health professionals who genuinely struggle with their own and others' frightening existential plight, and for all those activists who demand the absolute entitlement of dignity and respect for everyone, I offer my voice to inspire hope and to join with them in their continuing *fight to be*.

Part I

**My Lived Experience with Madness and its Treatment:
Surviving and Constructing Identity**

Chapter 1

The Personal Face of Madness

We only become what we are by the radical and deep-seated refusal of that which others have made of us. (Jean-Paul Sartre)

In 1966 I earned my Masters degree in clinical psychology from Temple University and later that year commemorated my twenty-third birthday in the seclusion room of a psychiatric hospital.

A graduation from academic restraint was followed by a descent into psychiatric restraint – a signature event marking my failed transition into adulthood. Being awarded a Masters degree was the culmination of years of half-hearted participation in an educational process that failed to meet my personal needs or professional aspirations. School, with its mind-numbing restrictions and demands for passive conformity, always collided with my need to be special. I hated school. Why did I have to adjust to the monotony and control of a classroom? The world outside promised exciting adventures. Inside, I was expected to digest information which I did not find helpful and then to present myself for judgment and criticism. I played at the school game and did little more than just enough.

My graduation would not be an official commencement launching me into the world of real work and responsibility, but rather it would set in motion a series of events that would force me to reconstruct my innocent beliefs about goodness, fairness and justice. I had to face the present. No longer could I think or feel that my life, happiness and self-confidence would magically appear at some time in the future. I was ill-prepared to leave the school womb, but I could not continue hiding in graduate sanctuaries. Some say mental health is measured by one's capacity to tolerate ambiguity. The capacity for tolerating my own inconsistent and undeveloped beliefs and values was extremely limited. My needs and desire for change were mirrored by the turbulence and rampant adolescent angst of the 1960s.

President Lyndon Johnson was implementing his vision of the

"Great Society" by putting in place social programs to form a safety net for people in need of assistance. The Vietnam War was escalating and our government was carefully managing the information being released to the public – but not too successfully. Seeds were being sown for radical changes in society's mores. Sexual permissiveness, the women's movement, black pride, hippies, war protesters and communes were inciting challenges to authority in all of its manifestations. Young people listened with unrestrained optimism to songs trumpeting the changing times. We watched the Beatles experiment with psychedelic music, drugs and mysticism. FM radio's enlarged presence provided an outlet for the new music and a primitive platform for communication, perhaps a precursor to future internet chat rooms and blogs. Just twelve years earlier, psychiatry had introduced clinical trials of Thorazine, the first of a long line of miracle drugs, into a Vermont state mental hospital. And it had been fewer than ten years since most of the country's state mental hospitals had stopped performing prefrontal lobotomies. Forced sterilization of "mental defectives" was still an acceptable medical practice. The deeply rooted tentacles of eugenics had not been completely severed from government programs.

The later half of the 60s exploded with conflict. Our country was sharply divided into opposing factions championing war or peace, conservatism or change, dread or hope. Values and morals once inviolable were now fair game. Youth shouted for change while their established elders dug their heels in and refused to be intimidated. The stage was set for psychiatrists to show their usefulness and build political muscle by entering into the fray as enforcers of social control. In 1969, testifying before the United States Congress, psychiatrist Bruno Bettleheim dismissed protests against the Vietnam War by students at the University of Chicago as misdirected attempts to resolve their Oedipal conflicts. He told the U.S. Congress that the authority function of universities symbolically represented the students' fathers and the protests arose from developmental issues, not genuine opposition to government actions. At the same time, radical thinkers like Thomas Szasz, R.D. Laing and Michel Foucault emerged to challenge the dominant mental illness paradigm. Yet, their intellectual critiques were not able to sustain the briefly lit flame of anti-psychiatry. Today, the theories and thinking of these iconoclastic giants are given no more than passing mention in psychiatric texts and are outside the awareness of most students studying to become mental health professionals.

Maybe the uncertainty of the times helped bump me off safer, more well-traveled paths. Maybe it started when I was still in grade school and I elected myself hero, rescuer, savior of my family. Or perhaps it was because the seams and membranes of my psychic coat were sewn from ill-fitting, hand-me-down intergenerational materials. Maybe I was always too attentive to the wrong cues. Or maybe too attentive to the right cues that others ignored. When I denied my sensitivity, I could function, but I lost too much of me. It seemed like I was constantly hiding from others and myself. I was good at seeing and feeling, but that seemed to be more of a weakness than a useful ability. I wanted to respond the way I thought I should. I criticized myself for what came naturally, and the voice inside told me, *You are not a hero thinking and feeling that . . . you are too soft. Think and feel differently. Don't be frightened. Look calm and cool. Don't be afraid or everyone will see the scared little boy and laugh.*

Not being able to subdue my feelings, I tried to hide them. I was not very successful. The more I tried to hide, the more anxious I became. I was constantly on guard. The hyper-vigilance fed into my overly sensitive temperament. I was unhappy, did not like myself and was desperate to find a way to deal with my anxieties.

Twenty-two years old, just prior to my first bout with madness, my self-respect eroding, I realized I had nothing of value to lose. I told myself that this avoid-embarrassment-at-all-costs mentality had to go. I wondered whether I could allow myself to screw up without being devastated. What if everyone saw me for the timid little soul that I truly was? But what would my life be like if I stopped hiding? What if I did not accept others' expectations and critical evaluations? Maybe, I thought, perception without the constriction of guiding principles would open me to wider and richer experiences. Co-existing within me was the excitement of expansive possibility as well as the practical fears of entering a realm of being that lacked the security of familiar habits.

I chose to accept the risks. I would see, hear and feel in a unique personal way that was suited to who I wanted to be and become. I abandoned the persona of the frightened boy who wanted to blend in, be approved of and belong. I made the fully conscious decision to not care what image I projected to people. If to not care meant being considered crazy, I accepted it.

Home for me was the Weequahic section of Newark, New Jersey – where Philip Roth grew up and found the inspiration for the characters he created in *Portnoy's Complaint*. The Weequahic section, once predominantly Jewish, was a kind of suburban enclave within the larger city. Newark was a changing city, with each new mayor talking about creating a "New Newark" that would end the suburban flight and re-energize the decaying inner city. Within a few years the urban riots that swept American cities would ravage Newark and send the remaining businesses fleeing for safer environs.

Chancellor Avenue, across from Weequahic High School, in front of Sid's Hot Dog Haven, was the hang-out where everyone met. There, on the street or passing by in cars, was my entire social network. The new me would be played out on that urban street stage. I wanted personal authenticity, but would the new me be genuine? I did not have to work very hard to draw attention to myself. The denizens of Chancellor Avenue had cravings for excitement which melded well with my newly emerging freedom. Being outrageous would be the driving theme of my new identity, a temporary antidote to chronic boredom, an entertaining distraction.

I recklessly peeled away inhibitions. Was I crazy? Crazy meant freedom. Although driven to be provocative, I believed that I consciously chose when to abandon restraint and decorum. I was not out-of-control crazy, just a crazy-acting, eccentric guy. Speaking my thoughts without censoring them, I began noticing the inconsistencies between what others were saying and what I saw them doing. I watched people enacting habitual sequences of mindless tasks, sleepwalking through life without awareness. I saw their more absorbing private musings, and I astonished onlookers with my insightful excursions into others' unconscious. I regarded the events with curiosity, letting the changes evolve. I had a naive trust that all would go well. I enjoyed the responses I was getting and I became the role I was playing. Years later in psychodrama training, I learned how to de-role, to shake off the remnants of an enacted part, but on Chancellor Avenue I could not throw off my new role when the dramatic skit ended. Not caring, giving up my ego, was deceptively difficult.

What started for me as an unstructured summer, a time of little responsibility while waiting to be drafted into the army, became the major turning point in my life story. I was astounded by and irresistibly drawn to the freedom I experienced during that drop-out summer. At first it was simply speaking without my usual tight censorship. With the directness came, for the first time, a lessening of the social anxiety and an ability to engage in relaxed conversation. I was able to be spontaneous. I seemed able to see and hear everything more clearly. I could smell and taste without passing every sensation through filters of self-evaluative judgments.

Experiencing my feelings without trying to change them allowed my intuition to come bubbling to consciousness. What was I to do with this power? Where was it coming from? I had never had so much energy . . . my eyes were opening . . . I was seeing things that others didn't see. So much was happening so quickly. *Right over there, don't you see it? . . . no, there . . . . it's gone now.* They never saw it but they were impressed by my vibrant energy, and to me, this translated as personal power. I felt as if I had become charismatic.

Change is a ghostly mistress. An apparition, tantalizing to the eyes, impossible to hold, frequently too elusive to be verified, but the glowing satisfaction she promises . . . how could I refuse to surrender to her charms? There was a point, a line in the sand, a boundary that I knew was dangerous to cross, that membrane set forth by society as acceptable reality. But the pursuit of possibility blinded me. I mistakenly thought I was ready for anything. I vowed to never return to the timid life. Freeing myself from bondage to my fears and inhibitions released a source of energy that was going to seduce me into believing I was capable of anything. Too quickly, the sound of freedom I heard reverberate in the breaking of my chains became an echo signifying a new bondage conceived in my need to prove my capabilities. Not caring, my doorway to freedom was lost in the Catch-22 of caring too much to be able to demonstrate the power of not caring.

Psychiatrists Carl Jung, R.D. Laing and John Weir Perry describe feats of courage and heroism associated with the descent into psychosis, and the struggles and necessary battles to survive and overcome.[3] Yale University's John Strauss, considered an authority on schizophrenia, tells how his perspective changed over the years. Once, he was a psychiatrist/investigator engaged in the diagnosis of weakness and psychopathology; later, he learned of the importance of looking at the whole person. Strauss speaks of the great courage he has seen displayed by people confronting their confusing and frightening inner realities while living under great stress in near impossible circumstances. Expressing embarrassment at what he calls psychiatry's "rubber gloves" approach to people, Strauss contrasts the methods of the biographer, who studies and researches a subject for years, with the absolute diagnostic and predictive statements expected of the psychiatrist after conducting a mere twenty-minute mental status examination.

I am not suggesting that the travails associated with madness can simply be explained as the adventures of heroes engaged in mythical quests to find their identities. But I do believe that each person's journey into and out of their altered states is unique and loaded with heroic possibilities. Our understanding of these quintessential human conditions is severely limited by the penchant for accepting facile generalizations.

Magical thinking, the attributing of causation to unrelated phenomena without regard for the evidence, does not distinguish psychopathology from eccentricity. Weeks and James speculated, "Objective cannot always be distinguished from subjective intuitions . . . . Thus under certain circumstances a person's grasp of reality may be made to feel false . . . . It has been said, uncharitably, that while neurotics construct castles in the air, psychotics live in them. This formula is not only unkind: it is wrong. It overlooks the essential role played by fantasy in human affairs."[4]

Are the correlations foisted upon us by science any less magical than the string of coincidences that are pathologized in psychiatry's definition of magical thinking? What part does choice and personal responsibility play in the progression from the ordinary to the extraordinary, from competence to incompetence, from freedom to protective confinement?

Friedrich A. Kekule, who had searched for many years to find the molecular structure of benzene, awoke from a dream with an insight that revolutionized modern chemistry. His dream of a snake getting hold of its own tail led to his discovery of the construction of the benzene ring. Robert Lewis Stevenson reported that his stories were created in nocturnal dreams by his little dream people and that he merely transcribed them when he was awake. Interesting that his "sleep brownies" gave him a story that recreates the popular split-personality misconception of schizophrenia, *Dr. Jekyll and Mr. Hyde*.

Brief flashes of insight illuminate the dots and dashes of human history. Those discrete visionary moments of clarity or artistic inspiration elevate us. But suppose you misinterpret the nature and ignore the context of those pure lucid moments. Or worse, the world doubts your credibility and rejects your new knowledge. During Nostradamus' lifetime, the regard for his visionary ability vacillated several times, alternating between reverential worship and heretical treason, depending on shifting political winds. Joan of Arc's prophesies were relied upon to guide her country to victory but later – the war won – she was sold to her country's enemies. Refusing to renounce her voices, and without her former political protection, she became a victim of the Inquisition and was executed for heresy.

The founding of any new religion breaks with the prevailing reality. Moses, Jesus, Gautama Buddha, Muhammad, revered and honored visionaries, were not conventional. Psychiatrist Havelock Ellis spoke to the vagaries of shifting contextual perspectives when he wrote, "Had there been a lunatic asylum in the suburbs of Jerusalem, Jesus Christ would infallibly have been shut up in it at the outset of his public career. That interview with Satan on a pinnacle of the Temple would alone have damned him, and everything that happened after could but have confirmed the diagnosis."[5]

The argument may be made that all religious beliefs are irrational in their orthodoxy since they make claims that go beyond scientific evidence. In the early days of the Society of Friends, when members felt the inner light of Christ shine on them, they were moved to loud outbursts and violent trembling from which the name Quaker was derived. Would considerations of madness detract from George Fox's legacy as founder of the Quakers? Like many great spiritual leaders who preceded him, he had to confront the inner and outer perils of self-examination in his absolute commitment to discovering truth. Is it possible to reconcile revelation with reason? Visions and other extraordinary phenomena continue to be reported throughout the world and, despite the scientific skepticism of the past century, the faithful remain convinced of their authenticity.

And what of the many great artists – those who have been seen in their lifetimes as being touched with "madness" and whose works have later come to be praised by historians as insightful masterpieces, capturing the essence of the human condition?

A story in the *New York Post* by Adam Miller titled "Psycho Theory on Birth of Jazz" would be subject to a different interpretation by me than that proffered by psychiatrist Dean Spence. He states that Buddy Bolden, widely recognized as the founding father of jazz, couldn't read music due to being schizophrenic. According to him, Buddy Bolden's need to improvise resulted in the technique we have come to know as jazz. Dr. Spence goes on to say that modern drug treatments would have helped Bolden, who died in 1931 in a Louisiana insane asylum.[6] Makes me wonder what Buddy would have chosen if he had been fully informed of the cost-benefit ratio involved in taking psychiatric drugs to cure his schizophrenia.

Feeling or being different, whether you see yourself as blessed with a gift or suffering a curse, sets you moving on an uncharted course. Too easily, stress, life circumstances, temperament and motivations can lead you to misconstrue meaning and misapply knowledge. With the combination of naiveté and desperation, and lacking supportive and empathic anchors, you might easily aggrandize this gift/curse and twist it into an overgeneralizing, all-powerful escape that is desperately needed to replace an undesired self and an accumulation of unsatisfactory life choices.

How do you react to being trapped? Do you permit the frustration and hopelessness to expand and permeate all parts of your being, to take over your whole life? Only twenty-two, I could not accept the inevitable conclusions that life events were pushing on me. I had a Masters degree in psychology, but had no idea what kind of work I wanted or was qualified to do. I had hoped to discover in my study of psychology a key to my personal transformation, but I found no door to unlock. With eyes closed, I stood frozen on the bridge from adolescence to adulthood. I desperately wanted to escape from the trap I felt closing in on me.

At that juncture during the summer preceding my first bout with generic madness, I believed I saw a vehicle that would carry me across the bridge. Instead of my usual caring too much about what everyone thought of me, I elected myself the sole judge of my value. No longer would I be a slave to the expectations and critical evaluations of others. I intuitively knew that along with the expansive possibility, confusion and fear might follow my head-first dive into a new realm of being. I glimpsed my doorway and path – not caring would set me free. I made the fully conscious decision to find me.

If you want something to happen, can you influence events, can you make it occur by the force of your thoughts, by wishing, or by focusing all of your energy? Taoist healing practices work by moving energy along meridians. Acupuncture has gained acceptance as a legitimate service, eligible for coverage by health insurance. Eastern traditions are interfacing with Western medical practices. Now, few challenge the importance of attitudes and emotions in determining the course and outcome of an illness. What is the power of the mind? Are placebos the little miracles that give us a taste of the psyche's power?

Stories of psychic medical diagnoses and unexplainable miracle cures are recurrent themes throughout human history. The disciples of Edgar Cayce and other proponents of alternative healing like Norman Cousins, Deepak Chopra, Bernie Siegel and Andrew Weil have challenged the medical community to be less dogmatic and to open up to other perspectives on health, disease and healing. Edgar Cayce, while in a trance, was the conduit of "divine" messages that enabled him to diagnose medical ailments and prescribe natural cures for 43 years. In the archives of the Association for Research and Enlightenment (the international organization founded by Cayce and his followers), there are documented 30,000 stenographic reports along with hundreds of complete case records containing affidavits by patients and physicians as to the accuracy of his diagnoses and the curative effects of his suggestions for treatment. Cousins' book *Anatomy of an Illness as Perceived by the Patient* and Siegel's *Love Medicine & Miracles* were best sellers that focused on the medically inexplicable part of the healing process. Their sales records indicate that a large number of the reading public are open and receptive to such themes. Cousins wrote about how he cured himself of an incurable disease by designing his own regimen of megadoses of vitamins and laughter. Siegel, a surgeon, writes about patients who get well even though they are supposed to die. Andrew Weil, author of numerous books and articles, has made holistic health and alternative healing practices accessible and more acceptable to the medical establishment and the lay community. The ubiquitous presence and success of Deepak Chopra is testimony to unmet needs. The internet has served to introduce a diverse audience to the potential benefits of non-traditional health and mental health practices.

Arthur Frank, in his book *At the Will of the Body: Reflections on Illness*, writes that the stories we tell ourselves are dangerous. He cautions us to choose carefully what narratives we live with and use to answer the question of what is happening to us.

What is the relationship between madness and altered states of consciousness? John Weir Perry, a psychiatrist who studied with Carl Jung and founded the alternative treatment center, Diabasis, suggests that madness may be nature's way of providing one with the means for renewal and the capacity to reorganize the self on a higher level. Can the quest for enlightenment described in the diverse paths of the mystics get sidetracked into the mental prison called schizophrenia? Zen Buddhist tradition describes the powers that so enthralled me as Makyo and dismisses them as the toys and games of magicians. E. F. Schumacher writes that there is no easy means of differentiating between infra-human and supra-human madness. He identifies a key marker of the Buddhist path as a high degree of inner calm and quietude which is known as vipassana or clear vision. The Zen master warns the disciple to guard against being seduced by illusions of power and becoming diverted from the more meaningful path. When too much emphasis is placed on the paranormal abilities that entice, it interferes with and clouds awareness. The egotism of pride and power, influenced by the need to impress, stagnates the growth process. To Christians, the elevated state of consciousness arises from some kind of encounter with a higher level of Being, above the human level. The universal advice of knowledgeable people in such matters is not to seek the extraordinary experiences that inevitably occur when any intensive inner work is undertaken. Schumacher informs us that those who have not had personal experience of a higher level of consciousness cannot understand the language of those who are trying to tell us about it, and therefore they conclude that the mind is disordered by madness.[7]

As the end of the summer of 1966 was drawing near, I pushed myself to experience all I could while denying and refusing to face the responsibilities that should have been demanding my attention – getting a job and the looming possibility of being drafted into the army. Instead, I decided to experiment with sleep deprivation. Would sleeplessness help accelerate the processes that were developing within me? How far could I expand my boundaries and control my bodily functions? I had read of yogis who could slow their heart rate and breathing to a point at which they could remain buried for hours, but I overlooked their years of disciplined study and practice. I thought that if I accepted no limits, I would become limitless. I began to believe that I could do whatever I wished with my mind. I could hallucinate whatever I wanted to see. I began projecting my thoughts onto a television screen. Watching television became a creative enterprise. It was easy to change the theme or direction of a program. Once decided upon, the new creation had a spontaneous energy of its own, as vivid as an eidetic image. Stored memories and images were spontaneously combining into various themes and patterns, needing very little conscious direction from me. Initially done just for fun, as I slept less, the images became more vivid and I became convinced that I had developed a valuable new ability. The experience seemed similar to lucid dreaming, that is, consciously controlling dream content while remaining asleep.

Lucid dreaming is a pleasant harmless experience if it occurs naturally while you are at home sleeping in your bed. But being able to experience such a phenomenon while I was going about my daily waking life required a major revision in my thinking. Fascinated by this new talent, I wanted to withdraw from the problems of the external world and spend my time enjoying the exciting imagery of my internal life. The adventure and thrill of my mind's creativity released a torrent of energy. The high I felt was self-sustaining. I moved deeper into my internal life, valuing its importance more than the external world. I paid little attention to my appearance or to social amenities. I let my hair and beard grow long and become dirty and unkempt. For a short time, I could get by acting the part of the absent-minded, eccentric professor involved too much in his projects to remember life's everyday concerns. That protective stereotype might have lasted longer had I not sought the recognition and affirmations of others.

In his book, *The Seven Storey Mountain*, theologian Thomas Merton writes of his admiration for the peaceful freedom of the Trappist monks. Rather than being lauded for accomplishments that make one rise above one's peers, the most successful monk is he who best blends in and is never noticed. Merton writes that the Trappist monk is free from the constraints of living in the projected imagination of others and thus having to submit always to their perceived judgments.[8] That summer, I was dabbling in that principle of freedom, but I lacked the faith, knowledge, discipline and commitment of the Trappist. I also lacked a community of support.

Without any training, guidance or cultural initiation rituals, I expanded and misinterpreted my new experiences. The freedom, excitement and adventure blocked out my chronic struggle with the unhappiness of who I was. I began to like me, and who I was becoming. I felt as if I was growing larger and larger. All of my past conceptions of reality were open to question and challenge. Feeling as if I could do anything made me feel that I was above criticism. The realities of my mind became stronger than any popular view of reality.

Regrettably, in seeking and needing the recognition and acknowledgment of others, I would become annoyed and then angry when my assertions of special abilities were challenged. Elliott, my oldest friend, believed me and tried to see what I saw. He sensed I was onto something and wanted to share the dreams, but he could not see the rapidly changing images in my mind's eye. Being with me so much, he witnessed the successes of the new me. He saw the extraordinary degree of perceptiveness. My heightened sensitivity to people enabled me to anticipate what they would say and their reactions. It seemed like I was reading minds. It was extrasensory. It was precognitive. I had nothing but naive labels to obscure, rather than communicate, the nature of my experience. Peering inward, I could explore the universe.

Precious are our memories. I wish I could say with conviction as most people easily do, "I'll never forget that." I have worked relentlessly to recapture and secure my lost memories. I have found some dim flickering lights in the foggy storage space allocated to that pre-hospital summer. I have mourned my losses, but I will not absolve or excuse responsibility for the psychiatric treatments inflicted on me and others. The few of us who have been able to survive insulin coma treatments and have regained the capacity to speak out must provide testimony to counter the newest, latest, greatest invasive "healing intervention" inflicted upon us "for our own good."

Elliott was my one solid link to that pre-hospital summer. He helped me retrieve lost memories. Elliott's own needs compelled him to believe in me. He too was frustrated by the conflicts between the world he lived in and the world he wished for. Flawed with an inability to persevere and discipline himself, he avoided dealing with life's demands. Food and drugs became his sanctuary. Big and funny, everyone liked Elliott but Elliott.

For the first few months after my discharge from the hospital, except for the evenings that Elliott would cajole me into going out with him I would live in a quasi-vegetative state in my parents' apartment. Silently accompanying him, I would see someone who looked familiar, but be unable to remember how I knew that person. Elliott's explanations left me grasping for a connection, looking for the elusive oh yeah, aha insight. Our years of experience growing up together allowed us to trust each other about as much as we were then capable. We had an easy, natural rapport, despite of or perhaps enhanced by the differences in our appearances, personalities and actions. Whereas I was skinny, shy and serious, he was a big hulking extrovert, with a flair for the dramatic and a gift for making people laugh. We seemed to sit at opposite poles: skinny and fat, quiet and boisterous, cautious and impulsive, college graduate and high school drop out. Yet there was more commonality than difference. Sensitive and insecure at our cores, we shared an unspoken deep understanding of each other. Frustrated in our childhood dreams to become professional baseball players, we shifted our fantasies to get-rich-quick schemes. Gambling cemented our bond.

It is a gambler's dream to have some kind of edge . . . better still to have the power . . . the intuition, the "right hunch." I was introduced to the quick late-night action of four-card monte when I was seventeen. Played in an old run-down warehouse in Union City, New Jersey, the monte game was usually populated with an assortment of seedy characters. The aura of danger and violence hovering around the players intensified the immediacy of the moment and ultimately would feed my paranoia. As in an old gangster B-movie, you were eyeballed through a peephole in the door in order to be admitted to the game. All of the players knew that there was some organized-crime involvement, at least to the extent of protecting the game with payoffs to the local authorities. Once in a while things would get hot, so the location of the game would shift and security would be tightened. For a gambler, the hopes, excitement, suspense and danger embody much of the appeal.

Winning at monte was completely dependent on luck, or so it seemed. Unlike three-card monte, the street hustler's game, this one was played by arranging four cards face up on the corners of a square with the house money resting in the middle. The players could choose one of the four cards and bet that a matching card would be drawn first from the deck. Wagers were made by placing the money you bet in a certain position on the table corresponding to the card which you chose to appear first. It was important to fold the corner of your bet money so that you could watch and identify it when it was time to collect. Bets were won and lost in a matter of seconds.

The magic of that pre-hospital summer has remained alive and exciting for Elliott. My spotty memory provides only barely remembered fragments. One of the few recollections I have retained was our one fantastic and frightening night at the monte game. That night I knew I could predict the order in which the cards would appear. Elliott and I went to the game as partners with a very small money stake and our usual hopes. I was in charge of the betting. Before the game began, I whispered to Elliott that I knew which card would come up first, and I did – time after time after time. I was confused as to the source of this power. I felt as if I were cheating, and was frightened by the anticipated reaction of the other players. I kept winning. Each time, I increased my bets, but resisted Elliott's urging to double up and bet everything on each play. I tried to avoid drawing attention to myself, but it was unavoidable. Other players began betting with me as the streak of wins built to six, ten . . . a dozen. One leather-faced old man with a stogie cigar stared at me and stubbornly persisted in playing the exact opposite of whatever I bet. Some other players stopped betting, and watched and whispered among themselves in Italian. The tension I perceived seemed to increase proportionately to the amount of Italian being spoken in the room. I was sure they were talking about me. The house had to replenish their money supply several times. Becoming increasingly more frightened, I told Elliott that we had better leave while we could. Elliott, who was always looking for the big score, tried to persuade me to make one more big bet, to bet it all. I was too scared and convinced him to leave with me.

My mind was racing as we drove home. As the daylight began to break through, fear and relief mixed with elation and fatigue. Flashes of light became images charged with electric energy. I asked Elliott if he saw the strange sights I was seeing on those empty streets. He tried, but could not.

Looking back, I wonder if the many phenomena Elliott and I remembered did indeed happen, or whether we were simply participating in a *folie a deux*. Was that monte game more than an uncanny series of coincidences? Explanation aside, the monte game pushed me deeper into my own private reality.

The sudden changes brought on by the act of opening up were confounding. Was I walking such a thin line that the simple decision to let go could set me adrift into a nether land that invited madness? Had I unleashed forces that were driving me to expand on and eventually become captivated by the heroic and messianic elements of madness? Or was this merely a stop on a spiritual journey that we should all be entitled to explore? Regardless of the interpretation, the new realities of my mind had become more important to me than anything else.

I wonder if I had had enough time to test myself, to experiment, to make the new toys a part of me, could I have worked it out? There was no structure, no discipline or mentor to aid my journey. I was in a foreign environment without a map, trying to convince myself and others that I knew the way. Their maps and strategies were useless for an expedition into a shadowy world where I had to create my own roads. Out in the uncharted, I was challenging a lifetime of admonitions to beware of the unknown. Later, I would be told with finality, "You are dangerously lost and cannot be allowed to stay where you are, or to try to find your way home alone."

My attempts to recall and make sense of the experiences of that pre-hospital summer were handicapped by the shock treatments and heavy medications. I yearned for the optimistic energy that was once available to me. I vacillated between remorse for stolen abilities and self-criticism for romantically remembering that troubled time with wish-laden fantasies. The path that I once traveled has fallen into a state of disrepair, become overgrown with weeds and remains hidden from my sight. The extraordinary and inexplicable may be a bit more acceptable now than in 1966, but I think pragmatic self-protection makes me unable to reconnect with that path.

Much to my chagrin, my introduction to madness followed the norm for my diagnosis; I was twenty-two when I was first hospitalized. According to the DSM-IV, "The median age at onset for the first psychotic episode of Schizophrenia is in the early to mid 20s for men, and in the late

20s for women."[9] Late adolescence/early adulthood is the developmental stage most closely associated with initiation into the diagnostic category called schizophrenia. The young person is expected to begin his real life. Although the cues are never pure and unidirectional, the prevailing theme of entering into adulthood demands action and devalues continuing preparation. Few escape the anxiety and ambivalence inherent in the necessity of resolving the independence/dependence challenge. Preparation is usually inadequate. Messages from significant others often pull in at least two directions. Success and failure may be interchangeable and frequently dependent on the changing perspectives and needs of mothers, fathers, friends and lovers. Realities that have been defined in loving contexts are not immune to society's unrelenting, conflictual, impossible demands. For those who cannot swallow the conventional interpretation of reality, who find the walls closing in and the pressure too painful, tiny spaces of relief can appear. Those little cracks offer the opportunity to reconstruct oneself. The possibility of acquiring the ability to alter one's personal universe can be hard to resist.

As a twenty-two-year-old, I had to interpret and attach meaning to a new set of experiences. The old way had not worked. I had not fit in. I could get by, but I was miserable. I chose to see unlimited possibilities. I chose to be outrageous. But once the line was crossed, could I return? Where was the line? My inability to let go of ego, my innocence, my lack of training and knowledge about alternative realities, made me vulnerable to poorly constructed explanations that set me tumbling down false trails and into exaggerated notions of self-importance. It is easy for the powerless, insecure and trapped to trick and seduce themselves.

Our western industrialized, information-overloaded society neglects spiritual mentoring, training and initiatory rituals. Perhaps traditional religions' reduced effectiveness in meeting the spiritual needs of young and old have made New Age themes like angelic guides, past life regressions, reiki healings, shamanism, crystal energy and astrology so attractive. But the inward journey, despite increasing public attention and acceptance, is still considered an undervalued fringe preoccupation. When you deviate too far, your choices and freedom are restricted.

Our culture dictates how far its members will be permitted to move beyond the designated safety zone before forced intervention is deemed necessary. The size of one's safe area is context-determined. Each person's primary social network lays down the micro-rules within the larger macro-rules of the family, job, school, religion, neighborhood, town, city, state and country. Some parents and teachers offer a context that allows children to test their boundaries and limits, while many only tolerate small deviations. The active child who can be the delight of one family may find that same activity level elicits the diagnosis Attention Deficit Disorder with Hyperactivity in a family that places a high premium on peace and quiet. Etched deeply into the family ethos is how much risk and disruption will be tolerated.

My family required a great deal of safety.

Chapter 2

Becoming a Mental Patient

Having stripped myself of all illusions, I have gone mad.
(Friedrich Nietzsche)

Ten years after my last hospitalization, shortly after my mother's funeral, my brother and I shared our grief and talked for the first time about my psychiatric experiences. We were able to listen and gain some new understanding of our respective perceptions and interpretations of my mad voyage. Sy grew up seeing only the still-water surface veneer; I was the proverbial bright younger brother who has it much easier than the one who came first – the one who gets all the unearned attention. He knew nothing of his brother's inner struggles. To be suddenly faced with an unpredictable, crazy brother was frightening. He could not understand how I could be so different than he had known me to be. After twenty-two years of living within the acceptable range of normality, my passage into schizophrenia was bewildering to me and my family.

Psychiatrists looking back at my history could perform a psychological autopsy and uncover warning signs of future mental illness, but those predictions could only be made after the label was already in place. Within our current state of knowledge there are no convincing predictors of schizophrenia. Even highly publicized physiological markers, including the most sophisticated brain scans, cannot be used to predict which is the schizophrenic brain. A desperately hopeful public has been seduced by a successful marketing campaign foisted upon them by the mental health industry. An unholy alliance between mainstream psychiatry and the pharmaceutical giants has marketed and represented advertisements as facts. The public is led to believe that scientists have discovered the biochemical mechanisms responsible for mental illness, and that with just one more, tiny step – the identification of the specific genetic marker – the new miracle drugs will be available. This quest to end the anguish and suffering of being human by re-engineering our biochemistry will be regarded by future historians as twenty-first-century fool's gold – not too far removed from Spanish explorer Ponce de Leon's search for the "fountain of youth" in sixteenth-century Florida.

Thin skin has been a mixed blessing for me. What helps me as a therapist, I hated as a child. When practicing psychotherapy, I am respected for my ability to understand and empathize with feelings that go beyond what is consciously expressed; the child receives no reward for feeling the denied pain of others. With my older, tougher skin, I work at calling up experiences from my past to connect with the experience of an *other*. These others' needs for acceptance, belonging and recognition, so prominent during my childhood, are easy for me to recall.

I was a child filled with dreams of unlimited potential. Every day I walked home from school with my best friend Steve. When he turned onto Aldine Street, I slipped into daydreaming as I walked the last few blocks home. In my reverie, I compared myself to Steve. He was a self-assured ten-year-old. I didn't like being jealous, but he was happy and popular, and was always allowed to do the things I could never get my parents to let me do. "But Steve's allowed to do it" never packed the persuasive clout with my mom that I knew it deserved.

I imagined Steve and I standing next to each other. I was taller, but I was too skinny. I hated the way my shoulder blades stuck out. Whenever I turned at an angle to see my back in a mirror, those bony shoulder blades grabbed my attention. No shirt, sweater or change of posture could hide them. Yet, with some work, I convinced myself that I was better looking than Steve. It was toughest on those days when I thought my nose was too big or when I hated my freckles. On bad days, my legs were too skinny, my teeth were awful, my hair too curly and the wrong color. Smarter was easy, that I was sure of; pretty sure, too, that I was a better athlete, kinder, braver and a better son. By the time I reached my front steps I was telling myself, "You're better than him. It's not fair now, but when you grow up it'll be different – the breaks will even out and you'll be recognized for how good you really are." The pep talks usually worked, except on those days when life reminded me of how small and powerless I was in the larger arenas of school, family and society.

I would fume and complain about school and our teachers. "Forget it," Steve would tell me, "you know how they are." But I could not let it go. I felt held back, not understood, not related to, not seen. I needed to be seen. I needed to connect with an understanding adult, a mentor. An interested teacher might have made a difference.

Funny how memories of our childhood disappointments can retain their emotional import over events which would seem to warrant more significance. All of the fourth and fifth grade classes were gathered in the auditorium listening to the announcements that preceded our weekly assembly meetings. One of the announcements caught my attention. A pupil would be selected to represent our school in a city-wide competition to be broadcast on the local radio station. The subject was prehistoric animals. I couldn't believe it – what an opportunity! I was an expert on dinosaurs. Busting with excitement, I knew that this was my chance to get recognition. I would get the respect I craved.

Mrs. Silver, the teacher in charge, was a stern, no-nonsense person, a stickler for rules who didn't seem to like children in general, and me in particular. A hard and threatening demeanor and a reputation for over-reacting to even a hint of mischief or silliness, Mrs. Silver was someone I regarded with caution and I tried not to misbehave in her class. She had punished me the previous week for laughing and talking while we were lining up to leave the auditorium. For my punishment I had been made to sit several rows away from the other students during the next two assembly meetings.

Mrs. Silver had a series of questions about dinosaurs that she would ask to help her select the student who would represent our school. I foolishly believed that if I could give the most correct answers, I would be chosen. At ten years of age, I was a strong believer in fairness. When I realized that she would block my participation in the contest and deny me my chance to shine, I fumed. I knew all the answers to the questions, but when I raised my hand she refused to call on me. I begged for her to give me a chance – only to be told to be quiet, that my poor conduct indicated that I was unworthy of the honor of representing the school. Frustrated, I finally began calling out the answers to prove to her that I knew more than anyone else. Mrs. Silver sent me to the principal's office to be disciplined

Rather than helping a child who was struggling to find his voice, Mrs. Silver deepened my resentment of authority. I withdrew back into myself. I would wrestle for many years with arbitrary authorities who dismissed my demands that fairness and justice had to guide one's actions.

Teachers exerted control that conflicted with my need to be independent. My little knee-jerk rebellions were the start of a pattern. I wanted the praise and recognition, but I resisted the passive submission teachers required. I did not trust my teachers. I was particularly sensitive to insincerity. Lack of caring, impatience with children, and general dissatisfaction with their jobs too often provided the context for their lesson plans. I couldn't quite figure out what I was reacting to, but I knew something was not right. What they said was often different from what I felt they meant. That feeling of inconsistency was one I experienced frequently as a child. The acute sensitivity to incongruity and hypocrisy intuitive to children seemed stronger in and more disturbing to me. My intuition, my gut feelings were difficult to validate with both children and adults. I felt that what I sensed was accurate, but when I responded accordingly, my perceptions and conclusions were denied or discounted. I eventually learned to be quiet so as to avoid the discomfort and embarrassment.

The powerlessness a child feels in trying to make his identity known in an overpowering, impersonal world can take many forms. The powerlessness directly arising from trauma, abuse and extreme neglect may also be borne in the day-to-day battles, usually lost, in which the child struggles for validation of his or her worth.

For a few years I worked as a psychologist in a school for children classified with severe emotional disturbance. I realized that I was envious of those troubled youngsters who wanted but resisted closeness. I was jealous of the teachers' and staff's attempts to develop caring relationships with the children. Remembering my own sterile educational experience, I wondered if I would have been better off if my behavior had been outrageous enough to get me a diagnosis. To my surprise, when I shared my feeling of envy at a staff meeting I was leading, others talked of similar feelings. Perhaps it was our personal identifications with deprivation that enabled some of us to be more giving to those whose education was entrusted to us.

The growing turmoil I felt seemed to find a home in my belly. I complained of stomach pains as far back as I can remember. Unable to find a cause or name for my illness, our family doctor dismissed my discomfort and attributed it to gas pains. I remember wondering if the pain I felt was the most severe that anyone could ever experience. I thought if grown-ups had to endure stronger pain than this, I would not be able to survive. I comforted myself by thinking that the pain was making me stronger and preparing me for adulthood.

My continued complaints made my mother seek other doctors' opinions. Finally, she took me to a stomach specialist, Dr. Kaplan, who would treat me for the next seven years. Dr. Kaplan had me admitted to Newark's Beth Israel Hospital for x-rays. There, it was determined that I had a stomach ulcer. The treatment he prescribed was a very restrictive, bland diet which I would follow from the time I was eight years old until I reached fifteen.

The following three months I stayed home from school, with no homework and only the responsibility of drinking a lot of milk and not cheating on my diet. During those three months at home, my mother saw to it that I had a glass of room temperature milk every two hours, and ate only day-old bread, bland unseasoned meals, no fresh fruits or vegetables, and no chocolate, candy or ice cream. I was compliant with my diet, not tasting chocolate again until I began cheating at thirteen and ultimately tossed all restrictions at fifteen. The pain had subsided, maybe from milk drowning, but more likely from a combination of special attention and the natural maturational process. Often I have wondered if I really did have stomach ulcers.

No one explained to me what it meant to have stomach ulcers. I was simply told not to tell any of my friends that I had ulcers. More secrets. I did not understand why I should be ashamed. Actually, it kind of made me feel special. Adults seemed to be amazed that an eight-year-old youngster could have an adult disease. At the time, stomach ulcers were believed to be a condition brought on by stress and tension, part of the price one paid for ascending the corporate ladder. Dr. Kaplan mistook my pride in being special for anxiety, and tried to reassure me and my mother by telling us that they had discovered even younger children with ulcers. I was not unique.

For some, childhood can be a nightmare; mine was not so extreme. My unhappiness was not difficult to see if one looked closely at the sad, under-achieving, preoccupied child. But overall there was more normality than abnormality. I was an active child who played and socialized with a steady group of friends. Even the continuous arguing and unhappiness of my parents were not of alarming proportions. Although introspective, fearful and easily hurt, I was able to navigate most of childhood's confusing conflicts.

My early conflicts were sparked by my search to understand and reconcile the inconsistent messages I perceived. Always, answers to the questions of fairness and justice belonged to the adult world. Being good and acting right never seemed to be enough. My conflicts with adults generally stemmed from my refusal to give in and go against something I believed or did not understand. Later, as a mental patient confined to a psychiatric hospital, my insistence on fairness would threaten my very existence.

The Jewish immigrant's dream, to improve one's lot through

education, was as deeply embedded a parental legacy as the color of my eyes. The twists and turns of high school were of little consequence; college was the imperative next step. I naively believed that joining the army was a viable alternative to the time-honored traditions, values and dreams of my family heritage; I thought that entering the army after high school was a good idea. In 1961, the world was not a dangerous place and the peacetime army offered some attractive options to a high school graduate. By making myself eligible for the draft I could fulfill my military obligations with two years of active duty.

I thought I articulated a convincing argument with my family. I knew I was not ready for more school confinement and in a convoluted way the army represented independence. Until then, I had unhappily drifted down the path my parents had assigned to me. One night after dinner, I told my mother I wanted to join the army after high school graduation. My mother's stunned reaction was quickly followed by a too-familiar wailing in Yiddish to God. Her chest-beating complaints and requests for God to help her understand why her child would do this were transparent. I knew those whys and accusations were for me, not God, to see the depth of her angst. I was not able to convince her of the advantages of joining the army. I suppose it really was just a trial balloon. I could not oppose my mother on such an important issue. Mom . . . .

You gave me so much, too much. You loved me so much, too much. You made me feel too important, too powerful. They are not just blaming accusations, but rather the acknowledgments of mixed gifts. I did so wish that you could have had your own life, that you had not sacrificed all parts of yourself for your children. Perhaps in some secret inner place you rejoiced at my unwillingness to give in. Was it really you who encouraged my little rebellions? I see so much of you in me. I cherish and am thankful to share that touching of souls that you cultivated with love. I hate those fears that sneaked in on the sleeves of your love.

I was fortunate and unfortunate. I had a powerful, loving, protective mother for security, but one who also inspired a guilt-inducing lack of boundaries and an inability to disentangle. I fought not to be engulfed. I needed my own identity. She needed me for her identity. The ambivalence of loving her dearly, and feeling suffocated, permeated my being. I lived the dualities and dialectics, with guilt riding on the *ifs* and *buts*. My too-strong childhood love carried the immense responsibility of having to compensate for her ill health and unhappy marriage. The prodigal son theme that guided me said that Mom would be affirmed, her life would have meaning, if I could perform some great deed. The public recognition of the greatness of her son would make her happy and set me free. If either of us had understood the implicit demands embedded in our interactions, we might have been able to avoid considerable pain. Years later, after my battle to separate was finally resolved, I could see that my mother did indeed have a strong, independent identity which she had packed away after her children were born.

Mother, you were the next-to-last born of eleven children. Your father died when you were six. Your mother, orphaned as an infant, had her first child when she was thirteen and her last when she was fifty-one. Grandmother was forty-eight years old when you were born. You came to this country, riding in the cargo hold of a freighter with your mother, your brother Jake and your sickly older sister who was to die five years later at the age of twenty. Uncle Hymie was the first one to come here, having fled from the Russian army into which he had been conscripted to serve for twenty years. Next was Tante Ida. She came to the United States in 1899 as a twenty-five-year-old, traveling alone by ship to a new land without knowing what to expect. Twenty-three years old when your mother died, you were consumed with devotion to her and devastated by her death.

My mother worked in a sweatshop as a seamstress from the time she was eleven until she married at thirty-five. My brother Sy was born when she was thirty-seven and I was born when she was forty-two. The bravery of the family, on the one hand, coupled with what seemed to be innumerable fears, posed a perplexing paradox.

My family always seemed so frightened, so vulnerable and so sensitive to persecution. Our heritage of being escaped Russian Jews, alone and different in a strange new country dictated fear, but I did not want to live that way. Fear, self-protection and martyrdom are antagonistic to warmth, yet somehow your warmth and compassion survived. I fought to deny the fears and be strong, but the result often came out wrong. It became stubbornness and rebellion. I tried to sacrifice the precious sensitivity that was my family endowment.

My inability to trust took many years to resolve. As a child I understood much that was happening, but I often felt like someone was trying to trick me. There seemed to be an enormous cache of secret information that was kept from me for my own protection. Of course, my imagination could construct something much more horrible than the simple truth. If you need so much protection, fears easily seep in and take up residence at a deep level of your being.

Hiding was a constant during my growing up. I was either hiding my own fears and insecurities, or trying to keep my parents out of sight. I wanted to fit in, to be like the other kids. My family's orthodox Jewishness became the representation of my problems. Yiddish was the primary language spoken at home. I understood Yiddish but I refused to speak it. I was afraid that if I let it come naturally to me, it would pop into a conversation and I would be ridiculed. I wanted to be an American.

During my doctoral studies, I was attracted to the newly emerging field of family therapy. At a post-doctoral family therapy institute, our class assignment – to do a family history – gave me a rationale to interview my relatives. The secrets resisted clarification.

I remember being in a foster home when I was about four years old. Mom told me she would have to go away for a while and I would have to live with another family until she came home. She explained that my father would only be able to take care of my brother, who needed to continue in school. After both my mother and I returned home, there was no discussion of that period of our family life again. When I inquired as an adult, no one could remember how long I was away, or why family (my aunt lived next door) had not taken me in, or for what sickness my mother was being treated. The direct questions made them uncomfortable.

As a child I was told that my mother needed an operation, and then she would need to be in a convalescent home to recover her strength. After my psychiatric experiences, although I never completely bought into the hereditary component of mental illness, naturally I wondered if that convalescent home was really a mental hospital. Putting together the bits and pieces, I now believe it was some form of surgery and recovery, but unexplained secrets do retain their ability to provoke the imagination.

Given the centrality of orthodox Judaism to my family, my parents' decision to put me in a Christian foster home is puzzling. I liked the family and seemed to have adjusted well to the separation. During the first months of my stay there, no one from my family visited me. Maybe they were told that if I didn't see them, my adjustment would be easier. It seemed to work.

When my father finally did come to see me, he told me that we were going to see my mother. My father waited outside while I rushed to gather up the jelly beans I had collected during the morning's Easter egg hunt. Excited about seeing my mother, I nervously gobbled up my jelly beans in the backseat of the car. When my father realized I was eating candy, he told me that it was a sin to eat candy on Passover. I felt awful for sinning and worse for wanting to finish the candy that my father had confiscated. Later, my mother assured me that it was not a sin because I hadn't known it was Passover. My father always confounded me and seemed to enjoy my and others' consternation at never knowing who he was or what he stood for. The little I knew about him came from his sister, whom we seldom saw.

Dad, you could have made life much easier for me . . . probably a too common refrain for sons and daughters. Mom was your responsibility, not mine. Your sister told me you never took another chance after you married Mom. You did not let anyone know who you were or what went on inside of you. Sometimes I would get a vague hint of your dreams, but your inconsistency would shatter any insight. In 1915, after your freshman year, you quit high school to see the world and try to make your fortune. You rode freight trains cross-country in your youth. You worked a ship to Alaska and almost lost your foot to frostbite. You never shared that part of your life. I only knew you as a graveyard-shift factory laborer in a job you hated. It would have been helpful to identify with that courageous and adventurous part of you. The only bits of advice you offered were: just keep nodding yes to your bosses on the job – yes them to death; and after I brought my girlfriend Sara to the house to meet you, on the way out you whispered to me, "Never let your wife drive your car." Double meanings, did he intend them? I never knew.

Tough, athletic and smart – an all-American boy, that's who I wanted people to see when they looked at me. But my mother only wanted to see smart, and that had to be in the school way. My heroes were athletes and rugged movie stars. Her heroes were the doctors carrying medical bags filled with the impressive tools of what was then the most respected and secure of all professions. We were not supposed to be physical, that was not for us. On the street, I was proud of my scrapes and bruises, the little badges of a rough ball game or the acceptance of a risky challenge. At home, I would hide a black eye by pretending the sunglasses I wore inside the house were just my way of being "cool."

My fight to reject the role that my family assigned to me came at the expense of my Jewish heritage. I had strongly felt spiritual needs, but my religious instruction was directed at teaching the observation of customs and traditions. I wanted explanations, insights or at least spiritual counsel. I could not follow role models whose contradictions between their professed beliefs and their actions were easy to see. My parents did not have the knowledge to answer my questions. My Hebrew school teachers focused entirely on teaching the necessary reading skills to follow traditions and prepare for Bar Mitzvah. Who am I and how do I fit into a world where I always feel like an outsider remained unanswered questions. My religious education did not confront the issues which were important to me – values, morals and justice, how to be a good person.

I wanted to know why I felt that I was different than the other children. On the surface, I could blend in, be like others, to fake belonging, but I was always a little out of step. I rarely felt at ease. Instead, I felt guilty for sinning against God and betraying my mother. God was always letting me down, and I was always letting my mother down.

My struggle to establish an independent identity was a consistent, manageable conflict as long as my status as a dependent child guided the limits of my rebellious behavior. Real adulthood, the next developmental stage, offered opportunity, freedom and dangerous risks.

Instead of seeing my schizophrenia as the inevitable culmination of a maturing pathological process, I see it as part of a search for identity, an attempt to realize potentials, a struggle to understand me in the universe. To confront or avoid my existential dis-ease, I faced a crossroad. The complexity of factors that went into my choice to seek answers in psychosis, rather than compulsive gambling, over-achieving, drug addiction, alcoholism or a life of quiet conformity cannot be simplified into cause-and-effect medical logic.

There are no typical schizophrenics nor, for that matter, are there any typical representatives of any of the major mental illness categories. Although professionals can find similarities between people that can justify assigning individuals to specific diagnostic groups, they must do so by ignoring important differences. Some of us voluntarily enter the mental health system to find treatment for pain. Others are forced to submit to treatments. Many are lied to, tricked or set up with a choice of voluntary status which is quickly changed to involuntary when the patient demands discharge. Regardless of the mode of entrance, all receive a diagnostic label which virtually assures a lifetime of searching to find an exit, that is, unless one's spirit has been bullied and bludgeoned into accepting the passive dependent role of the "chronic mental patient."

I believe that the very same characteristics that extended my hospitalizations and provoked the most severe and damaging treatments are also the major factors that enabled me to survive and transcend my psychiatric experiences. I would not be convinced to abandon my sense of being special. Perhaps my survival was supported and nurtured by my then unarticulated core belief in the integrity of the spirit. A Jungian analyst might call that an abiding trust in the ability of one's unconscious to know what is right. Most certainly I had, at least temporarily, been deprived of the opportunity to use my intellect to understand and formulate an action plan. They could reduce the raging fire inside of me to nothing more than warm embers, but I would use my stubbornness to persevere in keeping a spark alive. Now I know how fortunate I was that those in charge did not, as was within their power, decide to extinguish the fire completely. Whatever attributes I possessed, whatever work I later would do to develop my capabilities, begs humble deference to a higher plane, be it ascribed to God, karma or the blind vagaries of fateful luck.

I had never dreamed that some day I would be hospitalized for mental illness. Impossible. Where were the clues? I was different, but never in that way. Studying abnormal psychology in college, I made the rather typical comparisons between myself and the textbook descriptions of psychopathology, but I remained relatively unconcerned about being mentally ill. Back then we were taught, *"Under enough stress, given the right circumstances, anyone could become. . . ."* Acceptable as theory, but not something to worry about for yourself. "Crazy" was a word reserved for other people, far removed from the people I knew. Not me. They were the helpless and hopeless, completely out of it, cheated by fate, nameless poor souls who populated the abnormal psychology text books. Even during that pre-hospital summer of great chaos and change, I had no hint of what I was about to face.

As I look back I realize that I lacked the social skills that would have enabled me to play my new role successfully. By temperament shy and introspective, my new extroverted behavior was out of synch and incongruent with the responses I sought. I tried to dance while lacking any sense of rhythm. What at first may have been amusing to my social network began to become obnoxious. Disregarding social amenities, I too bluntly shared my observations and insights about people. My family became increasingly alarmed by my actions.

There must have been a great deal of agonizing within the family before the call was made. Were my problems serious enough to let down the family code of privacy? Someone had to evaluate how out of control I was. A family member, my cousin George, was the logical choice. He was a clinical psychologist who was fifteen years older than me. Too much was expected of George. He was asked to bring me back into the fold or at least provide some reasonable explanation for my actions. I knew very little about George. Our relationship did not go beyond small talk at family gatherings. Those interactions usually left me uncomfortable: I felt targeted by his critical eyes, as if I were under a psychological microscope.

My family resisted any attempt at reworking requirements for maintaining family stability. If one member of the family changes, the tension reverberates throughout the system and activates the champions of the status quo. They were obligated to fight whatever illness or alien force had removed me from the preferred family portrait. My behavior had gone beyond the family's tolerance for eccentricity. They demanded that I return to living in a manner that was acceptable to them, but unacceptable to me. I refused to go back to being a frightened little boy. I had to keep the powerful new me. George arranged for me to see a psychiatrist.

I looked upon my visit to the psychiatrist as a test, an opportunity to vindicate myself and get my family off my back. Cousin George and I sat stiffly, together yet apart. The small, too brightly lit reception room was clean, orderly and lacking in any personal touch. George was obviously uncomfortable and remained minimally responsive to my attempts to make conversation. At first I thought he was just trying to appear self-assured, but his measured responses hinted to me that he was soothing his own discomfort by being the psychologist here. Fear and pride had forced me to whistle in the dark too many times to be fooled by his posture. Eventually I lost myself in the picture of the forest scene hanging on the wall across from us.

The door to the inner office opened and a young woman walked out and hurried past us. She was determined to avoid looking at anyone and probably hoping in turn that no one would see her. Sitting there, I felt lonely and isolated. Seeing her discomfort triggered fear. Too late, I realized the danger of this impending encounter with a stranger who was about to change the trajectory of my life. An overweight, middle-aged man in a poorly-fitted, wrinkled grey suit appeared in the doorway to the two adjoining rooms. Quickly looking us over, he extended his hand to George and introduced himself. I stared at his bushy eyebrows. I searched his face for some indication of warmth or friendliness but found none. He nodded to me and motioned for me to enter his office.

I sat down in a chair across from him and watched as he very slowly, almost ceremoniously lowered himself into a leather chair behind his fortress-like desk. Like the outer room, his inner sanctum was cold and impersonal despite the family picture on his desk and the two perfectly shaped plants hanging beside the small window.

I began to sweat. The pressure was making me extremely restless. I struggled to sit still and not tap my feet. My skin felt itchy. I resisted scratching my scalp. I did not know what to do or say, but I was keenly aware of the need to be cautious. He looked me over. I looked him over. He did not speak. I did not speak. He sucked on a piece of candy; I had no candy and he didn't offer me any of his. I was thirsty and nervous. It seemed to be a test of wills. It was not a fair fight, or for that matter, a fair assessment. I waited for him to speak.

"Do you know what day and year it is? Do you know where you are? Can you name the last four presidents? Please count down by sevens from twenty. Do you know who I am and why you are here?

I became irritated, then angry, and only my anxious awareness of his importance to my future prevented me from giving in and letting out my anger. His bored air, demeaning questions and mechanized rote manner of relating to me smacked of an undisguised arrogant superiority towards a non-person. I was an object to be acknowledged, but unworthy of respect. He did not need to attend to the civilities owed to a real person. There was neither enough time nor the need for anything more than the face-to-face meeting required for a quick psychiatric evaluation in preparation for commitment. As a favor to George he had squeezed me in between appointments. Later I learned that his recommendation had been unequivocal: I should be taken to Newark City Hospital to be held there until I could be transferred to Fair Oaks Psychiatric Hospital.

Driving back with George, I wanted to talk, to ask him about what had happened, but I knew that nothing good could have come from my psychiatric visit. I was hoping George might think of someone else for me to talk with, maybe a therapist. Although I was very guarded about letting anyone get a look inside of me, I did have a lot of questions I could discuss. George remained silent. If he was aware of the inadequacy of my brief interview, he didn't show it. I was ignorant of the pre-determined verdict and the sentence that awaited me.

Silence, and the expectant eyes of Mom, Dad, my brother Sy and Elliott greeted George and me when we arrived at my parents' apartment. I absorbed the tense excitement I felt all around me. Their nervousness energized me. Everyone's anxiety and uncertainty made me feel the need to help them, to teach them how to tap into their latent potentials and grow. I thought if they believed in me, if I could make them see my new abilities, I could show them the path to a better life. *No, silly boy, it is your life that will be changed.*

The whole family was prepared to take whatever action was

necessary. They were bewildered by their inability to influence me. Elliott, too, was confused. He could not understand my beatific attitude when my family talked of committing me to a hospital. Elliott was trying to get me alone so that he could convince me to run away. I was too self-involved to understand his motive for wanting to talk privately. I wanted everything worked out publicly. What did I have to hide, I thought, as I foolishly deceived myself.

When I found out about the psychiatrist's recommendation, I was outraged by his audacity. "We never talked," I protested. "That psychiatrist knows nothing about me."

George, having discharged his uncomfortable family obligation, left and let the others wrestle with the decision. What my family saw as their desire to help, I perceived as ignorant interference. To me the problem was simple: I was able to exercise control, but I was unwilling to control myself their way. I did want to make everyone feel better, but I saw no solution other than to convince them of my competence. The problem was racing to its inevitable resolution. I defied family-society requirements; therefore, psychiatric intervention was necessary.

We discussed for hours. We argued for hours. My beliefs and theories did not make sense to them. I saw them trying to understand, trying to believe, trying to see some signs of what could pass for rationality in me. I had to convince them that I was not mentally ill, and apparently only one proof would be indisputable. I would show them by agreeing to go to the hospital with them. To demonstrate that I was not mentally ill, I had to admit myself into the hospital as a mentally ill person and then prove that I was not mentally ill. Elliott saw the trap. I did not.

Sy and Elliott drove me to Newark City Hospital. Elliott wanted to protect me but knew that I had made up my mind. He had the street sense I lacked, and realized that going to the hospital was a horrible mistake. My brother was intent on protecting me by getting me the recommended treatment. He was carrying out an important prescribed duty and would not be deterred from his obligation. Feeling the rising tension between Sy and Elliott and sensing they might come to blows, I reassured both of them. I talked about how I was beginning to understand the special role I would play in the great world changes that were about to happen. The intensity of the street lights combining with my swirling emotions scared me, but I believed if I gave in to my fears the world would face a major disaster. Everything was dependent upon my maintaining control. Each of my thoughts, emotions and movements kept the world in balance until the time was right for the great changes to occur. I rationalized my fears and converted them into irritation at Sy and Elliott. Their petty squabbling was interfering with my concentration on events that affected the entire universe.

We arrived at the hospital late at night. The nurse would not let Elliott accompany us through the admissions procedure. Elliott moved closer to me and whispered, "You have to get out of here now."

Again I assured Elliott that I was alright and would see him soon. He waited in the lobby as my brother and I were led into separate rooms. Despite sensing danger, I continued to convince myself that I was choosing to cooperate.

I went into a room with two attendants who would undress me, weigh me and assign me my new uniform, a hospital gown. I tried to focus on the acclaim I would receive when I was eventually vindicated, but I could not drive away the aura of violence that permeated this routine hospital procedure. No longer was I resisting loving, well-intentioned family and friends. I was encountering the uncaring efficiency and cold distance of hospital workers who were on guard for the unpredictable.

I was leaving the world where I had legislated rights and power, and entering a world where I had no rights. I was ambivalently holding onto consensually validated reality while struggling to understand my new place in the universe. Soon I would be introduced to the magnitude of the power vested in society's enforcers of reality. Besides taking my clothes and personal possessions, those two aides as representatives of the mental health system stripped me of the right to be treated with dignity and respect. My inability to accept their power to control me, and their unwillingness to define our respective positions in a mode other than dominance-submission, left no space for communication or choice. I said goodbye to being regarded as a person. My rights were suspended. I entered the horror-filled world of non-being; I became a hospitalized psychiatric patient.

Newark City Hospital was exactly what its name implied. In 1966 it was an urban hospital serving the poor of Newark. The psychiatric facilities consisted of a ward with beds assigned for emergencies: disoriented vagrants, alcoholics, drug addicts and assorted crazies like me.

I had been cooperative since entering the hospital. Yet, no one had spoken to me, just about me, as if I were an inanimate object to be moved and directed. All through an admitting procedure that took no more than twenty minutes, I felt the tension build. My heart beat faster, and my body pumped adrenaline and readied itself for the necessary fight or flight. But my mind dictated a different course. I offered no resistance until I became aware that they were going to strap me down to the bed. The two experienced aides did what they knew how to do best, easily overcoming my ineffective thrashing and wriggling while ignoring my verbal pleas. I had no impact on them. They just wanted to finish their job with no hassles. I could not integrate my specialness with their complete indifference. The realization of the mistake I had made in going to the hospital came crashing down on me: I was a prisoner.

As they were leaving, I asked them to remove the straps that tied me down. I told them that I could not sleep on my back. They ignored me. I insisted that I was only staying there to prove my sanity to my family. I explained to them that I could escape from their restraints through mental concentration. I let them know about my powers quite loudly. They laughed and waved goodbye. Their reality no longer suited me. I re-entered the world where I could do anything . . . except fall asleep on my back.

I freed myself from the first set of restraints. I should have stayed quietly in bed instead of proudly showing the nurse that I could escape any time I wanted. I believed I had passed the first test. They were so impressed that they held me down, gave me my first forced injection and then put me in four-point restraints. I fought to free myself. I strained, I ranted and raved, I huffed and puffed and blew my own house down. Too much noise; they moved my bed out in the hall so I wouldn't disturb the other patients on the ward.

From my new position I could see someone on night duty sitting a short distance away. It looked like she was operating a telephone switchboard. I asked her for help.

"Please get someone to take this off of me. I won't make any trouble."

No response.

"Please call someone."

Nothing

"Talk to me . . . help me."

Nothing. She would not respond to me. I needed her to say something, for anyone to recognize me and see that I was scared and hurting. I was still too loud. The nurse was called and she put another drug-filled needle into the fleshy part of my hip. As this drug began taking effect, I withdrew into myself. With the sedation came further disorientation and finally the loss of the passageway between my inner world and the world that society demanded I accept.

The myth of fairness, that right will triumph, took a beating that night. Yet that belief in fairness was so deeply rooted and central to my psyche that its call for justice would again and again interfere with my adaptation to the realities of survival in the world of psychiatry.

Being incarcerated creates its own sense of powerlessness. Absolute powerlessness, however, comes from the loss of credibility, first to others and then to yourself. My feelings and thoughts had no import. I was told what was best for me. I was judged by preconceived notions and made to fit into defined categories. And then the final verdict: "You are a paranoid schizophrenic."

I was not aware that I had become an unconscious inert object, to be transferred by ambulance to Fair Oaks Hospital.

I entered the abyss.

Chapter 3

Mental Patient: Learning My New Place

All he knew was that Dr. Franklin had never been anywhere that he had been, so he despaired of ever describing the things he had seen.

(from Force of Gravity by R.S. Jones)

They rode in silence to Fair Oaks Hospital, parents aching for the recovery of a broken child. One powerful certainty bridged their differences – their son would never be abandoned. Without knowing who was enemy or ally, a deadly threat propelled them on their mission.

Determined, unyielding tenacity was their strength. She was anxious, frightened, but above all, angry and intolerant of her own ignorance. He was unexpressive, appreciative of the control driving afforded. The car was his domain, the children hers. The unity mobilized by crisis muted years of quarreling. She would soon be asked to let down the walls of privacy that insulated and protected her family. The traditions and history of many generations made it impossible to trust the dreaded authorities. But the new danger required the summoning of strength from the deepest of human wells . . . a mother's resolve. Father would remain impassive; a lifetime of inaction would not be transcended. With an odd mixture of resignation and hope, they looked to the doctor for answers.

"What's wrong with him?" my parents pleaded. "He's always been a good boy. When will he get better? What should we do? How did this happen? Whose fault is it?"

The questions were for the doctor, but later would be asked of God. A broken foot was for the doctor, but a broken boy – who is to treat such a sickness? Their generation had witnessed the medical miracles of modern science. They regarded the doctor with reverence. Indeed, the doctor was royalty.

Doctor asked endless probing questions. She wished she could explain in Yiddish, but Doctor was a gentile; he would not understand her family regardless of the language. Still, she forced herself to try – his guidance was desperately needed. The immigrant's dilemma, the inability to

44

communicate in English, was always for her a source of pain and humiliation. She never forgave herself for her lack of education. Her husband's understanding of English could not compensate for his lack of knowledge about his children's lives. All he could do was help his wife understand the doctor's questions. As always, she would make the decisions. His typical response to crisis had been activated; defenses went up as he distanced himself from the outside world.

"He is a very sick boy," the doctor declared. "You must trust us to treat him in the way we know best; otherwise he could be in a mental hospital for the rest of his life. You have to follow our instructions and leave him to us or we won't be able to help him."

I forced my eyes open and tried to bring the room into focus. Harsh light, bare walls, shiny metal door; the room was too warm, the air heavy and stale. My skin was moist and clammy, sticking in places to a black mattress sealed in heavy-duty plastic. Why a mattress on the floor?

I lay there looking up at the high ceiling and felt the confusion turn into fear. Like its response to a never-drink-again hangover, my body was reminding me not to do it again. I felt my entire being rebel when I tried to muster the effort needed to stand up. I stared at the strange room and tried to remember how I had got there. My mind yielded nothing, days were missing. I tried to concentrate, but could not force back the memory. I was frightened and confused. I had lost time and events as if they had never occurred.

Bits and pieces came back to me. I remembered seeing a psychiatrist with George . . . arguing with family then . . . tied to the bed at city hospital, but nothing after that. My mouth and throat felt raw. What did they do to me? I gasped when I realized that I was naked and there were no clothes or anything else in the room. What are they going to do to me? I pulled at a door that didn't budge. I looked out the tiny thick window in the door, but saw no one within the narrow view it offered. My shouts bounced off the door as if they, too, were unable to leave the room. I walked over to the room's other window and gazed out at a walled courtyard, empty except for a heavily padded pole holding up a backboard and a basketball hoop. Panicked, I ran back to the door and yelled for someone, anyone to let me out. I kicked and pounded on the door.

"Help me, let me out of here. You . . . over here, come here. I'm in here . . . don't you hear me, can't you see me? You . . . stop, don't go. Just talk to me, tell me where I am. Come back. Open the door. Someone do something. I don't belong here, I didn't do anything. It's a mistake. Is anybody out there? Please."

I've got to figure out why I'm locked in here. Why am I being punished? I feel sick. This can't be. I must think . . . I can't think. Why won't someone talk to me? Why am I naked? Where are my clothes? I've got to do something. Are they watching me? Maybe it's a test. I can't take it in here. I need space to walk, to breathe. I'm suffocating in here . . . I'm going to die if I don't get out of this room. My throat's sore. I can't yell anymore. I need water. I can't just wait. They want me to yell. That's the test. They're watching to see what I'll do. They're trying to make me change, do what they want. I won't give in. They won't change me.

"Open this door. I demand my rights. You can't do this to me. I'll tear this room apart . . . I'll get you. You can't do this to me. Is there anyone there? You better listen."

"I'll be good."

"Please hear me."

Alone and isolated, me in the locked seclusion room; Mom and Dad trying to deal with the mystifying loss of a once promising son. We could have been worlds apart, but we were just in adjoining buildings facing our shared helplessness from different angles. Locked in that room, my family and I lost birthday twenty-three.

Waking stark naked in that tiny room was my hospital orientation. The heavy sedative drugs forced into me for my transfer from Newark City Hospital to Fair Oaks Hospital left me with only my imagination to make sense of what was taking place. My confused, frightened vacillation between anger and pleading would seem to be a normal gut reaction to such a bewildering situation, but I assume the hospital treatment team filtered their interpretations of my behavior through the formula they used to treat madness.

My panic and frantic reactions worsened my prospects of getting anyone to listen to me. The staff had a protocol to introduce the mental patient to his submissive role in the power hierarchy of the hospital. Locked in seclusion and heavily sedated, I fought with all of my might against giving in to the spirit-breaking power of the drugs. Each time a drug started wearing off and I again began demanding justice, fairness, a hearing, I would feel a brief surge of hope when the door opened, only to have it quickly dashed by the entrance of two dour attendants and the ominous presence of the nurse waiting in the doorway. The two attendants easily managed my ineffectual thrashing, and with her practiced professional calm, she stuck the needle in my butt and off I would go to a mindless space that I would never remember. It was my first lesson in a hospital curriculum designed to teach passive dependency through aversive training.

I recall looking through the tiny window in the door of the seclusion room at a fellow patient in his own, better appointed seclusion room across the hall. I could see that he had a larger window in his door and I saw him working on a jigsaw puzzle. His room had a bed and a table in it. I was envious. Why did he have more than me? Was I so threatening? No, more likely I was just another obnoxious nut who was being taught that he had no chance of winning this unequal battle.

Soon, I passed the point of being willing and able to force myself to abide by the principles of reason. I believe if someone had spoken with me before I reached that point, just listened to me and tried to understand without judging or commanding me to change, I could have responded. Compassion, warmth and understanding are effective. Some respectful conversation, some regard as a real person and I believe I would have avoided the more damaging treatments and shortened my hospital stay. Responding to "treatment," I withdrew to a place inside where I was inaccessible. I had begun to be fitted for my label: schizophrenia, paranoid type.

I am sorry my family suffered alone without any help in understanding the mystifying events that were occurring. My mother visited me during those first weeks I was in the seclusion room. I angrily lashed out at her. I could not understand why she was participating in my confinement. She could not grasp what the hospital was doing to me, and I could not see the pain behind the mask she was using to hide her emotions from me. She had to be calm and pleasant. "Don't upset him" were the instructions. Did they not understand how upsetting it is to have your mother act calm and unconcerned when you are fearful of losing the essence of your being? Each of us in our respective traps was ignorant of any options. I saw only her unwillingness to respond to what I was demanding. I vented my frustrations at her. She became the target of all of my accumulated childhood grievances. She had not given me a perfect life; therefore, she was not a good mother. My wish for an ideal father became my reality when I told her it was Dad who really understood me. The lowest of blows, to attribute caring and understanding to the one who was insensitive, while denying it to the one for whom it had powerful meaning.

For the next few months I fought all of their attempts to get me to change. At my meetings with hospital staff, they focused exclusively on changing my beliefs. They demanded that I acknowledge the irrationality of my beliefs. Each interview became an interrogation. It didn't matter to them what I believed, but rather they sought the relinquishment of my beliefs and an overt demonstration of my submission to their authority, as demonstrations of progress.

I was alone, afraid of everyone and everything. I sensed dark, inexplicable forces lurking everywhere, yet I was reluctant to communicate my fears. I needed to trust someone. But who? The doctor? My doctor followed the still-existing historic psychiatric practice of spirit-breaking.
Our doctor-patient sessions were conducted during morning rounds. The themes and interactions varied little and were always predictable. This stage of treatment would continue until I could demonstrate an absolute compliance to hospital authority that verified that my spirit had been broken.

"My boy, do you still think you are special? Show me your magic. Show me your ESP power."

Pausing to heighten the drama of his next words, looking pleased and self-satisfied, my doctor of the soul demanded, "I would really like to have more hair. Please be so kind as to grow hair on my head."

Dr. Diaz's challenges only occurred when he had his posse with him. They were a reliable audience, ready to laugh on cue when he turned to them with his familiar question, "Do you see any hair growing?" And turning again to me, "Show me your powers . . . grow hair on my head."

Rubbing his bald head, he would ask if anyone saw any new hair there and in response to a chorus of "no", he would signal his disappointment with raised eyebrows and a limp body posture. I tried a few times to explain ESP to my arrogant antagonist, but he was too enamored of his own theatrics to change the dialogue. I controlled my anger as I stared at him walking down the hall to apply his brand of therapy on another patient.

What did he see when he saw me? I felt as if he regarded me as less than the slimy left- behind trail of a slug.

Still, I persisted in holding out. If I gave in I would be destroyed. They would rob me of my soul and it would be as if I had never been born. The more they challenged my beliefs, the more emotional and antagonistic I became. They were teasing and laughing at me. I was powerless. I had nothing but the beliefs in my specialness to comfort me. I became less available to their reason and logic, and grander in my assertions and beliefs. I had to be endowed with such abilities for a spiritual mission. As the hospital staff became more aggressive and coercive, I fought against their "treatments" with the only means available to me, the willful and stubborn need to be self-defining. I countered their taunts by elevating my abilities. What began for me as simple psychic powers were metamorphosed in the hospital crucible – I was touched by God. Searching my mind for some explanation, something to make sense of the incomprehensible. I began to identify with Jesus Christ; I wondered if my persecution, like His, was a sign of my mission. Was I the new messiah? There had to be an explanation to make sense of these trials and ordeals.

Anger, whether justifiably appropriate or not, is considered belligerence in a psychiatric hospital. I imagine I was quite belligerent. I would like to think so. I was fighting for my life, my personhood. I could not give in and give up me. I took too long to recognize the rules of the game. Just be pleasant and answer the questions their way. Nobody cares what you believe. It's only a game, a job, a business. Who cares what you believe or what you feel. Tell them what they want to hear. Give in. Pay homage. Worship at their altar. It might have been easier if those inviolable rules had been explained to me and my family when I was admitted to the hospital.

The drugs drained me of the energy required to sustain my anger. Boredom and restlessness became my constant companions. My thinking and movements were slow, out of synch and clumsy. I read without absorbing the meaning of even the simplest stories or concepts. My mind and body seemed to be separate from my will, and my feelings were losing their intensity.

Although I was becoming more dull and compliant, and easier to control, I mechanically, almost rotely continued to hang onto my so-designated inappropriate beliefs. That ornery, stubborn refusal to say the "right" thing was what I would not give up. Looking back I see that self-defeating behavior, which got me the most radical and potentially damaging treatments, as necessary for me to maintain some tiny bit of self-respect. Those of us who have managed to recover from our treatments and experiences of madness, and whose lived lives have successfully refuted psychiatric predictions of dependent ineptitude, often find ourselves sharing our stories of impractical resistance . . . our cries for fairness, and our refusal to accept psychiatric pronouncements of what we must do and become. Our unwillingness to give up the fight to be in charge of our own lives was instrumental in sustaining the much-needed kernels of hope.

Less able to experience pleasure or joy, I needed to adapt to a controlled environment that was purposefully unstimulating. I had to deal with the excruciating boredom of the therapeutic hospital milieu. I became less able to hold onto a thought, connect events sequentially or summon facts from memory. Rationality was not one of my options.

I can only surmise from later reading the sparse progress notes in my hospital records that after a few months they gave up believing that the psychiatric drugs alone would work. I could not be medicated back to acceptable reality and the confinement was failing to curb my resistance. The drugs were wearing me down, but not working fast enough to satisfy the people in charge of my life. Most likely, in anticipation of the approaching expiration of the number of hospital days my medical insurance would cover they decided to move more quickly. Given that I had not progressed through the first treatment step, the breaking of the mental patient's spirit, they decided on a more powerful psychiatric intervention.

The next stop on the patient tour was electroshock and insulin coma treatments. I remember nothing of the electroshock treatments, and only learned of them when I had the opportunity on a future job to look at the summary of my hospitalization contained in my personnel file. Until reading in my file about the electroshock "treatment," I was only aware of the forty insulin coma treatments. I wondered if it was a mistake in my record since I had no recollection and it had never been discussed with me while I was in the hospital. Years later I found what psychiatrist Lothar Kalinowsky wrote: "Combined insulin and convulsive therapy has been used quite extensively and has become so much a routine in insulin units that a clear evaluation of insulin coma treatment alone has hardly ever been made since convulsive therapy became available."[10]

Prior to being hospitalized, I had never heard of insulin coma treatments or electroconvulsive therapy. My introduction to this treatment was what my mother told me during one of her visits. Too cheerily, she said, "Good news, the doctors gave you a complete physical, blood tests, everything . . . you're in perfect health."

Suddenly hopeful, I held my breath and waited for her to tell me when I would be released.

"They're going to give you a new treatment that will make you better and when they finish, you'll come home."

A few things were not explained to my mother and me about this new treatment – for example, what would forty insulin coma treatments do to me?

Like other families, mine was given a minimum of information. It was not necessary or useful to give me any information. I had no choice. To imagine thinking of this – the opportunity to be put into insulin-induced comas – as good news makes me wonder how my family could have been persuaded that such a procedure would be beneficial. What about the side effects, the potential brain damage, the memory loss and the risk of death? Was the insulin treatment described to them in the same glowing terms that once promoted the miraculous benefits of lobotomies?

Was my family carefully coached in what to expect? An ex-patient describes the too familiar manipulation of information one faces:

> There's one thing I want to tell you that my mother told me, when they came up to see me for the first time, after the first two weeks when I wasn't allowed visitors, the resident told my parents, 'Now Dorothy is getting shock. Now she's going to tell you she doesn't like it and that she doesn't want any more and that she wants you to take her out. Now this is perfectly normal. Everybody says that.' So my parents came in and I said, 'You know, mom, I'm getting shock and I really don't like it and I wish you would take me out,' and my mother went 'Good!' – just like they say when your baby learns to walk you say 'Great! That's exactly what's supposed to happen; the doctor told us it would.' She never thought to inquire, why does everybody who gets shock treatment not want any more? Why are you afraid of something you don't remember?[11]

A few years after my treatments were completed, insulin coma therapy was buried in psychiatry's version of a pauper graveyard – there to lie without a gravestone signifying its valuable contribution – like those other once heralded new magic bullet treatments for schizophrenia. Fortunately for me, when I became a mental patient, prefrontal lobotomies were no longer believed to be an effective procedure. Thorazine's entrance into the marketplace in the 1950s replaced the crude brain surgery known as lobotomies. But for the luck of timing, that I was first hospitalized in 1966, rather than several years earlier when lobotomies held sway, I might have joined the ranks of the unheard and unseen. Still better timing would have enabled me to avoid the damage and lost years resulting from the forty insulin coma treatments.

Being one of the treatment-resistant, rebellious, non-compliant irritants to the system's need for patients to be passive, I was chosen to become a member of the special elite group in the hospital, the insulin coma treatment group. Were my magical beliefs more dangerous than psychiatry's magical belief in the benefits of putting people into comas? How could physicians in 1966 have believed that depriving the brain of oxygen and randomly destroying brain cells was actually a viable treatment for schizophrenia?

Each weekday morning before breakfast we were herded into the grey surreal basement of the hospital, and directed to cot-like beds where we were injected with enough insulin to put us into comas. Accustomed as we were to the groggy effects of our other medications, and not fully awake, it just seemed as if we were going back to sleep. After we lost consciousness, our hands and feet were bound to prevent us from injuring ourselves. The purposeful destruction of our brain cells was far more acceptable than an accidental injury during the treatment.

Fear would suddenly appear at the end of the coma treatment when I was awakened into a semi-conscious state. I felt empty, my body a hollow shell without nerve pathways – set adrift and apart from my mind.

Panic! I can't move. Am I about to die? I can't completely open my eyes. I try to move. I cannot. A shadowy figure is near me, saying something. I am unable to understand what he is saying. The words become louder: "Swallow . . . drink up." He holds my head up and presses a straw between my lips. "Drink," he insists. I try . . . I must obey. With great effort I manage to get some liquid in my mouth. A sweet wetness trickles down my throat. I gag . . . I can't breathe. "Swallow it . . . swallow," is the incessant demand. I swallow and feel a bit more of my body coming to life. "Keep drinking," is the order. I try.

Starting to rouse, I squirm in the sweat-soaked sheets and weakly tug at the restraints. I search for something familiar to ease the panic. Immobile, awake in a nightmare, I cannot grasp who I am. I am barely me. I must finish drinking the sugar solution until the huge, bottomless container is empty. I am drowning in the liquid I drink. It is as if I am being pulled from my grave while gagging on fluid that is being poured into me. The presence of death feels as real as the voice pressuring me to drink the glucose back into my blood stream. I am tumbling into a vortex. I feel myself being pulled out by a stream of liquid . . . I hold on. I am bursting from liquid pouring and pouring and pouring down my throat. With absolute certainty I know that if I don't do something, if I do not fight, I will die. But for which side do I fight? I do not know whether life is drinking and awakening, or letting myself continue to fall to the bottom of the hole and ending this nightmare.

I struggle to free myself from the straps around my ankles and wrists, but the only reward for my efforts are the bruises whose origins I would later try to remember. I fight with all my strength. My observers see no fierce battle, merely the easily managed thrashings of an unruly child. A lifetime of tortuous indecision wavering between the poles of cooperation and rebellion, passivity and assertion, acceptance and challenge, were comically diminished in those battles. The unalterable fact was that I would only be untied when the liquid in the container was completely drained. The war, the life or death decisions were only waged in my mind. The outcome had already been determined and always mocked me in the same way.

Upon finally reaching full consciousness at the end of the morning treatment, I wait for the rest of the group to be untied. Next, we are herded into the showers for our second rude awakening. It is humiliating to have the attendant stand and supervise while we are hosed into consciousness. Once demeaning, after awhile the repeated treatments have drained the energy needed to elicit an emotional reaction to just another of the many dignity-squashing hospital routines.

Humiliation, associated with specific events, would fade with distance from the precipitating circumstances, but the feelings of powerlessness were ever-present and would stay with me for many years. An important element of my psyche was becoming inaccessible to me. As the treatment progressed I became more dull and zombie-like, experiencing occasional, uncontrollable onrushes of scattered emotions. The insulin treatments occurred five days a week for eight weeks.

Like most who have received shock treatments, I have only sparse memories of the experiences. Since the electroshock occurred while I was in an insulin coma, it is my imagination rather than the memory which makes me cringe at the thought of electrical current being forced through my brain to stimulate convulsive seizures. The ease with which medical practitioners can ignore evidence of damage from invasive cruel procedures makes me realize that anything can be justified or rationalized in the name of healing. Barbaric abuses in the treatment of those who have been labeled mentally ill have occurred throughout our history. A myth underpins the nothing-to-lose attitude which permits our western culture to approve almost any kind of psychiatric intervention: *Since the natural course of major mental illness (schizophrenia) is a progressively deteriorating, incurable life-long condition, any possible way of controlling its course is acceptable.*

Psychiatric survivors often confront memory deficits when trying to describe or understand what happened to them. Accounts of other first-hand experiences of electroshock are catalogued by shock survivor Leonard Roy Frank in his book *The History of Shock Treatment*. Seeing bits and pieces of our experiences described by others helps confirm the feelings we sense – that we have been violated. Seeing reminders of our suffering helps some of us reframe our experience from one of weakness, to bearing witness to the strength and courage we demonstrated in our survival. Above all, we are validated, able again to feel dignity and attain credibility by virtue of the experience we have shared with others.

Acclaimed author Janet Frame wrote of her experience with shock treatment in *Faces in the Water:*

> There is no escape. Soon it will be time for EST [electroshock treatment] . . . . Suddenly the inevitable cry or scream sounds from behind the closed doors which after a few minutes swing open and Molly or Goldie or Mrs. Gregg, convulsed and snorting, is wheeled out. I close my eyes tight as the bed passes me, yet I cannot escape seeing it, or the other beds where people are lying, perhaps heavily asleep, or whimperingly awake, their faces flushed, their eyes bloodshot. I can hear someone moaning and weeping; it is someone who has woken up in the wrong time and place, for I know that the treatment snatches these things from you, leaves you alone and blind in a nothingness of being and you try to fumble your way like a newborn animal to the flowing of first comforts; then you wake, small and frightened, and the tears keep falling in a grief you cannot name . . . .[12]

Another account of electroshock, under the heading "Let Him Feel It This Time:"

> Let me describe the most horrible experience of my life. I was injected with a muscle relaxant, while my mouth was plugged with a rubber tube to bite down on (so that I wouldn't bite my tongue), and an oxygen mask covered my face. Dr. Ames Fischer fitted the pieces of metal to my temples, and then he said in a sterile voice, 'Let him feel it

this time!' As the current went through my brain along with the rest of my body, I wanted to scream, but because of the muscle relaxant, I was paralyzed – I couldn't even close my eyes. I remember the next time that I was to have a treatment, I begged and begged, 'Please don't let me feel it this time!' I had fourteen of these treatments in the period of four months that I was detained on the fourth floor Acute Treatment Ward in Langley Porter.[13]

From Janet and Paul Gotkin's book, *Too Much Anger, Too Many Tears: A Personal Triumph Over Psychiatry:*[14]

I open my mouth and the scream surrounds me. My body a lurch and a scream of pain. I am impaled on a pain. A firecracker, pain and lights, burning, screaming, my bones and my flesh. I am on fire. Shorter than a second. The fragments of a bomb sear my body. Blue-white lights fiercer than God, going through me, my body, poor body, a contortion, a convulsion of ripping, searing. Pain incarnate. Branded. I cannot comprehend. Burning, burning, my fingers and toes, my limbs rigid with pain, stretched longer than the night. Shooting, shooting again, my body is charred. No breath. Hiroshima. The living dead . . .

At a point during my own series of coma treatments I began answering Dr. Diaz's questions in a more acceptable manner.

"No, I don't believe that I have special abilities."

"Yes, the medication is helping me."

"Yes, I understand that I have a mental illness – I am schizophrenic and I must take medication."

"No, I am not angry about being in the hospital."

"No, I no longer think I can sue the hospital."

He smiled and nodded his head appreciatively at my answers and my new attitude. Dr. Diaz saw clear evidence of a successful treatment outcome. The insulin treatments had reached critical mass for spirit breaking. My senses were dulled and large parts of my memory were inaccessible to me. I was becoming an automaton. He was impressed with my progress. I became a good hospital patient and acquired privileges. Docile and trustworthy, I had an unlocked room and after five months, my friends were permitted to visit me.

Elliott, Jack and Julian stood across from me in my room. We struggled to get a conversation going. They seemed even more nervous and ill at ease than I was. I couldn't think of anything to say. What could I say? We no longer shared any common experiences. My reflexes and thinking were excruciatingly slow. I was embarrassed to be seen in my forlorn, defeated condition. I had only one interest, one goal – to further my discharge prospects. All I noticed about them was that Elliott had lost a lot of weight.

They didn't take their coats off. A fragile voice gurgled up from a deeply buried place inside of me.

Please get me out of here . . . take me with you . . . do something . . . don't you see they're killing me.

I would not say it out loud. The game had become me. Appearance was everything. I won't look upset. I'm not agitated. I won't give anyone an excuse to put me back into seclusion, to stick more drug-filled needles into my butt and then have the series of shock treatments extended. I will be bland and harmless, a threat to no one. I was relieved that their visit was over quickly.

My friends had left. Too strong to control, the sadness and hurt swept over me. Despair momentarily overpowered the deadening effects of the drugs. I was unable to block out the rising pathos. Tears ran down my face. My body began to tremble and I fought for control. I had to find a place where staff would not notice me. I slumped into a chair before the TV at an angle such that those at the nursing station could not see my face. Crying in public is inappropriate.

The insulin shock coupled with the Thorazine and Stelazine did what the drugs alone could not accomplish. I was submissive. When I entered the hospital, I managed to salvage some pride by asserting myself. I was proud that the medical staff were disturbed by my lack of response to treatment. I believed that their failure to control me proved my capability and would lead to my discharge. Here was probably the most indisputable evidence of my poor judgment.

The hospitalized psychiatric patient is less of a person than a prisoner in the criminal justice system. If a prisoner screams in agony, his pain may be ignored, but the existence of the pain is not denied. When treated for madness, you have no credibility. There is no confusion for the prisoner: the crime demands punishment and it is not confused with treatment that is declared to be "for your own good" or claimed to make you feel better. The punishment for living in an altered state is covert and not acknowledged. Or as Janet Frame has written, "For your own good are persuasive words that will make a man agree to his own destruction." The best you can hope for as a hospitalized mental patient is favored pet status. Wagging your tail and licking the master's hand is good. Begging or barking too much signifies the need for more training. Good dogs have less trouble in a psychiatric institution and tend to be discharged more quickly.

Those in the insulin coma treatment group were required to participate in group therapy. It was a superficial group emphasizing the suppression of emotional material. You soon learned that group therapy was not therapeutic but rather a means of checking on your pathology. The less revealed, the better you were perceived. Sitting with my boredom in the group, I fought my restlessness and tried to look interested. The insulin comas were doing their job of slowing down everyone, suppressing psychic conflict as well as making us very uninteresting.

Our insulin coma group was special. We received preferential treatment and much attention. The specialness derived from our needing to be watched carefully to monitor the effects of the insulin and prevent us from spontaneously going into shock. Our mealtimes and diet were strictly regulated. We were ravenously hungry and needed to eat separately from the other hospital patients so that we could be served extra large portions of food and get snacks at regular intervals. Along with the snacks we were required to drink orange-flavored sugar water. As a result, for the first time in my life, I put on unwanted weight, most of which sought out my stomach. I went from 140 pounds to 170 pounds and my waist size increased from twenty-nine to thirty-four. My mind and body were becoming alien to me. My family said I looked healthy. I was beyond arguing the point.

Knowing that I was getting close to being discharged, I tried to be on my best behavior. Answer questions politely and correctly. Be as cheerful and pleasant as possible. Do not let anything get you too upset or too happy. It was easy to become an identity-less supplicant since I had lost my self-respect.

Many people taking the major tranquilizers do not like them. The drugs are promoted as anti-psychotic agents, but sedation continues to be the key "therapeutic" effect. Drugs from this group make the user uncomfortable, and often downright miserable. The discomfort and the odd behavioral manifestations associated with the drugs should not be dismissed as side effects. The numbing disinterest the taker feels is the primary effect of the drug on the mind and body. Common is a feeling of restlessness without the energy to discharge it. Depersonalization and a sense of standing outside oneself are often reported. Add libido loss, obesity and diabetes to the disempowerment associated with taking these drugs. When the Soviet Union existed in its most repressive incarnation, the major tranquilizers were considered to be very effective means for torturing and controlling political dissidents. Is it any wonder that there is so much resistance to taking these so-called anti-psychotic drugs? There is no danger of someone breaking into your house or mugging you to get money to support a Thorazine habit.

The toughest task I had during the last couple of weeks preceding discharge was to remain unemotional. I felt extremely sensitive and vulnerable, and was afraid of having an emotional outburst. I could go for long periods of time being dull and feeling nothing, but then periodically without warning, I would descend into a morbid sadness where everything seemed meaningless. At those times, the accumulation of months of helplessness, dependency and submission to the will of others left me with the sensibility of a small child. I could cry at the silliest, most trivial incident.

Although I had not been given a definite discharge date, it was apparent that I would be released when I completed the final week of the series of insulin comas. Just at that time I caught a common cold of the runny nose, sore throat variety, and I worried that the cold would prevent me from getting the two more insulin treatments to complete the series. I was devastated by the possible delay. I could not stop myself from responding to the onrush of emotions. Staff saw me crying, and this show of emotion made me a questionable risk. Could I be trusted? I needed to be observed in a more secure location. When I was told that the only space available was the seclusion room, my memories of that room caused me to become more upset. I pleaded with them to put me any place other than that seclusion room. No other observation room was available. The nurse promised me that it would be for one night and the door would not be locked. She could have told me anything. There is no obligation to tell the truth to the hospitalized mental patient. I had visions of beginning the whole hospital experience over again. I did my best to calm myself, to go along and play the hospital game. I went into the room without arguing. I stayed up all night watching to make sure that no one locked the door while I was sleeping.

Listening and staring at the door, I tried to sort out my thoughts. I could be made do anything in order to get out of that hospital. Had I lost my courage and integrity? I had no rights and the only way I could survive was to go along with their program completely. The next day they brought me back to my old room.

I asked about my impending discharge and whether my cold would prevent me from getting my last two comas. An eavesdropper overhearing the discussion could have assumed we were casually talking about dispensing two more aspirins. Don't worry, I was told, you already had them and your discharge is arranged. My relief was mixed with the fear that they would find out they had made a mistake and I would have to stay an extra week. I had been very carefully keeping track of my comas and how many were left before discharge. I had to believe I miscounted. I was confused. It must be a lapse in my memory. Actually, they had already arranged the discharge the week before and had settled the insurance bill with my parents. Our family's healthcare coverage for this hospitalization was about to end and without further insurance money, the hospital would have to consider the treatment complete.

I still am amazed that when one lies to the psychiatric patient the act is not judged negatively, but instead is justified as a necessary part of treatment. Ironically, those who are most sensitive and responsive to honest, genuine interactions find themselves humored and deceived in their quest for answers. Under the guise of protection, or more accurately, efficiency and convenience, honesty becomes irrelevant.

Once, a friend of mine told me about her close escape from becoming an involuntary psychiatric patient. Hers is a common story and although the players may be different, the scripts are frighteningly similar. After a serious suicide attempt, she was placed in a room at a general hospital with a round-the-clock nurse. She was expecting a friend to visit and wanted to call her to remind her to bring cigarettes. The nurse told her that there were no pay telephones in the hospital. My friend, a hospital social worker herself, knew there were available phones in the hospital and persisted in her request. Again it was denied. She began yelling and arguing with the nurse. She was very close to unwittingly bringing on the next intervention – restraints and sedation. Luckily for her, a resident physician passing by in the hall heard the commotion and went in to talk with her. When she explained what had happened, he gave her a cigarette and arranged for her to use the telephone. She was fortunate that someone gave her the respect and understanding needed to interrupt the spiraling process of disempowerment that occurs when one is denied even the simple truth.

Hospital patients learn that rules and regulations reign supreme. My reasons and logic could not stand up against the rules. When a rule is bent and adjusted to an individual's needs, is too much sacrificed? It is a wonderful acknowledgment of your personhood when a rule or regulation is made to fit you.

"But what will we do if everyone demands that the rules be bent?"

Seeing each person as a unique individual with differing needs is life-affirming. Why not listen and make independent context and person-based decisions?

"But I will be accused of unfairness, discrimination, prejudice. We must be consistent."

Recently I heard the above refrain while I was visiting a friend who was admitted to the crisis unit of one of New York's public hospitals, Capital District Psychiatric Center. My friend, a long-time and very effective activist for patients' rights, asked me to attend her treatment team meeting as her psychologist. The treatment team seemed to listen respectfully to what I said and appeared to ponder possibilities. However, when I suggested that she be allowed to go outside and get the sun and fresh air she repeatedly requested, the psychiatrist said no. She was uncooperative, and she would only be permitted outside privileges when her behavior met the standards established for her to earn that privilege. I suggested that maybe her behavior would improve if they made this special exception. The team leader countered my suggestion by pointing out that even if she were permitted to walk outside with an attendant by her side, they could not risk the possibility of her doing something outrageous or disruptive. I wondered out loud how shocking her behavior would be in the enclosed grounds of a state mental hospital.

As I left her that day, she asked the attendant for a cigarette. Although they were her own cigarettes that were being held for her, she was not given one. She was reminded that she knew the rules, one cigarette on the hour – she would have to wait fifteen more minutes. My friend leaned over to me and whispered in my ear, "Please don't leave yet, I'm scared."

Why couldn't she have a cigarette when she wanted one, when she needed one? They had a smoking room available. I suppose it's easier to regulate smoking on the hour. But does every smoker smoke on their time schedule? Arbitrary rules and control still dominate the transactions between staff and patients decades after my last hospitalization.

When will they learn that discrimination is not always the devil, and treating everyone the same is not the holiest of the mental health commandments? Following the rules is easier and more efficient. We can train rats to follow rules.

How well you follow hospital rules generally determines when you will be permitted to re-enter the community. My early rebelliousness resulted in extended stays in seclusion under heavy medication. My first excursions out of seclusion onto the ward were training trials. I was initially accompanied by Dwight, a large burly aide – no doubt his bulk and strength were desirable employment attributes. One evening we were watching TV when I innocently got up to change the channel. He moved quickly out of his chair and punched my shoulder. It didn't hurt much; the blow was just strong enough to let me know that I was required to ask permission to do anything, including leaving my seat – just another step in the rat's training.

After about seven months, the day of my discharge arrived. I shuffled into the office, physically demonstrating the hospital's successful transformation of anger, fear and defiance into apathetic compliance. My parents and I were to be interviewed and given instructions by the psychiatrist in charge of the insulin coma treatments. Ironically this man, who always seemed so amused by my quaint ideas, had appointed himself to be my outpatient therapist. I sank deeper into my chair, knowing full well I had no right to object to anything. Defeated and dejected, I was too weak to resist Dr. Diaz's recommendations. His mission was to convince us that I was an incurable schizophrenic. I was twenty-three years old when that prosecuting doctor, serving also as judge and jury, sentenced me to a life of, at best, controlled madness. With the smug certainty of a bookie, he told my family that my chances of making it without being hospitalized again were very slim. His medical orders were stated with an absolute authority that discouraged any challenge. Barely acknowledging my presence, he declared, "Your son will have to take medication for the rest of his life and should return to the hospital regularly for outpatient treatment. He should look for a job in a low pressure, low stress environment. He should make new friends and avoid seeing any of his old friends." Dr. Diaz was emphatic in alerting all of us to the chronic life-long course of my disease and explained how I would have to learn to live with my limitations.

My attention riveted on and could not get past, "make new friends." I was devastated, and fearful I would not be able to keep my old friends. I was ashamed, embarrassed, stigmatized. My already damaged self-image had plummeted to an unrecognizable depth. The heavy doses of Thorazine,

Stelazine and Artane made me feel like I was walking in slow motion under water. Dull-witted and slow, I was easily fatigued and constantly tired and sluggish. My memory was shot; I had nothing to offer people. In the poorest physical condition of my life, my ballooning weight had made me appear the clown in too small clothes which no longer fit. To say that I was feeling insecure about re-entering the world is a gross understatement. How was I to face my friends? How was I to explain what had become of me? Give up my old friends! I was sure they already had given up on me. And how did he expect me to make new friends? I needed all the support and acceptance I could get from my old social network. Perhaps Dr. Diaz realized that my old friends would not let me accept the finality of his verdict. I might become non-compliant.

Most disturbing was to hear him say that I would never be free of that oppressive hospital's control. To think of returning weekly to reveal any newly emerging hopes to my torturers was too much to keep suppressed, even in my quasi-comatose state. I wondered how this doctor could know so little about me. Did he have no comprehension of the condition I was in when he discharged me?

The hospital staff had trained me well enough to know that I should not say anything there. Later, when I asked my mother to let me find another therapist, she consented. I was surprised how easily my mother agreed with me. She, too, did not share the hospital's sense of accomplishment when they returned to her the shell of a once-promising son.

Chapter 4

The Personal Context of Recovery

Be always displeased at what thou art, if thou desirest to attain to what thou art not.
(St. Augustine)

The road back – to what? Recovery – from what? Was I sick? Am I cured? Is this the best it will get for me? I had to face the next step regardless of my lack of comprehension as to the what and why of the preceding steps.

In his book, *Beyond Culture*, anthropologist Edward Hall states that failure to fulfill one's potential can be one of the most devastating and damaging things to occur to a person. Hall continues, "A kind of gnawing emptiness, longing, frustration, and displaced anger takes over when this occurs. Whether the anger is turned inward on the self or outward toward others, dreadful destruction results."[15]

When I was discharged to my family in 1967, what we now look at as foundational principles of "recovery" from schizophrenia were outside the awareness and practice of mainstream mental health professionals. There was no plan, except drugs and maybe an attempt at some kind of psychotherapy. Stabilization and maintenance, not recovery, were the best possible outcomes. The development of a comprehensive community support system with its emphasis on rehabilitation would not be a treatment choice until the 1980s. Mental health professionals of the 1980s and 1990s proudly heralded advances and achievements wrought by their emphasis on recovery-based psychosocial programs. Yet I wonder if I was not fortunate in avoiding the price charged by many psychiatric rehabilitation programs – that is, living better with more supports, but in the bargain, always being a mental patient. My friend Rae Unzicker said to me, "I worked, because I had no choice. There were no psychosocial rehabilitation programs then, for which I am often grateful. I believe I still might be a mental patient if I'd had support for it."

Looking out the rear window of my dad's car as we rode off the

63

hospital grounds, I thought the parting images might elicit some pleasant feelings, but it would take much more to weaken resignation's governance of my emotions. I was confused and disoriented by the open spaces, the shifting light, the movement and the lack of predictability. Everything was fast and I was slow. The cars, the buildings, the people, they all seemed to disappear before I had the time to process and evaluate them. I was accustomed to living in predictable, slow-moving boredom. It was as if I had a hole in my perceptual organizing ability, like I was seeing things for the first time and not knowing how they formed meaningful patterns. I had to relearn useful habits that once had been automatic. It was too cold and too bright and I knew that I didn't belong anywhere as I bounced between two worlds. I was not scared, just uncomfortable and sad, very sad – and I felt dirty.

You're free . . . Free to do what? I had little energy. With big gaps in my memory, timid and fattened up on hospital starches, I was embarrassed by what I had become and uncomfortable alone or with people. I had lost too much of me. And I knew that the medical authorities could, at any time, again determine that I was incapable of taking care of myself. In fact, that was expected. I had a special name and label that could never be erased: paranoid schizophrenic.

When we entered my parents' apartment, I needed to be alone, away from their anxiety-generated happy talk. A bath was my escape and although I had always favored showers, I longed for the bath I hadn't taken in many years. I locked the bathroom door. I welcomed the power of being able to lock others out. I lay down in the bathtub, reached over to turn on the water and was startled by the shower spraying water in all directions. I grabbed the faucet, but only succeeded in drenching myself with too cold and then too hot water. The entire bathroom was getting wet. I tried to close the shower curtains, but in panic, pulled them down. My mother called out to see if I was okay. Yes, I was all right, I told her as I shut off the water, laid back in the wet, but empty bathtub, and to myself sobbed, *What will become of me?*

I had returned to my parents' home, an emotionally battered boy-man needing a safe place to gather strength and heal. The unhappy, intense, inwardly searching son had become a sluggish, dense dullard. Trained to be submissive, I felt the spunk, the challenge, the willingness to fight had been quieted. My parents had been frightened by the impulsive unpredictability of the confrontational son they had sent to the hospital, and although they were saddened by the lifeless son who had been returned to them, they wanted to believe progress had been made; above all, they needed to be hopeful.

One possibility held out some hope – psychotherapy. Again, cousin George was asked to be our expert consultant. I assume my parents had valued George's previous efforts and thought that he could recommend a good therapist. Mom and Dad were probably convinced that the hospital had saved my life. George, who had gone through many years of formal character analysis, was enamored of psychoanalysis. Unable to think of any local therapist capable of seeing such a difficult client, he recommended Dr. Robert Marcus, a psychiatrist in Manhattan.

Needing to go to Manhattan for therapy reminded my parents and me of the severity of my condition. I did feel some pride at thinking of myself as too challenging for any of the local New Jersey therapists. For me, New York had always been the city of important people, skyscrapers, money and excitement. On childhood visits to the city, I enjoyed the feelings of light-headed awe when I tilted my head back to look at the tops of the giant buildings. I was intrigued by the stimulation, fast pace and the freedom and opportunity of life in the big city. So often intimidated in handling life's little social interactions, I was surprisingly at ease and adaptive to the unexpressed laws of big city survival. Perhaps the hospital had not completely destroyed my drive to be special.

Dr. Marcus' office was across from Central Park in an upscale building with a proper doorman. Mom, Dad and I felt out of place. While we waited in his reception room, I wondered what you say to a high-powered New York psychiatrist. Surprisingly, a rather ordinary looking man stepped into the room and introduced himself. Instead of the sophisticated doctor I had expected stood a tall, pale and tired looking man who did not seem to pay much attention to his appearance. He had a friendly face. I was relieved, even a little hopeful. I thought he might be OK. Dr. Marcus interviewed me alone, then talked with my parents, and finally called all of us in together. I was willing to see him for therapy and my parents liked him, but Dr. Marcus said that I would need to be seen at least twice a week for an indeterminate number of years. We would not be able to afford his fee. As an alternative, he recommended a social worker, Mrs. Susan Warner, who would see me at a reduced rate. Dr. Marcus agreed to work as a consultant to her and supervise my medication.

It was a mistake for me to be in therapy with a woman. I needed a man to identify with and to have as a role model. Even in my emotionally battered condition I felt uneasy with the decision that was made for me. I wonder why Dr. Marcus, after meeting with all of us, lacked this insight.

The next week, when I went to Manhattan for my first appointment with Mrs. Warner, I was glad my parents had stayed home. At least I was capable of going to the city alone. Arriving early, I was disconcerted when Mrs. Warner answered the door bell herself. I saw a middle-aged, conservative-looking woman who must have worked at appearing bland and asexual. She told me that she was finishing her last appointment and would see me in a few minutes. I sat and waited in one of two straight-backed wooden chairs in a long and narrow foyer. From there I could see the door to her consulting room at the end of the hall. To the left was a large folding ornamental screen that blocked access to the other rooms. I wondered if the rest of the apartment was her living quarters. During the years that she worked with me, I never felt that it was permissible to ask personal questions of her.

At exactly my scheduled time, she emerged from her office and as she had no doubt done many times before, Mrs. Warner formally introduced herself and directed me to sit on a couch in front of double windows facing an antique writing desk. She sat in a stiffed-backed chair against the wall just to the left of the doorway (Later, during my studies to be a therapist, I learned that some therapists chose to sit in uncomfortable chairs to guard against falling asleep. I was probably one of those sleep-inducing clients). Mrs. Warner conveyed an air of professional distance which tapped into my feelings of being unworthy and inferior to her. I wondered how she could possibly understand who I was and the impact of my experiences. How could she help me? I knew that I had no choice. I had to believe. On the psychoanalyst's blank screen of her presentation, I projected the propriety and disinterest of my elementary school teachers. Later, during one of our therapy sessions, when she asked me what kind of fantasies I used during masturbation, I could not shake off the absurd incongruity. Did schoolmarmish Mrs. Warner really think I was capable of suppressing my need for privacy and opening my sexual imagination to the analytic judgment of a detached observer?

Trained in psychoanalysis, Mrs. Warner was committed to that one exclusive model of psychotherapy. Her style of therapy demanded cool, aloof detachment. But for me to trust anyone, warmth and understanding were required. At that point in my life I needed encouragement, support, advice and helpful suggestions. Her system dictated a treatment structure that required the patients to adjust, not the therapist. She was only comfortable treating me in the method she had learned, but I needed a guide, an understanding ally. I could not relax and let down my defenses with her.

Mrs. Warner's therapy model viewed the failure of therapy as a reflection of the patient's inadequacy or resistance. As this was my first experience of therapy, my ignorance precluded awareness that something better or different was possible. The feeling of helplessness – admitting to yourself and another that you are unable to help yourself – that accompanies the start of therapy is greatly magnified for the recently released hospital patient. At my initial session, when I saw that the couch had a padded headrest, I asked Mrs. Warner if I was supposed to lie down. Mrs. Warner, with unintended insensitivity, increased my feelings of insecurity, telling me that lying down was for patients who were able to free-associate and could benefit from formal psychoanalysis. Bludgeoning my fragile self-esteem a little more, she informed me that when my ego became strong enough, we would begin psychoanalysis. From this beginning I felt the hopelessness of the task that lay before me. I would require years of work in preparation to develop the ego strength to do the many years of the real work of psychoanalysis. I did not ask her to tell me how to live in the meantime – while I built up my ego. Then again, I thought, at least she won't tell me how to run my life. But I would later realize that although she would not tell me what to do directly, she would, subtly, inject her values into our therapy.

Too often, therapists ignore their patients' strongest feelings and attempt to squeeze them into rigid systems. Did my therapist have experience with people like me – other "schizophrenics"? Others who had had insulin coma treatments? What had been her clients' outcomes? Questions I could not pose then, but am curious about now. How many Mrs.Warners were treating my fellow travelers? I was unaware of other options. As the person most strongly affected I was the least capable of objecting to my treatment.

Many therapists have had the experience of being a client as part of their training. Based on their own therapy, one would expect more empathy towards what another goes through. Is the lack of genuine empathy a result of the formerly powerless wanting to forget their past feelings of helplessness once ascending to power? Could it be that their experience as clients granted the comfort of escape, of rationalization . . . "It's only part of my training?" Yet despite the shortcomings of mandated therapy it is better than current training practices. Today, there is movement away from therapists engaging in self-examination as part of their training. Best practices formulas and cookbook models for short-term treatments under-value self-understanding's importance in the protocols for effective treatments.

Now, I am able to see the many weaknesses of my psychotherapy. At the center of my being, I burned with rage at how I had been treated in the hospital. My therapist coolly reflected and interpreted my free associations and dreams. I was bitter from having my experiences and memories wrenched from me. My therapist wanted to explore my libidinal fixations. I was unable to cope with the insecurities, fears and embarrassments of day to day living, but that was not relevant to her treatment plan. What would happen to me when I became able to feel the depth of my anger and pain? Would I turn it inward against myself or strike out at others? Or would I be able to use the returning energy and emotion to learn and transform the experience – to sublimate it in service to others? If sublimation was Mrs. Warner's treatment goal, her route was much too long and circuitous. I had already lost too many years.

I dreaded going to my psychotherapy sessions. I couldn't think of things to say. My brain was convalescing, slowly recovering and perhaps compensating for the coma-inflicted damage by building new neural pathways. Mrs. Warner interpreted my silence as resistance. I suppose she did what she knew best. It was too bad for me that she lacked the creativity and imagination to adapt her inflexible system to my needs. Beneath her therapeutic facade I sometimes thought I saw brief glimmers of compassion.

As would be expected, I formed a transference relationship with my therapist. How could I not ascribe to her feelings that more appropriately belonged to my mother? To the psychoanalyst, transference is the catalyst for effecting healthy growth. It is a way of undoing or redoing unhealthy connections. The client transfers a mixture of unresolved needs, traumatic experiences and unconscious ambivalent feelings toward significant others to his therapist. Mrs. Warner was going to make me transfer to her, whether I liked it or not, whether it was good for me or not. As a result I had to break away from both my real mother and also a surrogate mother figure. One was smothering me with love, the other with analytic interpretations. I needed someone who could be open to feeling and empathizing with my pain. I needed the depth of understanding and unshakeable support that would allow me to risk reconnecting with hope and possibility. It hurts to allow yourself to be truly touched by the pain of the troubled, but it is an essential part of the healing growth process. To be able to trust someone to touch the delicate part inside of me that still remained intact required a special person. My therapist was not that person. A therapist cannot be "the therapist" for everyone. But the best therapists have great respect for their patients' strengths as well as their vulnerabilities; they are also aware of the limitations of their own skill and knowledge.

At my first appointment with Dr. Marcus for medication management, I complained about the drugs I was taking. He agreed to try me on lower doses and evaluate the outcome. Three months later, the next time we met, I told him that I was doing better with the lower doses of medication and that sometimes I even forgot to take them. He agreed to try to wean me off all medication. I think he realized that I had been gradually reducing them myself and that it would be better if he supervised the process. Six months after my discharge from the hospital I was completely free of medication. There was a slight increase in my energy level, but my thinking was still dull and my concentration poor.

Hopeful of a full return to my pre-hospital condition, I became obsessed with retrieving my memory and coming to an understanding of what had happened to me. I tried to discuss my feelings in therapy, but Mrs. Warner resisted adapting her therapy program to my expressed needs. She brought all topics back to analyzing my childhood experiences and role within the family. My participation in psychotherapy became an obligation in which I invested less and less energy. More important to me were my reflections on that pre-hospital summer, recollections imbued with glamour and grandeur. Maybe Mrs. Warner saw my attachment to idealized memories as harbingers of latent grandiosity. I desperately needed a way to overcome the dull and empty boredom, and hoped I could return to feeling intellectually sharp and capable. I believed I had a right to be angry. In my fight to ward off despair and persevere, anger and hope were my allies.

Socially, I was extremely awkward. Not being extroverted to begin with, I became more and more inwardly directed. I tried to reeducate myself in psychology, but nothing I read addressed my needs and concerns. The few authors who offered alternatives that challenged the dominant paradigm were too difficult to understand. Their discourses on theory were not relevant to my pressing need to understand and somehow integrate my experience so that I might restart my life. I needed people who could relate to my experience to demonstrate through their lived lives that it was not my destiny to exist in this constricted way. In 1967 there were no self-help groups for psychiatric survivors. Activists decrying the treatment they had been subjected to in mental institutions had not yet made their presence felt. The sparse body of literature written by former patients was hard to find. People who had been able to make it back after being "mentally ill" rarely disclosed their histories.

One inescapable fact followed me everywhere – you are a mental patient. How can you value yourself after being judged by society as too crazy to roam the streets unsupervised? My engagement with madness began with my attempt to separate and clarify my sense of self, to change my dependency on the approval of others. I had tried to allow myself to be considered crazy. Now I needed to prove myself sane. Regardless of the passage of time, accomplishments or personal growth, I believed that I would always be evaluated against the context of a *possible* future psychotic episode. Was it an indelible title, once affixed, always there to define and explain me?

Frequently I would run into people I remembered, but whose names I could not recall. No amount of mental effort enabled me to connect with how I knew them or what our relationship was like. Most troubling was not knowing who was or was not aware that I had been in a mental hospital. I did not know how to respond to old friends and acquaintances. Were strangers able to tell that I was a mental patient? More immediately, I had to deal with the problem of finding a job. How would I present myself in a job interview?

In the job search, my Masters degree in psychology was more of a handicap than a help. It gave an illusion of knowledge and competency that I did not possess.

Why, the prospective employer would want to know, do you want a job that is so far below the skills demonstrated by your academic degrees? All of my studies had prepared me to continue to be a psychology student. Even without my hospital experience and my debilitated condition, I was ill-prepared for the job market. Now, I viewed myself as weak, inadequate and confused. Most of the time I felt as if I was living without the requisite skills to pursue any goal of my choosing . . . even if I could think of one. The long-held dream of becoming a doctor of psychology seemed less possible than winning the lottery. My thoughts and emotions shifted inexplicably and seemed unrelated to situation or circumstance. Much of the time I was preoccupied with mental inventory-taking to determine if I was regaining my memory. The vision of a future with unlimited possibilities had come to a screeching halt.

Because my family innocently believed that I could get a job because of my education, I was supported by their optimism. I was very quiet around the house. I was very quiet everywhere. I had nothing to say and little that I thought would be of interest to anyone. I was doing nothing and had no enthusiasm for anything. Somehow my parents were able to disregard my disabled condition.

I went for several job interviews in computer programming, marketing and personnel, fields I knew nothing about and had no qualifications for. Yet I tried to believe that if I was hired I would learn what was needed. Being rejected was a relief. Not too far from the surface was the knowledge that I was too slow-witted to take on any learning challenges. But I remained conflicted about letting go of my own high expectations to excel. You're educated, you're bright, I would tell myself over and over as I approached the interviews. Meaningless, empty words; I couldn't pump myself up for a few minutes, let alone truly believe my self-propaganda. I hated the picture I knew I presented as a job applicant . . . nervous and unsure, gaps in my employment background, unable to carry a conversation and an inability to demonstrate any degree of enthusiasm. After repeated failures, I went to the state employment service. There, I was interviewed by Lenny, an old high school classmate. We talked about the days we used to play basketball on the playground. He told me what some of the people we both knew were doing, who was married, where some were living, what kind of work they did.

What did Lenny know about me? I was embarrassed. He must have noticed how odd I looked with my protruding belly and poorly fitted clothes. Did he wonder about my stiff movements and the funny look in my eyes? Who would he tell that he had seen me?

"Hey, you won't believe who I saw. Yeah, Bassman. Do you know what happened to him? He looks awful. He was looking for a job. I always wondered about him too. It figures, he was always kind of strange."

I went through the motions of explaining to Lenny what I had been doing for the last year of my life. On previous interviews I had made up stories to cover the gap in my resume. For one interview I had made the mistake of saying I had been in a mental hospital. I was applying for a computer analyst training job at New Jersey Blue Cross. Since I was insured by them, I thought that the company would have access to my health insurance records, so I admitted to having had a nervous breakdown. I thought the interviewer would move on to other questions, but she surprised me by asking what had caused the breakdown. How could I explain what I did not understand? I told her I had been in an auto accident in which my two best friends were killed. The shock and guilt had overwhelmed me and I became extremely depressed. I thought she would let the subject drop there, but she wanted to know more. As I made up details I realized she already had decided not to hire me and was just satisfying her curiosity. Perhaps I had some need to confess to having been a patient in the loony bin.

I gave a simpler account of the missing year to Lenny. I told him that I had used the time off to travel. He probably knew the truth. My military draft status was another issue that always came up at job interviews. I explained that my history of stomach ulcers gave me a 4-F classification. I hated lying; I always felt like I was doing something very wrong. Lenny suggested that I apply for a job at the Essex County Welfare Board.

In 1967 the Essex County Welfare Board was hiring just about anyone with a college degree. I was relieved to learn that the only requirement of the scheduled group interview was for the applicants to fill out a few basic employment forms and show proof of having a four-year college degree. I was hired one week later. My family had mixed feelings about my new job. The pay was poor and the status was low, but on a more practical level, everyone knew that I needed to be working. My mother was concerned about my safety working in impoverished areas of Newark but did not make a big issue out of it. Intuitively they knew that work was very important. Meaningful work would have to wait.

At the Welfare Board, a one-week job orientation was followed by the assignment of a sixty-client case load. It was a thirty-five-hour week, one half day in the office for paper work and supervision, and the remainder of the time spent in the field. I quickly learned that the typical caseworker spent about two hours a day in the field and called it quits. Some workers would just call in for messages in the morning and not go into the field to work at all on most days. It was a full-time job that could be managed easily part time.

I fell into the pattern of working about fifteen hours a week, but always with traces of guilt. Lacking the counseling skills and requisite practical knowledge did not prevent me from chastising myself for not providing more assistance to the welfare clients assigned to me. Though still groggy most of the time, I was nagged by the feeling that I should be doing more on the job. Years of lofty aspirations engendered a resistance to resigning my life to skating by as a minimally performing welfare worker.

When I first started working for the Welfare Board, I secretly envied my clients. I wanted to stay home as they did. I didn't want to have to deal with the world. I was jealous of their simple, seemingly pressure-free existence. Filled with my own struggles, I could not see their daily battles. Anything that was not me was appealing, and their hopelessness seemed oddly matched to my own. My ignorance and tunnel vision became frighteningly apparent one memorable day on the job.

Barely awake and in my usual inattentive state, I made my

customary phone call to the office to see if I had to do anything. If not, I was planning to go back to sleep for the rest of the morning. However, several supplemental checks to clients, requiring their signatures, needed to be personally delivered and were waiting for me at the office. I dressed quickly, had coffee, and planned on delivering the checks and then returning to bed. On my way, I stopped at the corner candy store for cigarettes and heard some news on the radio about minor disturbances between the police and residents of Newark's Central Ward. I heard it, but it didn't actually register until much later. I drove to the office and picked up the checks without stopping to talk to anyone. More people were in the office than usual, and conversation was more animated and intense, but I was in too much of a rush to listen to anything being said.

Riding down Springfield Avenue, I noticed that the street was overflowing with people. Far too many people for that time of day. There was electricity in the air, high spirits and laughter everywhere . . . like a street party. I saw people walking in and out of stores, not through doors but through shattered windows. Everyone was loaded with loot, carrying appliances, televisions, clothes and groceries. I kept driving. Several policemen stood around watching, almost as if they were there to direct pedestrian traffic. The first of the Newark riots had begun. I kept driving. I rode by, watching without comprehending what I was seeing. Intent on delivering my checks, I drove directly to my client's house with a full-scale riot happening around me.

The shocked look on my client's face when she opened the door and saw it was me was my first inkling of the magnitude of the situation. Asking me what I was doing there, she nervously looked over my shoulder while quickly pulling me through the doorway and into the living room. Overcoming her initial shock at seeing me, she signed the affidavit to receive her check. And then we sat in the eye of a riot, talking formally in our absurd caseworker/client relationship. She described the day's events and told me how she and the children had hid under their beds and listened in fear to the gunshots, the shattering glass and sirens. While we were talking, I heard raucous laughter and loud voices coming from the hallway. The teenagers who boisterously ran into the house carrying televisions and radios were stopped cold by her shouts to alert them, "The welfare man is here!"

I finally opened my eyes to what was happening, quickly excused myself and left, appropriately frightened as I drove away.

Everything considered, my job was good therapy for me. Despite my guilt and mixed feelings, my supervisor consistently praised my job performance. I was incredulous of positive evaluations in a job that rewarded mediocrity, but I knew that at times I did try to make a difference. It was common knowledge that the most dedicated workers were the ones who were most often in trouble at the Welfare Board. Not being able to risk losing the job was everyone's justification for sliding by with minimal effort. Like everyone else, I told myself that the course of least resistance made a person the most highly esteemed worker. Those caseworkers who tried to get a little more done, who challenged the system, were not the favorites of the welfare bureaucracy. Being new to the bureaucratic game, I came very close to getting burned the times I tried to do a little extra.

One such time, I responded to a call from a landlord claiming that my client had not paid her rent in three months. He threatened to evict her unless the current month's rent was paid. Ranting about his tenant's complete lack of responsibility, he wanted her rent to be paid directly by the Welfare Board. I explained that this could not be done, but I was willing to bend the rules by personally delivering the check to her when he was present. As arranged, I delivered the check to my client, but the landlord did not have enough money to cash it. We agreed that I would give the landlord a ride to his bank to get the necessary cash, and come back with him to settle the rent bill. When we returned, she met us out on the street in front of her residence, and as soon as he gave her the money minus the rent, they began shouting insults at each other. Suddenly my client, a hardy six-foot-tall woman, punched the face of her rather thin, diminutive five-foot landlord. He responded in kind and the two of them tumbled to the ground flailing away. A crowd gathered to cheer on the fight and chase the wind-blown money that had scattered during the fracas. I separated them just before the police arrived. The policemen chuckled in amusement as they listened to me tell of the afternoon's events. My supervisor did not find it humorous.

My job as a Welfare Board Caseworker was a convenient dead-end job with little gratification and the ever-present knowledge that I was functioning far below my potential. Much of the time I felt lost and aimless. The future looked bleak and I generally felt vulnerable. I was guarded about my past, and my lack of openness made social situations uncomfortable.

My friendship with Elliott kept me going. I was nurtured by his belief in me and his certainty that I would get better. He gently pushed, teased and cajoled me into being with him and doing something other than staying home. Without his support I would have had no access to any world beyond home and work. Elliott put himself squarely and solidly in front of the threatening onslaught of overpowering despair. We continued to share our gambling connection, but as much as he tried to get me out to meet people, my heart was not in it. I always felt like an outsider unable to react to an inside joke. Elliott patiently explained the obvious. His acceptance and lack of criticism prevented me from withdrawing and becoming housebound. But when we would visit old friends or new acquaintances, it was as if I wasn't there.

One night, only a few months after my release from the hospital, Elliott and I were hanging out with some friends we had known for many years. Elliott was off to the side talking with Isa and Linda when I realized that I was late taking my medication. Isa was interested in the pill bottle that she noticed me take out of my pocket. All three of them had begun moving past smoking pot and were starting to experiment with other substances. I told Isa that it was Thorazine. She asked me what it did, and I said I was supposed to take it and really didn't know if people got high from it. I gave one to each of them and didn't think much of it until I ran into Isa a few days later.

She said, "How do you stand that stuff? I slept for twelve hours straight and woke up more tired than I've ever been. Throw that shit away."

It was probably the best advice I received that year.

Gambling was, at the time, the only way I could socially interact as an equal. I looked forward to playing poker. It was stimulating, a safe way of socially relating, and it provided a sense of immediate accomplishment and reward when I won. A great part of gambling's appeal lies in the aliveness of the moment, the here-and-now action reflected in the kibitzing, the teasing, and the rivalry. Important were the affirmations of manhood, the macho message that permeated all the transactions and gave me the feeling of belonging. You had to take your chances and risks when you gambled: the higher the stakes, the greater the excitement. While I was gambling I could escape my problems for hours at a time; all that mattered was the immediacy of winning. The high of having a lucky night, when the cards fall right and you are able to control the game – it was a pleasant vacation. To one feeling so powerless, the promise of power inherent in winning made poker very important to me. Gambling also seemed to be connected with my pre-hospital summer. It was almost as if I could revive or remain close to the feelings I sought.

With Elliott there for me to lean on, I avoided social isolation, but often I felt the need to be alone and withdraw into myself. On weekends I took refuge in the anonymity of walking the streets of New York City. There, but not there, I walked and observed. Watching people and the quickly changing chance transactions diverted my mind from its search for insights that never surfaced. Always I was hopeful that a magical connection would be made and the light would come back into my eyes. Between the scenes I saw, my mind's ruminations were narrated by self-pity.

They look at me walking, but they don't see me. No one knows how much I try, how much I long to move outside myself, to open my senses and relate to the world. I will keep getting smaller and smaller until I disappear. No one cares . . . .

The little boy's high-pitched squeal of delight jolted me out of my private reverie. I turned to see a toddler soaking up his mother's loving attention. I was transfixed, unable to turn my gaze from their radiant beaming faces. I wanted to become the child, feel his feelings and innocence, to shed my baggage and start fresh.

Sensing an intrusion, Mother gathered the child to her. The sudden change deflated me, but I tried to force out a non-threatening smile. Mother's cold evaluative look made me retreat. Pushing on to look for new images, I walked more quickly and hoped her cautious, suspicious eyes would not stay with me for long. And so another weekend passed.

I was constantly searching for something or some way to change myself. Primarily I hoped that my psychotherapy would provide a means of change, but I increasingly became disillusioned. I listened to others talk of their therapy relationship and was jealous of their progress. Much as I had gnawing doubts about my therapist's competence, I more strongly questioned my own ability to evaluate her. Recognizing that she was not helping me, I alternated between blaming her and myself. I wanted very much to believe it was working, but knew that it was not.

I called cousin George to discuss the possibility of changing therapists. I had so thoroughly bought into being unable to make independent decisions that I thought I needed permission to make a change. George, who like my therapist was analytically trained, ascribed my difficulty to resistance and assured me that the therapy process takes time. I had over a year invested in my therapy and the anxiety of beginning anew convinced me to stay. It is difficult to admit to yourself that you are not being helped and that you have wasted all that time. I needed to believe in my therapist's ability.

The unequal nature of the therapy relationship gives the therapist an opportunity to misuse power. Most of the systems of psychotherapy have made it easier for the therapist to affix the responsibility and blame for failure on the patient. It takes specific abilities, skill, personality traits and experiences to coalesce into making a good therapist. You don't become a good psychotherapist by learning a system of psychotherapy, you simply become a competent technician. Warmth, compassion and willingness to reach out and step into another person's pain cannot be studied in the same way one learns mathematics.

George did not help me switch therapists, but he did give me an important lead on getting back into the field of psychology. As I look back, it amazes me how little I knew of my chosen profession. George explained that I needed a one-year clinical internship in order to work as a psychologist. The State of New Jersey offered such an internship along with a stipend for training within state psychiatric facilities. I applied and was accepted.

Concerns about memory gaps and social awkwardness were temporarily set aside to allow space for the resurrection of an old dream – to be a psychologist. I had been a seventeen-year-old high school senior when Mr. Green introduced me to the study of psychology. A short stubby man with a mustache, his wild grey-sprinkled curly hair imbued him with a charismatic presence that captivated me and my classmates. Mr. Green's melodious voice resonated with his boundless enthusiasm for the subject he taught. He had an unshakable belief in psychology's promise – how this field would change the way we understand the human condition. Leaning on his cane, Mr. Green, unlike my other teachers, walked between our desks, stopping to look at us as he spoke. His optimism was compelling. Here finally, I thought, was a class that could help me address my discomfort with myself. I could learn to understand me, learn what made me so anxious, learn what made me feel so different and unable to fit in. I saw the answer to what I would choose to study in college, but my career path to becoming a psychologist was not what Mr. Green or I could have envisioned.

I resigned from the Welfare Board and was pleasantly surprised by the reaction I received. My co-workers and supervisor seemed genuinely happy that I had the opportunity to begin a new career. Apparently I had been so self-absorbed in criticizing myself and being aware of my deficiencies that I had blocked out the progress I had made.

Chapter 5

Becoming a Psychologist

Education consists mainly in what we have unlearned.   (Mark Twain)

I was one year and eight months removed from my hospital discharge in September of 1967. Although clothed in hope and possibility, I still worried that others would see me performing my rhythm-less dance with anxiety and uncertainty. I felt reassured that I was now able to concentrate well enough to read with understanding and retain concepts. My mind was becoming more lively, more able to grasp and integrate new information; I felt more intellectually capable. My social skills and my interactions with people lagged behind. A little bit of a sense of humor was peeking out from my turtle-like self-protective stance. Yet, ever vigilant of having my secret discovered, I regarded myself as a fraud, only acceptable when I was able to hide my true self.

The psychology internship at Greystone Park Psychiatric Hospital represented a new beginning. What lay ahead was unknown, but I was hoping that when I passed through this new door, I could lock out the preceding nightmare forever. Troublesome questions shouted for attention. Should I take this risk and give up my easy job at the Welfare Board? How will I react? Will memories of my hospitalization interfere with my ability to work in a psychiatric hospital? Will I be able to perform the job duties expected of me? Will I be able to learn and remember as well as I once did? Can I control my fears? Ready or not, I had little choice but to try.

It was forty minutes into what I was told would be a forty-five minute ride when I saw the small discreet sign, Greystone Park Psychiatric Hospital. The road snaked its way through a landscape of verdant woods. I watched with wide-eyed alertness, anxiously looking for my first peek at the hospital.

The haunting, ominous looking buildings of Greystone were aptly represented by the lack of warmth in its name. Set on the sprawling grounds of a beautiful, rural area of Morris County, New Jersey, the brilliant colors of the flowers, the lush green grass and the open spaces contrasted sharply with the hulking, uninviting buildings. I passed grazing cows and a few milling people who seemed remarkably similar to the cows in their stolid, straight-ahead indifference to their surroundings. I mused at how the cows, sedate by nature, and the patients exuded an easy rapport in the sharing of their hospital grazing grounds. Later, I would be shocked to learn that some of those placid, stiff-gaited people had been lobotomized. I walked to the building that housed the psychology department. Once inside and walking down the long, pale green corridors, I became light-headed. I fought the urge to turn and run back out the door.

Dr. Birjandi, the director of the psychology department, greeted me warmly. In contrast to my cautious, reserved manner, she was vivacious and radiated vitality. While we talked, she answered phone calls, responded to various interruptions and returned to me without missing a beat. She apologized for the interruptions, but for me, any breaks from the scrutiny of the interview were a great relief. I was intimidated by this powerful woman who was capable of juggling half a dozen projects at once.

The interview went smoothly. I was able to conceal my background without tripping over my explanations. Although my discomfort seemed to go unnoticed, Dr. Birjandi could not have missed seeing my anxiety. She was too sharp; indeed, her intelligence and perceptiveness impressed and frightened me. I knew that I could learn a great deal from her, but I was also afraid of her power to help or hurt me. Dr. Birjandi accepted me as a psychology intern and I felt the pressure attendant upon this opportunity. I had to succeed.

From the start, I set about the task of pretending to know what I was doing while frantically trying to learn everything I could. Despite my academic credentials, I lacked adequate preparation to undertake the internship. If I had indeed learned anything of utility in my Master's program, it had been forgotten. I was beginning from scratch.

Driving to the hospital for my first day on the job, I battled my insecurities. I was sure everyone would see my nervousness; I was on the edge of panic. Once at the hospital, I controlled and hid my fears by asking a lot of questions. Two hours into the morning, a moment of truth arrived – it was time to go onto the patient wards. My heart pounded, my stomach became queasy. I tried to ignore the nausea and make my face expressionless.

As we climbed the stairs, Dr. Birjandi talked about the ward we were visiting, what patients were there, whom to notify when coming to see a patient on the ward, and how this particular ward fit into the overall hospital structure. Although it was only one flight of stairs, I was breathing heavily by the time we reached the landing. I tried to keep her from noticing. Maybe she would just regard my uneasiness as new intern anxiety, but I worried that she might see beyond that and discover my damaged psyche. I was consumed with hiding my weaknesses. Dr. Birjandi took a large imposing set of keys from her purse and unlocked the ward door. Stepping across the invisible threshold, I was momentarily suspended in both worlds, and belonging to neither. Feeling weak-kneed and vulnerable, I fought to steel myself, to push down my conditioned responses to the locked door and the watchful attendants and nurses. Most of all, I was frightened of being unmasked by the patients. They would recognize me as one of their own, point their fingers at me and let my secret out . . . he's a patient pretending to be a professional.

As soon as we walked on the ward, Dr. Birjandi animatedly began engaging the patients we passed in the hall. With her drawing all the attention, I felt the pressure ease. Watching her very closely, I tried to follow her lead. My bright cheerful "hello's" and "how are you's" sounded hollow to me but seemed to fit well with the rest of the surreal theater of the ward. That day's fears diminished; I had passed the first test, but it was many years before I gave up my fear of being discovered and re-confined on the other side of that locked door.

During those first few weeks, I gave myself many pep talks. I encouraged myself with the idea that I could understand more than someone who had never experienced psychosis, that I was in touch with a special understanding not available to my colleagues. Although intellectually I believed in the possibility, I was not yet ready to draw on my experience. Many years of integration were needed before I could use the insights garnered from my journey into madness and my hospital experiences.

Fortunately, I began to get more comfortable. I seemed to fit as well as the other interns. The insecurities and learning goals we shared created a bond of camaraderie that drew us together. I began to realize that they did not know much more than I, and also discovered that my sensitivity could sometimes overcome the deficits in my technical knowledge. As my confidence increased, I obsessed less about memory gaps and focused more on what I was learning. My hopes and dreams of earning a doctorate in psychology reemerged. I was proud to tell people that I worked in a psychiatric hospital as a psychology intern. People's interest and curiosity about my work gave me something to talk about. Answering their questions defused some of my shyness.

Inwardly, little of substance had changed. I was learning new job and social skills, but my problems remained virtually the same. A false sense of adequacy was making it easier for me to keep my mask in place. New learning was filed in a walled-off intellectual domain and was not integrated with my emotional needs. Still unable to effectively separate from my family, I felt a sense of inadequacy hovering close by. An inordinate need to please (my mother and surrogates), my need to challenge authority, my need to be different-special-great, and my fear of another mental breakdown were perpetually present, regardless of accomplishments. At core, a fine filter attuned to letting in and accepting only that which could be negatively interpreted seemed to envelop me. I had to change the pattern of the filter; instead, I was simply changing the experience that entered the filter. My psyche continued to be more receptive to the negative messages.

During the internship I developed an interest in sensitivity training and encounter groups. I discovered that I had a natural affinity for group therapy. My ability to tune into several people simultaneously was a boon to group work. This quality that contributed to my being labeled paranoid was a treasured ability for a group therapist. When paranoid, you are exquisitely, almost excruciatingly, sensitive to nuances of behavior. The sensitivity is real, but problems arise from the distorted interpretations of what is perceived. In leading or participating in groups, I could easily attend to the many individual and group vibrations. For me, vibrations, a catch word of the late 60s, had been a problem for years. I was picking up more information than people were consciously or purposefully transmitting, and when I reacted to it, I found myself responded to as if I was out of line. In groups where the goals are to be sensitive and tune in to the feelings of yourself and others, my reactions were validated. Groups gave me the permission to be real, to reveal things I couldn't say one-to-one. The group was a venue where a safe form of intimacy could be practiced without the responsibilities and demands of a full, ongoing relationship.

I read whatever I could about the sensitivity and encounter movement. The humanistic orientation was appealing and the promise of spectacular results in a short time appealed to me. I became increasingly resentful of the slow, deliberate pace of my own therapy. I learned of the therapeutic value of self-disclosure, modeling, touching, and the physical expression of emotion. I felt cheated by the detached analysis of my therapist.

Ironic that at the cutting edge of the new wave of progressive therapies that I was drawn to was the Esalen Institute. Learning of Esalen stirred memories of my pre-hospital summer when, during that whirlwind time, I was writing and audiotaping my philosophical and spiritual insights. At a party where I was talking about my new ideas, someone there suggested that I try to connect with Esalen Institute where they were exploring concepts similar to mine. With only the director's name, Michael Murphy, and an address of Big Sur California, I sent a package of my tapes and writings. In my naiveté, I did not know that Big Sur was a place and not an address. Often I have daydreamed of how my life could have been different if I had sent my material to the proper address. Would one of those humanistic therapists have understood what I was going through and invited me to study at Esalen? Could I have avoided being hospitalized and being labeled schizophrenic? Now, more importantly, I wish that I could see the material I sent and learn what I was thinking during that turbulent time. I wonder where that lost mail ended up and whether it was ever opened.

The growth-based human potential movement appealed to my need to circle back to a time when I was exploring other dimensions of my self. Enhancing the attraction of the new therapies were the lifestyles of the practitioners. The sexual freedom, colorful dress and rebellious attitudes toward societal norms attracted me. I wanted to participate in the promised here-and-now aliveness, the intimacy and unbridled optimism. Traditional psychology and psychiatry did not help me. Here was my chance to change, to grow, and in the process attack a mental health system that had wounded me.

I let my hair grow long, grew a mustache and attempted to identify with the counter-culture of 1968. I tried to be less concerned with fitting in. I began to revel in being colorful and drawing attention to myself. At the end of my six months at Greystone, I was getting looks of disbelief from the rest of the hospital staff. When challenged at the ward door, I enjoyed the reactions of the attendants when I showed them my keys. Letting myself be different was a significant step in my development, but it would once again prove to be a perilous path.

New Jersey's one-year psychology internship required six-month cycles in two different facilities. Finally comfortable working at Greystone, I did not want to shift work settings for the second half of my internship. I was uneasy with the recommendation for my new placement. The chosen site, Overbrook Psychiatric Hospital, was too close to where I had grown up, too reminiscent of all its nicknames – the Brook, the loony bin – and the various childhood taunts and teasing we used in my old neighborhood.

At Overbrook, the hospital buildings were closer together, more reflective of limited space than the larger, more expansive grounds of Greystone. I approached my interview at Overbrook with a very different attitude than six months previously at Greystone. The progress I had made and the assumption that the interview was merely a formality lessened the pressure. Perhaps it was my reluctance to leave Greystone that made me dress too casually for my interview, and refrain from getting my hair trimmed so as to look more presentable.

The chief psychologist, Mrs. Brunnel, appeared to be a little put off when she first saw me. She was less dynamic and more deliberate than I expected. I mistook the slow pace of her interviewing style for a lack of perceptiveness and I was not as guarded as usual. When she asked me if I had any special areas of interest in psychology, I revealed too much. At first I said that I was so new and inexperienced that I was still exploring and learning all I could. She pressed on, insisting that there must be something that piqued my curiosity. I bit the bait.

I talked about parapsychology and the new research studies of extraordinary phenomena at Duke University. Actually, I had only read one article and was reaching for some topic to discuss. I told her about my curiosity, about the heightened sensitivity of people who experienced paranoia and how it related to the tests of paranormal ability being researched at Duke. By her questions I guessed that she was interested in the subject, so I continued to speculate about possibilities. I didn't realize that she was exercising her skill at diagnostic assessment. I mistakenly believed the interview had gone smoothly.

The next week Dr. Keen, the director of the state intern program, called to set up a meeting with me. I was stunned when he told me that Mrs. Brunnel had grave reservations about accepting me as an intern at Overbrook. Her stated reason: As an intern I would be expected to assess and treat teenagers, work which would be compromised by my rebellious and adolescent-like look and what appeared to be a counter-culture affiliation. She also expressed questions about my stability and vulnerability, given my interest in paranormal phenomena. Dr Keen, who liked me, tried to soft pedal the negative critique. Despite his reassurance, I was frightened. Was it really so easy for someone to see through my facade in one interview? Dr. Keen told me that if I still wanted to go to Overbrook he would arrange another interview to clear up the confusion. He suggested that by cutting my hair and dressing conservatively, I could satisfy her. And if not, there was an opening in another hospital in the southern part of the state. He also suggested that I consider availing myself of the unique learning experiences that come from working with the difficult prison population in a corrections facility.

I was upset and hurt by how easily Mrs. Brunnel had tricked me into letting my guard down and revealing too much of myself. I became angry and wanted to prove her wrong. She joined the list of women whose perceptions I had to change. Instead of accepting placement in another similar hospital, I chose to finish my internship at Bordentown, a maximum security correctional facility. Bordentown was the last stop in New Jersey's correctional system before the young offender "graduated" to state prison. The population was males between the ages of sixteen and twenty-six.

I had chosen the tougher test. As soon as I parked my car and approached the main building, I recognized the folly of my decision and wondered why I consistently did this to myself – made everything harder than it needed to be. This was no place for the timid. Guards in uniforms, bars, the air thick with suspicion and tension; I felt like I had to wear protective hip boots to wade into this bad dream. I cursed myself for being afraid. I cursed myself for the stupid compulsion to prove my courage. I wished that I could just let myself choose the easy way once in a while.

During my job interview at Bordentown, I was matter-of-factly told that my appearance would cause me problems. I did not take it as a personal criticism, but as a reality of working in a prison. I was told that long hair was an open invitation to be taunted by the inmates about your sexual preferences. The inmates were constantly fishing for a weakness, and any difference in appearance or manner was used as ammunition. I heeded the good advice; everything went but my mustache. Possessing less than six months of self-confidence, I elected to see if that meager foundation would survive the rigorous test that lay ahead. Once there, I quickly saw the inmates' adroitness at zeroing in on anything that could be used to heckle and manipulate staff.

I had to learn the prison rules for behavior. Advantage and leverage were sought in what ever way they could be gained, with fear and intimidation being the dominant methods. Everyone had their antennas attuned to weakness, or what could be turned into a weakness. Maybe you need to be helpful, or want people to like you or need to have people think you're fair – your personal proclivities were excellent entrances; nice guy, tough guy, friend, hero, or a need for love, gratitude, respect – whatever the need or value, it is the inmates' profession to find you out. They are experts who have studied, polished and perfected the art of manipulation. After initially being conned like any other rookie, I learned the essential rules of the game. My adaptability was gratifying. I was passing the test. Surviving and flourishing in such a threatening environment lifted my confidence. Yet underneath, the fear of being discovered and exposed as a fraud remained solidly entrenched.

A strong need to test myself and overcome challenges was ever-present. Each challenge I overcame enabled me to put greater distance between me and the hopelessness of my diagnosis and prognosis. Functioning in difficult situations reinforced my feelings of strength, but I was pushing too hard and too fast.

During the second half of the internship, my interests continued to shift. No longer were my goals exclusively centered on becoming strong, cool or tough. Consciously, I was beginning to value sensitivity and the expression of emotion. Intellectually, I could accept that it was alright for me to feel deeply, to be sensitive to pain within myself and others. At a deeper level, I had not given up my ideal image of being the strong male, stoic and brave in all situations. The new here-and-now therapies emphasized the guts it took to be real and let down your guard. Ironically, I strived to be open without being able to reveal or talk about the most significant event in my life.

The nagging anxiety that hovered around my secret became fear when I saw Harvey waiting in line outside the professional offices for his six-month classification review.

Harvey and I, not quite friends, had traveled in similar social circles and grown up in Newark knowing the same people. He had become heavily addicted to heroin and was serving time for the numerous burglaries he had committed to support his habit. I was sure he knew about my psychiatric history.

As soon as I saw him, I hurried back into my office and shut the door. I needed time to think. Even if he hadn't seen me just then, I knew that I wouldn't be able to avoid him for the next four months. I reached inside for as much courage as I could summon, dressed myself in an attitude of confident authority and walked over to talk with him. I inwardly cringed when I saw his face light up in recognition. So adept in scheming, Harvey had to be plotting his next move while we traded amenities.

My new supervisor, Paul, had a light, easy demeanor and whenever I sought advice he was available and helpful. Unlike in my relationship with Dr. Birjandi, with Paul I did not feel I had to guard against revealing weakness or pathology. I needed to know how to deal with the potential problems Harvey could create, so I struggled with how much to reveal to my supervisor.

I told Paul that one of the inmates was a childhood friend and that I expected him to try to manipulate me into doing some favors for him. I asked him how he would handle it. Paul was supportive, but I wondered how he would react to what I had not told him, that is, if Harvey started telling everyone that I had been in the loony bin. My mind raced with imagined scenes of merciless ridicule when the inmates added their newly created names to the many ways of calling me nuts.

Predictably, the very next day, Harvey had concocted a reason to request an interview with me. After some small talk about the old neighborhood, and whatever happened to so and so, he asked me to bring him some pot. I had worked there long enough to understand that it wasn't necessarily the pot he wanted, but to test me, to see how far he could push me. Harvey wanted to have me in his pocket. I refused and it worked. When Harvey's ploy failed, I was surprised that he just let it go. Why he didn't pursue it further is a mystery to me. But for the remainder of my internship, Harvey's presence was a threat. I knew that I was one small step away from being discovered.

Everything was going better than I had dared to expect. I still had dead spots in my memory, but essentially my mental acuity had returned. The unique world of prison life, the anecdotes shared with new co-workers, broadened my life experience and gave me some interesting material to bring up in conversations. Seeing others show interest in what I had to say encouraged me to be a little more outgoing. I was gaining confidence in my ability to think and reason, but in social situations my shortcomings were most apparent. Small talk was difficult; heavy, serious conversation I could handle and enjoy, but casual conversations remained awkward.

I had a public life and a private life. The person I let others see was the bright, quick learner with a dry sense of humor who cared about people. The private person was fragile, hid his insecurities, and dwelled on his inadequacies and failures. I was ashamed of my past and felt dishonest about never revealing my secret self – who I really was and how I truly felt.

Self-protection clashed with my need to connect with people. I fought the inclinations to be guarded and closed. Sometimes opening too wide, sometimes closing up too tightly, I could not find a balance. My spontaneity always suffered. When too open, I became impulsive, when closed, my silence made me appear sullen. Desperately wanting friends, to share, relate and touch, I fought a continuous struggle with my defensiveness.

Upon completing my internship I faced the prospect of seeking full-time employment as a psychologist. Unlike my previous job hunt, this time I knew what I wanted and was prepared for the position I sought. I was offered a job at both of my internship placements, Greystone and Bordentown. I chose the former. Prison work was too nerve-wracking and I felt a kind of calling to work with people confined in a mental hospital.

My job as a staff psychologist at Greystone Park began in February of 1969. Richard Nixon was the newly elected president of the United States. The country was severely polarized by the Vietnam War. Young people were revolting against the established order. Outlandish behavior was stretching society to its limits and in six months a sea of young people would gather at Woodstock, New York for a rock and roll concert that would become a defining event for the 60s generation.

My psychotherapy was going nowhere. I wondered if Mrs. Warner cared at all about anything that happened to me. Was I any different than anyone else who came to see her? Did she think of me at all after our sessions or was I only 6:15 to 7:05 every Tuesday and Thursday? She gave me virtually no feedback; I needed a lot. Whether she intended it or not, I perceived only criticism from her. Instead of feeling connected in a trusting therapeutic relationship, I felt like I was reporting to my parole officer. It was farcical the way she tried to be non-judgmental, to not give me advice. It would have been OK for her to give me her opinion or be critical, but not while presenting herself in that impossible role of unbiased observer. Her dishonesty was returned in kind: I held back, I didn't tell her things that I thought would evoke her implicit disapproval.

Now, I believe that it is the therapist who breaks the rules, the one who moves beyond his or her model system, who is most effective. I have often heard people say that they made the greatest progress when their therapist reached out to them in an unexpected way, when some boundary was broached and some non-exploitative personal human contact was made. Too much is made of the importance of inflexible boundaries that do not take context into consideration.

When I was an intern at Bordentown I needed to get up at 6 a.m. to drive sixty miles to work. Two days a week, after work, I would drive to Manhattan for my therapy sessions. The additional thirty miles made it a tense one-way drive of ninety miles into New York City. I would leave work at 4 p.m. to drive to the city for a 6:15 appointment. If traffic wasn't heavy, I would arrive at about 5:45, in time for a quick couple of slices of pizza for dinner. My frustration at her depersonalized approach to me reached its limit one night after a particularly tough drive. A snowstorm had caused a traffic delay at the Lincoln Tunnel and added an extra hour to the ride. I did not reach Mrs. Warner's office until all but five minutes of our scheduled appointment had expired. She saw me for those five minutes without extending my session at all. Having worked as a therapist, I understand scheduling problems. Perhaps if we had had a stronger relationship it would have been a minor issue, but I thought a three-hour drive, the snowstorm and being late only once in two years warranted some special consideration. I saw it as another instance of her lack of caring and unwillingness to bend. She made it easy to collect grievances.

My therapy thus continued to confound me. My attitude toward therapy seemed to parallel the attitude I had had toward school. The interest and commitment of teachers and therapists always fell short of what I needed.

Shortly after I began full-time work at Greystone I made plans to move into my own apartment. I'd been living in my parents' three-room apartment with very little privacy. Yet, Mom became upset when I told her I was moving out. She acted as if I had betrayed and deserted her. In her belief system, a son moves out to marry or to be a bum. My brother followed the rules. He was twenty-seven when he married and left our parents' home for the first time. Moving into my own apartment was a big event for me. Finally, I would be independent.

Supporting myself on a limited income and paying for twice-weekly therapy sessions made money very tight. Shortly after I had begun working, my therapist had raised her fee. Later, when I told her I was going to move into my own apartment, she told me she was going to again raise my therapy fee. The implication was that if I could afford my own apartment, I could pay a higher fee. I was stunned. I thought we had been working on my becoming more independent. My salary was roughly about the same amount that I had been making as a Welfare worker. When I objected to her intended increase, she reminded me that I was paying a reduced rate for therapy. That reduced rate was a sore spot for both of us. It seemed like the only times I saw her at all energized was during our discussions of fees. I worried that I would always be operating at my budget's limit since she would raise my fee anytime I earned a raise. I felt strangled by the prospect of a lifetime in therapy without ever having any discretionary money to spend. We went over my finances and she insisted there were more corners I could cut to save money. After an entire session in which we did nothing but go over my budget and talk about a proposed raise in fee, I seethed in anger on my ride home. Frustrated, I made out my budget in minute detail with a thick-stroked black magic marker and mailed it to her. Something must have clicked; she began my next session by agreeing that I could not afford a higher rate right then, but added that when my finances changed, she would increase her fee accordingly. Her pressuring me about money became another impediment to our relationship. I could not get beyond the subtle message that I was somehow cheating her. If you are going to charge people a reduced fee, it is important to let them keep their dignity, rather than undermining your clients' pride and self-esteem with constant reminders of your charitable generosity.

(Much later, when I established my own psychotherapy practice, I made a vow to myself: If fees ever become so important to me that they influence my feelings toward my clients and how I conduct my therapy sessions, I will close my private practice.)

Still, I could not break away from my therapy. It would have been an admission that I had wasted all that time and money. I argued with myself, and convinced myself that I had improved. I speculated that she was deliberately provoking me, that it was really a therapeutic maneuver designed to get me angry enough to be assertive. I found all sorts of rationalizations for continuing with her. I was afraid to end therapy.

Upon my return to work at Greystone, I again let my hair grow long. The psychology department had expanded and split into two groups: humanistic/psychodynamic and behaviorist. The hospital was also in the midst of a scandal. Newspaper stories had exposed patient abuses involving prostitution and illegal drugs. The hospital was undergoing a reorganization and it seemed like all of the senior staff were vying for power. Dr. Birjandi was feeling the pressure. She appeared harder, more distant and impersonal than I had remembered her to be.

Once again I was energized by the excitement and challenge of what was happening around me. I blocked out my conflicts and at work I was able to focus my energy on learning and trying out new ideas. The increase in size of the psychology department had led to a kind of sibling rivalry among psychology staff – the mother being Dr. Birjandi. The competition resulted in each of us becoming involved in some creative projects. I began doing several groups with young, newly admitted patients. I received praise and encouragement for my work. Feeling more competent,

I again began to think of applying for admission into a doctoral psychology program, believing that my prospects for admission were enhanced by my work experience. I was putting distance between me and my mental patient identity. Not quite a fresh start, but I was finding my way back to a road with possibilities.

In 1969 at Greystone, and probably typical of other state psychiatric institutions, the roles of social worker, psychologist and psychiatrist were rigidly delineated. The psychiatrist had absolute power and responsibility for the patients. All decisions required his approval. The social worker was the right arm of the psychiatrist. Of the professionals on the hospital staff, social workers often had the most significant impact on the quality and course of the patients' hospital stays. The social worker was usually the one who made treatment and discharge possible. The most capable social workers had the psychiatrist's ear and knew the intricacies of the hospital and proclivities of staff. The social worker was seen as non-threatening and someone to work out the tedious planning and liaisons with families and other community placements.

The psychologist's Doctor-PhD title was perceived to be a threat to the established pecking order. The psychiatrists tried to keep the "greedy psychologists" from usurping their power. While the two camps fought for power, the social workers were unofficially responsible for the patients. Psychologists did their testing, conducted group and individual therapy, but only had limited impact on the patients' course of stay in the hospital. Psychologists at Greystone remained isolated from the main workings of the hospital, generally staying close to their department and having patients brought to them. They rarely went on the wards and were usually far removed from the daily lives of the patients.

The psychologist role began to change when behaviorism produced a new methodology that could be applied to patients in a hospital setting. Psychologists rode this new vehicle into the back wards and established behavior modification programs. These seemed to be an improvement but not as grand an intervention as hoped for and promoted. I had serious reservations about the behaviorists' rigid mechanical approach. I was alienated from a system predicated on reinforcement schedules, while ignoring feelings – a method that did not enhance human dignity. I did not have the intellectual concepts to challenge what appeared to be the new panacea, but I knew these artificial token economies left a lot to be desired. It felt wrong.

I was most intimidated by the psychiatrists at Greystone. Somehow,

I believed that they had some special knowledge which enabled them to peer deeply into human behavior and personality. Although I was afraid they would see through my act, more likely they did not see through anyone. The psychiatrists were too busy with their own charades. Many were inadequately prepared for their jobs and incapable of any other medical employment. I found them to be cold, unscrupulous, lazy and self-serving. It was not uncommon for them to take advantage of both patients and staff. The psychiatrists who had been there for many years had accumulated considerable dirt on each other. Maybe I make too big a leap by such sweeping indictments of psychiatrists and hospitals, but I don't think the conditions or staff predilections I encountered were unusual for that time period. Throughout the history of mental patient care, the public hospitals have served as training grounds where research is conducted, where reputations have been made and where basic human rights have been violated.

In the unlikely work setting I found myself in, I was thriving. Life was beginning to look good. I had a job I liked which also provided a source of learning. My confidence had increased. I was engaged in establishing relationships with people. The pursuit of a doctorate in psychology seemed to be a genuine possibility.

Too late I would realize that the good feelings were set precariously on a very fragile foundation. I needed more to time to understand and integrate my fledgling strengths and accomplishments. Underneath sat many years of insecurity. Shifting values needed clarification. I avoided thinking about my chronic fears and anxieties.

Chapter 6

Not A Straight Road

To dry one's eyes and laugh at a fall, And baffled get up and begin again.
(Robert Browning)

Pairs of opposites like freedom and order cease to be antagonistic at a higher level, the truly human level. Where love and compassion intervene, where there is real self-awareness, opposites are transcended. For E. F. Schumacher, it is not a matter of logic, but the main concern of existentialism, that experience must be admitted as evidence – and without experience there is no evidence.[16]

The denial of your experience, the assault on your beliefs and the repeated demands to accept your fate – that you are mentally ill – puts you in a war that you must fight to win. Once diagnosed with a major mental illness, you are told that you must learn to live with your mental illness. And because of your mental illness, outside experts will judge the acceptability of your experience, interpret what you feel, and profess to be more knowledgeable than you as to what is best for you.

Almost three years had passed since I was released from the hospital. Each day I surveyed my memory and searched for signs of improvement. Spotty as my memory was, I saw enough progress to be optimistic. I was understanding what I was reading without repeatedly pulling my attention back to reread sentences. My thinking was attracted to and stimulated by new ideas. Logical sequences were no longer mazes that tortured me with evidence of what I had lost. My hand tremors were becoming less evident. While playing sports, I began noticing that I had more energy and endurance. I had returned to my pre-hospital weight. I was even considering quitting cigarettes. Lost possibilities were reappearing. Yet, lurking rather than vanquished, the too familiar fears darted in and out of my consciousness.

I was pleased by my rudimentary but overestimated understanding of the politics that played out in my workplace. Greystone was going through another of its many reorganizations. Patients and personnel were being reshuffled to protect and benefit those in charge. The top administrators were each taking turns assuming the position of Medical Director just before they retired. It was a convenient way to beef up their pensions and avoid accountability before the newspaper reporters exposed the next breach of propriety and ethics. This old boys' network managed to stay one step ahead of the newest scandal by playing musical chairs with the leadership positions. I saw them as an odd fraternity of burnouts who opted to relinquish whatever dreams they may have once held in favor of safety and the power to rule the lives of those they regarded as helpless and hopeless.

The psychology department, housed in a small self-contained wing of the Reception building, had it its own haughty sense of identity, an *esprit de corps* based on self-assessed intellectual superiority. The psychologists believed that they were the best and the most unappreciated of the professionals working at the hospital. That theme was fostered and nurtured by the psychology department director, who was always fighting for recognition of the merits of herself and the rest of the psychology department.

Although I liked Dr. Birjandi and believed she liked me, I was ill at ease in her presence. Perceptive and knowledgeable, she probed every interaction as if all of life was part of a therapy session. Dr. Birjandi was a confusing person to me during an unstable time, another powerful woman from whom I needed approval and whom I didn't quite trust. I tried to adjust to the discomfort of dealing with women who exercised implied or explicit power over me. The deeper, more pressing concern was whether I would ever be able find a woman to love and who would love me back.

Intimacy was the next frontier. My dilemma: how do I build a full and genuine relationship? I was twenty-five years old and I desperately needed more than meaningless sexual liaisons. I wondered if I would ever get married and have children. Who would be able to accept me with all my baggage? How would I ever get by the insecurities and secrets? Would I ever shed my paranoid lack of trust in myself and others? Would I always be alone?

After I was released from the hospital my leisure activities and social interactions were almost exclusively limited to childhood friends. During my psychology internship I began cautious forays aimed at getting to know new people. I developed a comfortable rapport with Larry. He was a fellow intern who a year prior to his internship had worked at Greystone as a social worker. The experience we shared as interns and our similar goals led to a friendship. We played tennis together and began to socialize after work. He was a good-natured, former big-time college football player who was sensitive to people underestimating his intelligence – seeing him as just a large ex-jock. Married and having a young son, he drew my admiration with his stability. Like me, Larry dreamed of completing his studies for a doctorate. When we finished our internships, we both returned to work at Greystone and became closer.

During one of our lunches together, Larry told me that he would be starting a new job at Overbrook hospital, where he had completed the second six months of his internship. Mrs. Brunell, the chief psychologist, wanted him to come back and offered him a chance to earn more money. The incentive of higher salary and a shorter commute convinced him to change jobs. I felt bad that my friend was leaving but took advantage of the opportunity to ask him to do something that I had been thinking about.

"Larry, you know Sara pretty well, I've seen you talking to her. Do you think you can set up a way for me to meet her?"

He teased me a little, and then said, "I'll ask Sara and a couple of other social workers to go out to lunch with us. It'll be a good way for you to connect with her. What do you think?"

Four of us, Larry, two female social workers and me, were about to leave for lunch when we were approached by Salvador Maretti. Dr. Maretti, a psychiatric resident, invited himself along. We all looked at each other and acknowledged with rolled eyes our discomfort at not being able to exclude him. Dr. Maretti had a well-deserved reputation for his crude attempts to waylay and inappropriately touch women who worked at the hospital. On the way to lunch, he did his impersonation of an octopus, insisting upon squeezing between the two women in the backseat of Larry's compact car.

I was upset that Dr. Maretti's non-stop inane chatter made it difficult for anyone to get a word in, other than responding to him. Fortunately, shortly after we began eating, Dr. Maretti remembered that he had only ten minutes to get back to the hospital in time to testify at a court hearing. Hoping that he could get a ride, he insisted on paying the check for all five of us. By that time, we were fed up with his act and told him that we were going to finish our lunches. He ran out of the restaurant mumbling that he would hitchhike.

The laughter and joking about the image of Dr. Maretti hitchhiking relaxed me enough to talk and determine Sara's interest in me. Only when I was certain of a woman's interest could I relax my fear of rejection and move forward. Sara was twenty-three, two years younger than I. She had a vivacious, bubbly personality and lots of enthusiasm. I found Sara attractive and some of the experiences we had in common, like working on a job where both of us had our own versions of rumors and gossip, provided grist for conversation. I saw that Sara was interested in me, and it did not take long before we became lovers. Next, though, I needed to learn how to become a full participant in an intimate love relationship.

Like Sisyphus I pushed my way up the mountain, but for me, instead of the boulder, I pushed a label, a diagnosis that had the power to drain my strength and weaken my resolve. As I climbed the mountain I saw a world that was looking brighter each day and a promising future. I had a girlfriend, a job I liked, and a chance of getting my PhD, but underneath, pushing me back down the mountain was an unpredictable shroud called schizophrenia. As I felt better, my dreams expanded, yet a recurring doubt gnawed at me. I posed the question to my therapist: "What would prevent me from having another breakdown?"

I sought assurances, but instead Mrs. Warner pointed out signs to watch out for: "Over-confidence – thinking you can do anything – is a warning, something to carefully observe. Be alert for feeling too good about yourself or feeling exceptionally upbeat and energized . . . and of course sleeping problems."

I hated her over-cautious approach. Could I not feel good without worrying? Her answers suggested that the next episode was there, dormant and ready to spring if we were not watchful. Mrs. Warner's advice burrowed deeply into my psyche, and many years elapsed before I could automatically resist the urge to examine good feelings for hidden seeds of pathology.

My therapy certainly was not a haven of encouragement and support as I became increasingly impatient and distrustful of my therapist. Resentful of having to report my experiences to her, I saw her as an intruder who was constantly interfering with my life and goals. She did not share my excitement or interest. I felt criticism from her and I, in turn, found myself more and more critical of her. She was a risk-aversive authority figure with whom I could not identify.

In my sessions I revealed less and less. I fed my self-esteem by identifying with the freedom and idealism of the 60s. Whether I wanted to discuss the reshaping of a personal value or the discovery of an author that represented and articulated my evolving new beliefs, her lack of empathy was obvious to me. Always detached and striving for objectivity, she steadfastly adhered to her psychoanalytic training. I resented the way she smothered my enthusiasm.

And despite all my misgivings, I sought her approval. I needed to be liked . . . to be the "good boy" . . . to be the best . . . to make my mother proud. I had to win her over. The space within me reserved for approval was immense. How do you make Mother and your Therapist happy? My need to separate from each of them had to be resolved.

Perhaps my therapist was aware that I had stepped into a new transition. Maybe she saw it as a harbinger of the familiar regression expected of schizophrenics after a period of remission. Whether it was regression or progression, there was an interrupted developmental process I had to move through. Again, unaware of my destination and without enough preparation, I would find myself in the raging, uncharted waters of another altered state.

Vibrating in the rhythm of life, relishing those precious moments of immediacy when I was able to open the windows of perception, to breathe – letting out the stale experience, tasting the fresh air of possibility, I exalted in those inspiring feelings of wakefulness. The spontaneity, the intuition, the lack of inhibition, and the energy were coming back. I would not restrain my excitement. Still not having learned to exercise discipline, I abandoned caution.

I embraced the new surge of energy I felt and fantasized about future possibilities. I can only speculate on what was the catalyst. Perhaps like someone recovering from the flu after feeling so bad, the return of health and energy, by contrast, makes you feel euphoric. Or put another way, why do you bang your head against the wall? Because it feels so good when you stop. Should I have known that my renewed glimpse at the hero's quest would be seen as the return of madness? I misjudged the extent of my freedom.

Elliott might have been able to warn and protect me, but he had moved to Los Angeles the year before. Exuberance made me repeat the same mistakes. I revealed too much to my family and to my girlfriend Sara.

One night while I was driving Sara home, I told her about having been an inpatient in a psychiatric hospital. Why? Maybe I saw that we were getting more deeply involved with each other and needed to see how she would react. Maybe I thought it was better for me to tell her than to have her find out in another way. The secret was weighing me down. She quietly listened, asked a few questions and thanked me for telling her. Sara said it didn't matter, but she was not ready to deal with that level of openness. Our relationship began to subtly change.

How could I expect her to understand when the many layers of me were yet to be integrated? My struggle to define my identity was a barely started, dynamic process complicated by a lack of my own understanding of my encounter with madness and my psychiatric treatment.

Often I have looked back at this period of time and think about how things could have been different. I think of what I could have done to protect myself. I think of what my family could have done differently and how an enlightened mental health system could have provided support. What if I had been advised by a savvy support group of ex-patients, psychiatric survivors who had been through the experience and had learned how to swim in the rough waters of altered states and developmental crises, who had also learned how to avoid triggering the most negative knee-jerk reactions of families and their armies of professional mental health soldiers. Maybe those psychiatric survivors could have convinced me of the folly and more importantly, the consequences of proselytizing to loved ones when you are struggling with new and unpredictable changes.

I was trying to live and project a new self-image before the changes were processed and integrated. Throughout my life, I viewed myself dialectically, in a strong-weak fashion. Buried in the weakness was strength, but always under the dominion of fear – a fear that I was at core fragile. As a consequence, my new self-confidence, colored by wishes and fantasy, led to a paradoxically greater and lesser connection with the world. I performed better at work and socially, but lacked grounding. Without roots, I flew off in all directions, excited equally about everything and rejecting whatever did not enhance my self-perception. The eccentricity and creative spontaneity of my behavior was once again reinforced by people's reactions to me. The more outlandishly I acted, the more interest people showed in me. I fed on it and I became more self-possessed, less in touch, and more unwilling to bend to others' demands.

My family saw dangerous changes in me. It was happening again: He's not sleeping, he's too excited, too boisterous, too unconcerned about our opinions. Playing on my girlfriend Sara's doubts, they pulled her into their plan. Convinced I needed help, they were determined to convince me that I was becoming mentally ill.

Tired from several nights of interrupted sleep and unaware of my family's strategy meetings, I decided to take the next day off from work, sleep late, and change my regular therapy appointment that week from Thursday to Friday. I didn't know that my family and Sara had talked about the alarming changes in my behavior, and also had called my therapist.

Once the process started, it moved very quickly.

I agreed to Sara's request to accompany me to my appointment to meet Mrs. Warner. Without realizing it, I was setting the stage for an alliance between Sara and my therapist. First my mother and now my therapist-mother – was this meeting uniting the three of them into "Giant Mother" from whom I could never separate?

Riding into the city I felt as if something extraordinary was about to occur. It was both exhilarating and frightening. Listening and watching, I was like an animal in the wild who was on high alert, sniffing the wind for signs. Once in Manhattan, the over-stimulation of what I saw – all the people and mini-dramas – began to overwhelm me. The magnitude and intensity of the city's energy assaulted and flooded my senses. The boundaries between my internal world and the external world of people and objects were disintegrating. Out of sync, isolated, I was trapped in a time-space warp, feeling I knew things that others were denying, but having no control over the unfolding events.

I tried to explain to Sara what I was experiencing, but I could see that I was only pushing her further way. She tried to redirect our conversation to neutral topics, but I always brought it back to the disjointed hypotheses I used to explain what I perceived and she did not. By the time we reached Mrs. Warner's office, Sara was having a hard time hiding the incredulity with which she regarded me. She asked if she could talk to Mrs. Warner alone. Foolishly, I agreed, thinking by showing I trusted her, she would be reassured. I waited for her in a part of the apartment I had never seen. It was the secret area I often wondered about, behind the Oriental screens that divided Mrs. Warner's living space from her professional offices. I looked at the antique wooden furniture, the delicate art objects on glass and brass tables, and scanned the titles on the bookshelves to see what she read. My therapist had successfully made herself into a blank screen. Who was she? What did she really think of me? I sat very still and thought that I would try my best not to touch anything.

When Sara finally came out of the consulting room, I knew that I had lost her. I tried to make eye contact. Our intimacy was gone. To me, her eyes betrayed the fixed gaze of someone in hypnosis. Sara was no longer my ally. Alone, I would have to face a rising tide of unshakable opinions that would wash away any of my choices, in favor of others' decisions to envelop me in a protective shield – for my own good. My therapist was not going to enter my world and Sara was regarding me in a set way, unreachable by anything I had to say. She was like a new young social worker or student nurse going into the hospital ward for the first time. She was prepared to not be shocked by anything. She would only see and respond in the manner she had been taught was appropriate.

Mrs. Warner, disturbed by her discussion with Sara, arranged for me to have an emergency consultation with Dr. Mandel. My therapist did not talk with me, try to understand my point of view, or even try to see first-hand if Sara's perceptions were accurate. I realized that during my three years of therapy she operated under the assumption that I could become psychotic at any time. Was she case managing me, waiting for it to happen? How else could she so easily accept Sara's story, the view of a complete stranger? No need to talk with me – it was simply the validation of an already known fact: schizophrenia is a life-long illness. I swore at myself for being so stupid as to get involved with this Park Avenue therapist . . . for being so passive and dependent . . . for obediently making the twice-weekly trek into New York City for two and a half years.

As I waited with Sara in Dr. Mandel's reception room, I felt two opposing tensions that I could not reconcile, my extreme sense of urgency and the necessity of patiently waiting. I tried to focus on what I needed to do and how I could get Dr. Mandel to take my side.

The allotted fifteen minutes was not enough time to prove my sanity or for him to arrest the alleged onslaught of psychosis. Unlike in our other meetings, I felt a coolness and emotional distance between Dr. Mandel and me. As I sat facing him, the sounds of the ticking clock took on gigantic proportions. I thought my responses were being timed and paced to evaluate my lucidity. The clock was the Deity that governed our interaction. The ticking of that clock seemed to get louder. I noticed each of Dr. Mandel's furtive glances at the clock. I thought he too was aware of the desperate significance of each moment. I did accurately sense the importance of the clock, but I misinterpreted the meaning. It was simply my fifteen minutes being carefully timed.

Dr. Mandel went quickly to the point. "You may have to spend a short time in the hospital." He said "short" with a bit of extra emphasis, elongating the "sh" sound.

I tried to get him to see the problem differently. "As soon as I get some sleep I'll be fine. I'm just over-tired."

Hoping that his mind was not completely closed, I asked for sleeping pills. He appeared to listen to my request, but would not prescribe sleeping pills. Instead he prescribed Thorazine, explaining that it would help me sleep and also calm me down. I felt myself sliding backwards down the mountain at out-of-control, breakneck speed while watching my future slip away. What I had built up over the last three years was coming apart. I would be back at the beginning, at the bottom of the mountain, a psychiatric casualty who needed to be periodically hospitalized. I tried to mobilize my strength and not accept the verdict, but the threat of hospitalization undercut all my attempts to pull myself together and pushed me further into my own version of reality.

When I returned from New York, I called my mother to tell her I was taking medication from the psychiatrist to help me get to sleep. I was afraid Dr. Mandel would call to alert my parents and I felt that it would be better if I spoke with them first. Mom began to wail to God in Yiddish, not accusing me directly of doing this to her, but in her indirect manner making the guilt-inducing message clear. It reminded me of the all times while I was growing up that she had blamed my behavior for making her sick. She calmed down some when I told her Sara was with me. She liked Sara and thought highly of her.

As the evening wore on, I tried to get Sara to see my point of view. She kept trying to get me to go to sleep. I became more worried and irritable as the night progressed. The tiredness had turned into restless energy. I told her I did not want to sleep and wouldn't try. I wanted to prove to her that I was all right, but I could not prove it to her if I went to sleep or, for that matter, if I did not get to sleep. Sara wanted to call my parents. I made the mistake of telling her to go ahead.

I don't know what my mother, father and brother expected to find when they arrived at my apartment or what they thought they would be able to do. I felt like I was being attacked and needed to defend myself. My autonomy was at stake. They were united in their mission, the psychiatric orders were primary – get him to go to sleep. Despite having taken the Thorazine, I knew I could not get to sleep and I didn't want to lie in bed trying. My insomnia was their proof that something was wrong with me. But I reasoned that if I did not try to fall asleep, I would not fail.

The sad, outrageous farce, so frequently enacted for too many of us, was following its too common script – to be pressured to do the impossible. Four people in my apartment, thinking they could get me to sleep by ordering me to go to bed. How could I lie there inviting sleep, while in the adjoining room they would be discussing strategies that would change the course of my life? I should have been frightened but instead I was angry. They insisted on telling me what was right for me, what I had to do. I saw only the stripping away of my autonomy. They would not listen. They did not understand that the worst way to approach me was exactly what they were doing – bullying and ganging up on me. They were unable to shift tactics so we went round and round. I had to defend myself. Our voices kept getting louder.

The police peered through the slightly open door to my apartment. They were assessing the situation before they made their presence known to us. Startled, we quickly became quiet and attentive when the two policemen politely asked for permission to enter my apartment. They said that neighbors had complained of a loud argument taking place.

"You know, it's three in the morning, what's the problem?"

After listening to all of our explanations, the two cops moved to a corner of the room, talked and then came back to us with their decision. They told me that I could go with them to voluntarily sign myself into Overbrook Hospital or I could spend the next few days in jail and wait for a court-appointed psychiatrist to evaluate whether I needed to be involuntarily committed to a psychiatric hospital.

I was stunned by the narrowing of my options. Up or down, turn right or left, I had to accept their decision to take away my freedom. It was a sickening punch straight to the center of my being. I frantically searched my mind to find a way out. If I went to jail, I would miss work and lose my job. I reasoned that if I went to the hospital voluntarily, I would be able to sign myself out the next day and since it was the weekend, I would not miss work and arouse suspicion. I remembered that Larry worked at Overbrook and thought that he could help me. My senses were on high alert, acutely aware of the dangerous trap that had been sprung. Desperate, my thinking was guided more by hope than rationality.

As I rode in the police car to the hospital, everything I valued in myself was disintegrating in the undeniable reality of impending hospitalization. In that car, I felt the crushing weight of despair. I had lost my chance at a life. A failure was what I was and would always be.

Chapter 7

The Hospital Crucible's Second Lesson: Learn or Die

Adversity in immunological doses has its uses; more than that crushes.
(John Updike)

Arriving at the tightly sealed hospital, our motley group stood on the lawn, peering at the gate to my personal hell. I felt panic closing in on me. The too humid night had neither moon nor hope illuminating the path. The two cops slapped at mosquitoes and complained about having to wait in the sweltering heat for someone to wake up and do their job. I knew what was lurking behind those darkened windows. The cops' impatience and confusion about the admission procedure gave me hope. I prayed . . . give me another chance . . . no one is here . . . let me go . . . I'll be good. Please.

A security guard pulled open the door, mumbled a greeting and motioned for us to follow him. We were led into a large, dimly lit room and shown where to sit. When the guard turned on more lights, I looked around the room for a way out. I restrained my urge to let myself float up above the slow-motion crash I was witnessing. I fought to stay grounded. Both cops stood at arms' length on each side of me. My mother, father and brother sat in chairs bolted to the floor on the other side of the room.

My family were participants in this nightmare, but somehow had convinced themselves that this was a place where I would be helped. I felt the pulsating walls straining to contain years of accumulated terror. I breathed the despair of too many violated trusts dripping from the ceilings. I couldn't have been the only one who smelled the mixture of vomit, urine and Lysol. Was I the only one feeling the primal fear that permeated this madhouse and its inhabitants? I tried not to let anyone see how scared I was.

Too soon, a man emerged from one of the darkened corridors and identified himself as the doctor in charge. He made no attempt to be friendly or cordial when he asked the cops to identify the patient. After a brief evaluative glance, he led me to a desk, produced a form and started asking me questions. His sing-song speech betrayed a less than half-hearted attempt to connect to the soothing professional voice he had rehearsed in school. I looked at a tired, impatient man. This soul doctor, in the past more aptly named alienist, did not honor his responsibility as gatekeeper of my future. From him I felt no interest in the specific me who was in front of him.

In a foolish twist of logic, I thought I could protect myself by not answering his questions. Reacting to my silence, the doctor turned to my family for basic information needed to complete the admission papers: date of birth, allergies, education . . . and the question that would seal my indictment, "Was he ever in a psychiatric institution before?" Sy gave him the information he wanted while I sat in a corner and feigned disinterest.

Fine, I couldn't be held responsible for what my brother said . . . easier for me to deny it in the morning. Say it was his mistake.

I realized the folly of my ploy when the doctor prodded me to sign the voluntary admission form. I squirmed at being cornered. The cops wouldn't leave until I signed away my credibility. I have often wondered what would have happened if I had not signed it.

Two hospital aides came for me. One was tall, thick-bodied, with a barrel chest and very large hands. The other, of medium height, was soft and overweight. They were the soft/hard personification of the lifelong conflict I struggled to integrate. Neither made eye contact. Talking only to each other, they barely acknowledged my presence as they led me through the maze of tear-soaked corridors. At our destination, a tiny examining room, I was told to strip. Then after being weighed and measured like a slab of meat, they ordered me to put on hospital pajamas.

I felt the immense gulf between me and the aides, just as if we were standing on opposite banks of a river that was far too vast for the shouts from the other side to be heard. Whenever one of the aides did say something directly to me, it was as if he was addressing an alien species. Nothing I said was related to in the way I intended. My role in the unfolding drama was chosen and scripted by others. The shorter, soft one was in a good mood, frequently laughing as he spoke. I thought he was poking fun at me. More and more absorbed and insulated by my personal crisis, I became less able to recognize that others' actions were not always centered on me. As I tumbled and careened through my purgatory, the aides hardly noticed or cared. Their lives had few points of intersection with mine. They may as well have been laughing at me, for my destiny was in the hands of strangers. I had to listen and obey.

I was escorted into a dormitory room with too many beds, arranged in narrow rows with only enough space for people to pass between if they shuffled along sideways. The stale air and assorted bodily smells made my skin itch. I saw shadowy outlines of my new roommates and heard the uneven choruses of heavy breathing interrupted by sputtering snores. The aides working quickly in tandem set up a bed for me and left with their final order of the night, "Go to sleep."

Ironically, the Thorazine had finally kicked in and bludgeoned me into sleep. Morning came too quickly for me. The intrusive, too strident voices of the aides urging me into wakefulness melded with the sleepy gurgling of forty patients stirring into unwanted consciousness. It took several minutes for me to rediscover how truly lost I was.

After those few hours of sleep I was awakened to participate in the ward routine. Believing that I had had a full night's sleep, my fatigue was temporarily masked. My biological clock fooled, I felt energized for a short time before the residual effects of the Thorazine and exhaustion resurfaced and forced me to face my weariness. I had difficulty interpreting what was going on inside and outside of me. When I realized where I was, I recognized the importance of rising above the emotional turbulence and presenting myself well. All my actions had to be in the service of my prime directive: Get the discharge process started.

To walk into a hospital ward as a new patient shares elements with other experiences – new kid on the block, first day at a school, beginning a new job, first time attending an APA annual conference without knowing anyone. Learning the overt and covert rules as well as discovering the pecking order are difficult enough when you are functioning well, but imagine how the problems are magnified when you don't want to break into the existing order and routine. I didn't want to blend in. I had to be steadfast in my conviction that this was a big mistake.

The lessons drilled into me during my first hospitalization were going to be taught a second time – that stability and sameness are the priorities of a hospital, that hospitals worship routines, that patients in a mental hospital are similar to staff in their needs for predictability. Conformity is good. Obedience is good. Passivity is good. Invisibility is good. And deviance from the rules is bad. Change is bad. Questions are bad. Thinking is bad. Surprise is very, very bad. There would be no discharge and quite possibly no life should I this time not assimilate this lesson, and thereby fail the hospital test.

The patient can make his vulnerability tolerable by accepting and claiming as his own the hospital routines. The predictability supplants freedom of choice, but gives him the illusion that he has some control over his fate. The more capricious the blows life deals, the more compulsively one tries to control life's little events. The powerless, be they hospital patients or homeless street people, try to exercise domain over their collections of empty matchbooks, chewing gum wrappers and the paper bags they use to organize prized discards – anything that can be predictable and controllable.

My first plan – to set myself apart from the other patients, to show that I was different and didn't need to be in a mental hospital – was an ineffective strategy. The irresolvable conundrum: how do you prove that you don't belong? If by reasonable conversation, with whom? The hospital staff and the general public share similar beliefs about mental illness. They expect patients to appear logical for short periods of time, but when you say the magic word, the trigger that unleashes the pathology . . . the "Niagara Falls" of Abbot and Costello's slapstick comedy, then you'd better watch out.

In their classic skit, Costello is in a prison holding cell where he begins a conversation with his cell mate. They share their woeful stories and get along well until Costello's new friend begins talking about his wife running off with another man to Niagara Falls. Just saying the words "Niagara Falls" sends him into an uncontrollable fit of violence that is only relieved by his thrashing of Costello. After throwing him around the jail cell, his energy expended, he picks up Costello, brushes him off and apologizes. He explains that he is fine until hears those "two words." Of course, Costello says, "You mean Niagara Falls." And the whole farce is set loose again.

The humor vividly captures the dilemma felt by former "mental patients." They can look and act normal for a long time, but other people still believe, even expect, that if they hear their personal "Niagara Falls," the explosive outburst is sure to follow. Once crazy, you forfeit the right to be trusted. You must be unremarkable in appearance and actions, and even years of unblemished behavior does not entitle a vacation from scrutiny. Anthony Perkins in the last scene of Alfred Hitchcock's movie thriller, *Psycho*, sits in a chair dressed as his own mother. Viewers now know that he is the psycho killer. A fly buzzes around him, and we listen to his voice-over thoughts: *I'll just sit here and show them that I wouldn't hurt a fly*. The consistent message – crazy people can be cleverly deceptive.

If only I had known the enormity of my task, the impossibility of instantly asserting my sanity. If only I hadn't felt the intense urgency, the panic of needing to leave before the weekend was over, the exaggerated importance of reporting to work on Monday. My education and training as a psychologist was more of a hindrance than a help; indeed, little in my background had prepared me for these dark nights of the soul. In fact, I put more pressure on myself by thinking that I should have special expertise. My identity was confounded by the white slacks and brown corduroy sport coat I had worn to the hospital. Who was this new person on the ward? The other patients were confused by my clothes, my manner, and my assertion that I was a psychologist. Some felt it was a hospital trick. Others believed me, but most were not the least bit interested. The varied responses increased my own confusion and kept me mentally alternating between roles of patient and staff person. I mistakenly thought that some of the patients were people I had known outside the hospital, spoke to them of common experiences and called them names that were not their own. When the nursing staff saw the heightened energy and restless pacing on the ward, they blamed me. From there, it was an easy jump to see me as a trouble maker.

My plan was to sign myself out of the hospital as soon as possible. In a self-righteous authoritative manner, I informed the nurse of my status as a voluntary admission and requested my discharge. No one took my request seriously. I asked to see a doctor to authorize my discharge. All in due time, I was told. It was the weekend; everything had stopped. The nurse and the aide passed between them knowing glances and a disembodied voice soaked in syrupy parental patience let me know that I would get no special consideration. "But," I insisted, "I have to get out this weekend. Monday is too late, I'll lose my job. I'm a psychologist . . . I work at Greystone Park Hospital."

Again the look and the insincere, "Sure, sure, we'll take care of it." They pretended to believe me but they didn't do anything. Easier to agree with me and then go back to what they were doing. I needed help. I asked to use the telephone to call my friend Larry.

I hesitated and struggled with the decision to call Larry. I needed an ally, someone to advocate for me, but I didn't want Larry or anyone I knew professionally to know about my psychiatric history. I knew that all credibility would vanish once my past hospital record was discovered. They allowed me to make the telephone call.

It was Saturday morning and Larry had just finished jogging when I reached him. I explained my predicament as best I could. Still wearing his running clothes, he came right over. Larry was the first person I had talked to in days who genuinely listened and tried to understand, but he looked bewildered. I'm not sure how I expected him to get me out of the hospital. A staff psychologist in those days was not an influential or powerful person in the hospital hierarchy. My pleading must have seemed irrational to him. He tried to calm me down, reassuring me that I would probably be discharged when the weekend was over and the normal paperwork and procedures could be carried out. I sensed his uncertainty and discomfort. Here I was, a friend, a peer, suddenly a patient begging for help in the hospital where he worked. How could this be? What could he do? How vulnerable and threatened did he feel?

Years later, Larry told me that he had steered me in front of an open door and turned away. He had tried to subtly direct me to escape, to run from there. This was Larry's answer to the moral and professional dilemma I had placed before him. But I couldn't run. I had to get out the "right way." If I escaped, how could I return to my job? I was applying to doctoral psychology programs and could not seek admission as an escaped mental patient. Seeing Larry made me feel a little safer. I convinced myself that I was okay and that they would have to acknowledge this fact. Above all, I was sure that I was a voluntary patient and could sign myself out.

Only a few hours after Larry left, my confidence weakened and my sense of urgency increased. The day was slipping by with nothing happening. I realized that if I waited patiently for the doctor to see me, I would have to stay until at least Monday. Once the work week started, I would be exposed, the psychologist/mental patient's secret would be out. My career as a psychologist would be over before it had really begun. I could not sit back and passively accept what was happening to me; rising waves of panic had to be controlled. Once the day shift left, I had no chance of being released. I would be confined to the hospital for that night, maybe longer. Desperate, I began making more frequent and forceful discharge demands to the nursing staff.

The norms of patient behavior require the patient to stand passively by the nursing station door and politely make requests in a passive, calm, respectful, soft voice . . . to do the patient shuffle. At the door of the nursing station there is an invisible line that patients are forbidden to cross. You wait there until your presence is acknowledged, then you are granted permission to speak. It reminds me of how pack animals demonstrate an absence of threat before a more dominant animal by rolling on their backs and assuming a submissive position.

I hated the game immediately. However, I quickly learned the rules, which are taught well by the nursing staff. First, you are chastised for passing the imaginary line that symbolizes the many distinctions between the empowered and the powerless. Next, rules and procedures are explained to you. After that, you are politely listened to and humored. Your request is denied while you are bathed in smiles and condescension. Your second approach, if you follow the rules, is met with more smiles, a show of listening, agreement and usually a cursory follow-through to the request if it is simple – maybe for a toothbrush or a piece of your own candy. During your next visit to the nursing station you are trained to wait while the staff person takes care of several trivial tasks – rearranging some papers on the desk, organizing pencils or paper clips – a lesson in priorities is demonstrated. Gradually, as the visits and requests continue at the nursing station, you are met with longer waits, annoyance and disapproval.

I had to do something, so I raised my voice: "Don't ignore me." I was angry. I would not be manipulated and molded into a shape that was not me. No one responded to me. I was no longer a person, but instead, a representative of a class of people, a mental patient. The reaction I got was not what I wanted. I had dared to demand attention on my terms. To the staff it was confirmation of my pathology, and a ready-made explanation of why I was in a mental hospital.

My refusal to conform set in motion an accelerating downward spiral. The more demanding I became, the less attention was paid to me. All of my requests were ignored, and I knew that I could only get attention if I was outrageous. I lost sight of my purpose, discharge. I began fighting the denial of my personhood. I began fighting for the other patients on the ward, too. I saw myself as the people's champion, fighting for everyone's rights. I was sucked in, fighting the "good war." I was losing touch with my goal and becoming a martyr. There was life and death urgency to this battle. But to the hospital staff, I was just another nut to be oriented and put in place.

The more I pushed, the more blatantly I was ignored, until I did the unthinkable. I stepped over the sacred imaginary line. I put one foot into the nursing staff office. I was stunned by how quickly they shifted from disinterest to action. The aides grabbed my arms and began dragging me off. I went limp and wouldn't walk. They lifted me up, each aide holding an arm and dragging me off to seclusion. I assume there was a standing order from a physician authorizing emergency injections of Thorazine. A nurse came in and while my arms and legs were held down, she gave me an ungentle stab in the butt with the needle. My clothes were taken from me. I was left naked in a seclusion room with nothing but the plastic-covered mattress and the cold, hard floor. No explanations were given. The therapy of conformity had begun. And I was back in seclusion.

I was devastated. It was Fair Oaks all over again. Had I made no progress? Was it my destiny to spend a few years deceiving myself with illusions of adequacy, only to have my independence and dignity arbitrarily smashed by uncaring strangers? What was happening to me? There I was, locked naked in a room, with Thorazine making its way through my body. Fright, pain, outrage and anger pulling and buffeting me in dizzying combinations. Confused, fighting to hold onto my perspective, I could not keep track of time. How long was I locked in that room? Was it hours or days? Those lost days have never been recovered. The loss of my memory during my previous hospitalization worried me and I feared a recurrence. I searched for reference points, anchors to attach to memories for safekeeping.

After an unknowable amount of time, the doors to the seclusion room finally opened. An aide muttered something and left. *What did he say? Did he say follow me? The door is open. I can walk out. Did he say visitors are here to see me?* I walked out to find them. I only realized that I was naked when I saw the reaction of the student nurses. By the time the aide came back with my clothes, I had stirred up quite a commotion. He cursed me and pushed me back into the seclusion room.

I screamed for my rights: "Let me see my visitors!" I was informed that I was too upset to be permitted visitors. For not heeding their warnings and threats, I was given another shot of Thorazine and spent the rest of my time in the seclusion room fighting to maintain control of my mind and thoughts. I was most afraid of losing all that makes me who I am. Who would I be without my memory? When I was no longer able to yell, I withdrew into a corner of the room and sank to the floor in despair. My anchors were lost and what remained of my time orientation drifted away as I sank into a state of disjointed emptiness.

I spent my next days, I do not know how many, in and out of seclusion but fighting back enough to get two or three forced shots of Thorazine daily. My feud with the nursing staff escalated as I frenetically tried to get someone to listen to me – my plaintive cry, "I want to talk to a psychiatrist."

A pattern emerged. I would make my request in the morning. The nurse made a big show of writing it down. I did not see a doctor. Lunchtime came. I made my request again; it was recorded again. Nothing happened. Usually after an hour of pacing, my next request became more demanding.

I became angry and challenged whoever was in authority by breaking some minor rule. A shot of Thorazine and the seclusion room quickly followed.

It was impossible to tell how long each stay in the seclusion room lasted. Often I felt like I was suffocating from the stale air, enclosed space and heavy feelings of oppression pushing down on my chest. I fought the mind-deadening effects of the Thorazine, but my capacity to think through each crisis was diminishing rapidly. The drugs were not yet effective enough to keep me from struggling, but had sufficient power to deprive me of the ability to construct an effective strategy. In my panic, reason was replaced with fear. I wondered if they would ever let me out. I felt trapped, helpless and at the mercy of people who did not give a damn about me. I worried that there would be a shift change and that the new staff would not know that I was locked in seclusion. Imprisoned forever in the seclusion room, it would be as if I never existed. I imagined myself dying in a fire. Or coming down with a deadly disease from bacteria that lived in the foul air of that room. I became progressively more confused and frightened. My anger energized me, but it was counter-productive. I found it impossible to relate to a hospital staff whose phoniness and condescension seeped through all of their interactions with me. Only patients' responses that demonstrated passivity and compliance were acceptable. Some of the patients seemed cute to them, like amusing pets. I could not allow myself to relate in that way. I was their peer and would only relate to them in that manner.

I had the most confrontations with a nursing supervisor named Minter. She was of the *One Flew Over the Cuckoo's Nest* ilk, running her wards with despotic, steel-fisted intolerance. Nurse Minter was determined to make me knuckle under and obey her. She seemed to take sadistic pleasure in personally jamming Thorazine-filled needles into me. An image has remained with me, of her entering the ward at seven A.M. on a rainy, cold day, wearing high black leather boots. She stomped around the ward all morning in those boots. Her speech and movements were always too loud and fast for patients heavy with medication. That day, the sound of her boots shouted out her arrogant imperiousness. It was the first time I called her by the name patients mumbled under their breath, Nurse Hitler. I received my Thorazine shot very quickly that morning. I believe I saw her smile at me as she closed the seclusion room door.

What motivated her, I probably will never know. Feuding with her seemed to satisfy my twisted need to challenge an unbeatable tyrant. I funneled all of my anger at one evil adversary. She seemed to take particular delight in the execution of her job – to maintain order, and demonstrate power by squashing resistance. She was my scapegoat just as I was hers, but she had the benefit of choice. All she had to do was sit down and talk with me, to accord me the dignity of dialogue, and then I would have had the choice of bending or not. But I was treated the same as everyone else, dispassionately. She had no need or desire to extend special treatment, regardless of the possible benefits.

When I was admitted to the hospital I was exhausted, frequently paranoid and emotionally quite labile. Initially, I was able to set aside those problems to pursue my hospital discharge. Every part of me was mobilized for that one goal. Actually, I was clearer and more focused than I had been for the several days preceding my hospitalization. I fought to prevent my darkest fear from being realized – becoming known as a "cronk" to the staff, schizophrenia, chronic type for the official clinical file. Initially, I had pulled myself together for one last-stand battle to prove my sanity. But without help I could not sustain my effort at rationality. Society's soldiers, the guardians and keepers of chronic normalcy, will not allow you to move in and out of reality at your own discretion. The hospital workers spoke with one voice, "You will return the way we tell you or not at all." One cannot be cured or fully recovered in a system that only recognizes the possibility of remission.

Predictably, I started to slip when I accepted the social structure and patient relationships on the ward. I was a patient. If I wanted to talk with anyone, if I wanted to get information, it would have to be with my fellow patients. There I would seek comrades in arms. Looking for support, I found other wannabe hippies. My long-haired allies deepened my confusion. Identifying with their problems, struggles and misinformation widened the gulf between the hospital staff and me.

Jim, who was a couple of years younger than I, shared some common experiences with me. He was intelligent, into meditation and seemed to know his way around the hospital. I liked Jim, but more than that, I needed him; he was the only person on the ward who understood and responded to me. Problematic was Jim's ability to understand my half-finished thoughts and sentences, because this served to push me further into idiosyncratic ways of relating to others. I was stuck in a time warp. I would respond to something someone said a split second before they said it. I was always at least one half-beat out of step. As if there had been a sudden flash, like a camera flashbulb, time would freeze and I would see some action or hear some words or sound a few seconds before it would happen; a fraction of a second later, the event would occur. It was as if I was in a movie and there was a brief pause programmed into the projector. I was getting more confused daily and my fears increased. Jim seemed to be the only one who could, at times, synchronize his rhythm with mine and understand me. The Thorazine shots and the other medications became a heavy overlay on the entire process. I thought of myself as trapped, just outside normal time. Everyone except me seemed to be moving in slow motion. I was unable to slow down and prevent myself from tripping in between other people's movements.

The first weekend passed without my getting the opportunity to see a psychiatrist. All my yelling about being a voluntary patient and demanding to sign myself out was to no avail. My undoing was my lack of understanding of the procedure. Are you really voluntary when that status is dependent upon your abdication of your right to refuse to comply with treatment? And when you attempt to exercise your right to request discharge, you learn that your status can be easily changed from voluntary to involuntary. My rights as a patient were few; I was guilty – insane, until I could prove otherwise.

Monday came and went without me. Tuesday, I got word that a psychiatrist was on the ward. I did not get a chance to talk with him. He conferred with the ward staff at the nursing station and went over patient charts. He saw no patients that day; he was too busy spending the half-hour allotted to our ward making notes in patients' charts and approving medication orders. I requested an interview. I pleaded for an interview. I demanded an interview. I banged on the office door . . . seclusion and more Thorazine. I lost Tuesday.

I think it was a couple of days later that I again heard that *the doctor* was on the ward. There was also a buzz that he was seeing some patients. It was just a medication review, questions for a few selected patients, but the door was open, and I thought I could get through to him. I caught his attention and asked if he would talk with me. The aides began to usher me away but he stopped them and asked who I was.

Then, a magnanimous smile and, "You'll have the opportunity to talk with me the next time I'm on the ward."

I asked, "When will that be?"

"We shall see . . . maybe Friday."

My stomach sank; another day and a maybe. Slipping more, sliding down, no place to secure a grip; my ability to stay focused on discharge had allowed me to mobilize some degree of lucidity, but it was no longer working. Confusion grew daily, fed by my anger and exacerbated by the medication. I felt alone, isolated, unable to communicate or understand what was going on around me. Staff related to me as if I was crazy and only saw the behavior that reinforced their belief system. Most of the other patients saw me as different, not belonging within their structure. It seemed as if everyone was trying to squeeze me into a box so that I could fit their expectations. I felt as if I was in a dream, another kind of reality or dimension, separated by some invisible barrier. I was in a place where only certain messages or interactions could pass through the barrier. None of the things I wanted to communicate could penetrate the barrier, only the mistakes, negatives, non-affirmations of me could get through.

Everything connected with hospital confinement fosters regression. You are there because you are unable to see to your needs, or because you are a threat to others. Obviously, you cannot be trusted and must be monitored. How can such a negative stance help a person become more competent?

My parents were the first visitors to see me. They were permitted only a brief visit so as not to upset me. It didn't work; I was upset and the visit was cut short. Mom brought me food and clothing, but she wouldn't talk until I ate and changed clothes. I'm not a child, I protested. I was not about to talk, change my clothes and eat at the same time. I needed to talk first, convince them to take me with them. My mother insisted that I change my clothes first. I grudgingly agreed. Next I had to eat. I objected, she insisted; I conceded. Finally, in different clothes and having wolfed down the food, I begged them to get me out of the hospital. They told me they could not, it was up to the doctor. I became angrier and more frustrated. I asked for money for cigarettes. They said they could not leave me money but had arranged to leave me cigarettes, as per the nurse's instructions. The hospital staff told them that I was not allowed to keep my cigarettes, but they would hold my cigarettes and allow me one cigarette an hour. I could not tolerate so much supervision. I grew incensed . . . my parents were told to leave, as I had become too agitated. But how could I not act like an unruly child?

When it was decided I could again have visitors, Sara came to see me, bringing a box of cookies she had baked for me. I asked her to do something, anything to get me out of there. She listened but did not respond. I could see her ambivalence. Her picture of me was shattered and she was busily constructing a new image. With very little input from me, the new image was formed from her own internal needs to make the incongruous pieces fit. What had happened to her former boyfriend and lover? I had very little influence, not even enough to talk her into getting me a pack of cigarettes. The rules were set and she would not break them. No one would break the rules. They were inviolate. I was furious and hurled the box of cookies against the wall. I suppose I should not have vented my frustration and anger at her. I frightened Sara, more evidence that I needed to be confined, controlled and monitored.

An angry, tense person grabs you by the throat. Do you look into his dilated eyes and giddily say, "Isn't it a beautiful day?" A man fleeing from his burning house hysterically screams an appeal for help. Should he be ignored until he calms down and makes a civil, polite request for aid? If your internal house, your gut, is burning, should I demand that you relax because I know you will feel better when you do? Would you be crazy if my lack of acknowledgment provoked you into becoming more agitated? Which one of us would be denying reality?

Okay, my parents and Sara were not going to do what I demanded, but they could have validated my feelings.

Don't get me cigarettes, don't get me out of the hospital, but don't stay so damn calm. I'm not the only one feeling strong emotions. Don't let me yell at you while you pretend that you are unaffected by it – that is not the road to rationality. If you want me to be sane in your world then show me that my feelings are not operating in a vacuum. Validate my emotions with an honest reaction, don't humor or patronize me. The more you ignore, the more outlandish I become in trying to elicit a reaction that matches the feelings I express. I would not keep yelling if you honestly responded to my outbursts.

I needed to know that they were feeling and not just talking. I responded to emotions, not words. Emotions had substance – told me that I had impact, that I could influence others. The calm words were lies. The calm was a lie.

During my first month in the hospital, I met the rabbi who paid brief visits to the Jewish patients. There was something about him I immediately liked. I intuitively knew he was not part of the hospital staff and could be trusted. He would talk with me for a few minutes, and before he left, when no one was looking, he would slip me some boxes of cigarette samples. His visits had a clandestine air to them – as if he wasn't supposed to be there, like he was a secret agent visiting a prisoner in a foreign jail. I don't remember what we talked about, but I looked forward to his visits. He didn't ask anything of me, and in turn, he was one of the few people of whom I did not ask anything.

I started praying to God for help. As I was uncomfortable with organized religion, prayer had not been a part of my life since I was a child. Perhaps I was drawn to prayer by my interactions with the rabbi, but more likely it was my need to make some sense out of this frightening, disabling experience. I learned that as a Jewish patient I could go to Chapel for Sabbath service on Saturday mornings. The rabbi told me I should make my request to attend and it would be honored. Until then, I had not been permitted to leave the ward.

I went to the service and prayed and cried. I asked God to help me. After the service some volunteers served sponge cake and grape juice.

I went again on the following Saturday. Getting off the ward gave me relief. The service helped to counteract the feeling that I would die on the ward, that my existence would be simply erased and forgotten. Contact with people who were not part of the hospital staff temporarily allayed that fear.

When I discovered that there were Catholic services on Sunday, I decided to attend them also. I hoped that they too might help to overcome my sense of isolation and confinement. Perhaps I needed to feel closer to God and spiritual feelings, or any higher power that I could implore to help me. But I was uncomfortable participating in the unfamiliar Catholic service and didn't experience any of the good feelings I had during the Saturday service. Unlike the warmth I felt from the rabbi, the priest was cool and aloof. I felt guilty that I was betraying my religion and thought it was wrong for me to attend the mass, so I stayed away from future Catholic services.

My interview with the psychiatrist finally arrived. He immediately began asking pointed questions designed to enable him to quickly fill out the required mental status evaluation. I tried to explain the circumstances and events that had led to my hospitalization, telling him it was not necessary for me to be in a hospital and pointing to my lack of sleep as the reason for the unusual behavior leading to the hospitalization. He did not listen for understanding. He tuned into key words and disregarded context. He was a detective looking for clues. Dr. Detective was looking to fit me into a category. I was a design, a jigsaw puzzle; squeeze the pieces together and make them fit. I was mixed up, but I could see we were playing the game of life with different rules and that his already predetermined ending meant that I lose. He was responding only to those items that supported hypotheses with which he was familiar. With him owning all of the power, no rapport needed to be established. I had waited all this time to present my case, to have a dialogue, only to find myself being grilled. What day is it? I didn't know what day it was. Let me shoot you up with Thorazine, put you through a strange unnatural routine, lock you in seclusion on and off for days. See if you know what day it is. I was angry. I became belligerent with Dr. Detective and would not answer his stupid questions. I can still see him furiously taking notes, labeling me hostile, belligerent, paranoid. He fits – psychotic! For the mental patient, there is no justifiable anger.

I saw no option but to continue asking to sign myself out. I asked the staff. I constantly asked my visitors. No one would listen and I just became angrier, more of a nuisance; so, more shots of Thorazine to control my behavior and an increase in the dose of my twice-a-day medication. Acquiescence and docility were the pills I could not swallow. Your mental health evaluation was dependent on how well you adapted to procedure and how few problems you created. Deviance from the rules was inexcusable, and the rules and regulations covered all situations. No one walking in the ward corridor between six o'clock and eight o'clock, no crossing the imaginary line at the nursing station, no one in bed after six o'clock in the morning, no opening the windows, no matches. No dignity!

My will and independence were under attack. Why did they have to try to break me? Throughout my hospitalization I waged a battle to maintain my sense of who I was. The last three years of struggles to define myself were being threatened. A major portion of my identity was tied into my long hair and rebellious image. Yet, the appearance I sought to maintain, with its emphasis on outrageousness, worked against me. I wanted to be considered normal by the staff, but on my terms. I would not cut my hair. When the hospital barber came on the ward, the staff would grab my arms and mockingly pretend they were going to force me to have my hair cut. I was not amused. Later, as part of the surrender of my will to fight, I let the hospital barber cut my hair. Although I thought my emotions were too beaten down, too deadened to feel much, I felt the loss strongly. It was as if the last bit of will and self-determination had been crushed. Did I have too much fight, too much energy, or was I merely a nuisance who inconvenienced the hospital staff? I was a disrespectful pain in the ass.

Fear and power are paramount in a hospital. I sensed that the doctors were frightened of the patients; you could almost smell the doctors' fear. I am not sure whether it was a fear of mental or physical attack. Or maybe the threat was the exposure of their charade of being competent and knowledgeable. They were uncomfortable with patients. On the other hand, the nurses seemed to be acclimated and comfortable in their ward routines and stereotypical responses. They were automatons who made few decisions; their primary responsibility was to keep the routine going smoothly. At best, the patients were pets, to be cared for, trained and controlled. Genuine person-to-person interaction was minimal.

When you live on a psychiatric ward, it is important for you to understand the importance of being on good terms with the psychiatric aides. Since they have the most contact with patients, their moods and attitudes determine the quality of life on the ward. It seemed to please them to be in control, to exercise so much power, and to be superior to those in their charge. Typically, the aides were poor, uneducated members of minority groups holding down more than one job. Frequently they were tired, wanting only not to be bothered. Patients were nuisances, unless they were amusing or had some extra money. A simple request for a match to light a cigarette was generally met with a glare and other signs of displeasure. Too often, they relieved their boredom by teasing and baiting patients.

Everything becomes primitive in a hospital; food and cigarettes are treasures to be hoarded. My nature was to share, to be concerned about others. In the hospital, such behavior is considered being unable to take care of your own things. Selfishness and stockpiling are encouraged overtly and covertly by the staff. How can so much control and programmed helplessness foster one's development into a competent, independent person? The chance to be different, deviant, experimental, allows growth. Hospitals stifle growth.

I remember Steve, a fellow patient who was too heavily drugged to write letters to his girlfriend and asked me for help. For a few weeks, every day, I wrote the letters he dictated to me. Then one day, after completing a letter, Steve told me that it was the last letter he needed me to write. He told me that he was being discharged the following day. I couldn't believe it. He was getting discharged before me. How could that be? I was certain that anyone could see that I was in better shape than he. What about me? I stepped up my demands for discharge. He couldn't even sign his name to the letters I wrote. It wasn't fair. Why? Seclusion and Thorazine again – soon I would not be able to write.

There was no fairness, logic or justice. I saw other patients being discharged, and when I compared myself to them, I knew that I was in better mental condition, at least I thought I would be if I could get released.

I kept asking why.

Some patients had been there longer than I. Some had a place to go. Some had a doctor to see once they got out, a wife or parents pushing for discharge. I would not accept those explanations. What did I have to do? Why weren't my parents pushing for my discharge? Once again, my parents were told by a hospital doctor that I was a very sick boy with a serious disease. *A wrong move, anything rash, and he may be in need of hospital care for his entire life.*

It was not too long before the hospital became my world. The more trapped and confined I felt, the more magical my thinking became. In my mind I saw what I wanted. I made things fit, made them acceptable. I interpreted events based on my needs. And I became crazier. It was difficult to write, talk, or even find the energy to pace the hall. I was uncomfortable standing, sitting or walking. Boredom was constant. Each agonizing minute stretched interminably and was indistinguishable from the preceding one. I couldn't stand the food. I couldn't read. I forgot familiar phone numbers. I could not concentrate on anything for more than a few seconds. Fearing for my life, I sank deeper and deeper into myself.

How was I to get out? How was I to survive? I had to knuckle under to their demands, let them make me better on their terms. I had to make myself go along with their treatment program. I had to learn to be obedient. I had to be weak.

I could not accept or play the part of a mental patient and resisted all forms of therapy. Four of us – the four who were not allowed off the ward for activities – participated in the on-ward art therapy. The art therapist provided a break from the ward routine, but from the start I had problems relating to her. Mrs. Mills struck me as a frustrated actress. She would just about swoon as she entered the ward, and her exaggerated struggle to carry her art supplies would alert a selected volunteer that she needed male help to manage the last few steps. Mrs. Mills was thirtyish, blonde and slightly overweight, but pretty. The other guys thought she was sexy – my diminished sex drive made me indifferent to her charms. Mrs. Mills wore a soft neck brace some days that on other days was absent. That collar bothered me because I felt she used it for sympathy. I was perpetually irritated by her disingenuous, cloying manner of interacting. Mrs. Mills' voice alone was a grating irritant to my nerves. She spoke in an upbeat, contrived style that made me feel as if she was addressing children. Most annoying was her use of the word "groovy"; she thought she was being 60s hip, but that was not her.

I rejected her psychoanalytic interpretations of my artwork. I could not write legibly yet she was telling me that my artwork was beautifully expressive and groovy. She was making an effort, but she was ill-suited for this kind of work. Mrs. Mills repeated the things she had learned in school but she could not see and respond to the unique individualized needs of the person. After she left the ward, the other guys in the group criticized me for arguing with her. They told me to forget her bullshit and go along with it . . . After all, she wrote reports. I tried, but I could not get through a whole art session without getting irritated with her and expressing it.

In contrast to Mrs. Mills was the genuine caring of Ken, my music therapist. He would come to the ward, lugging his portable record player and albums. Ken was blind and his ability to self-sufficiently find his way around the hospital, coupled with my suspiciousness, caused me to wonder if he could really see. With time, I learned to trust and respect Ken and look forward to his visits, especially since I could bum cigarettes from him. He listened, tried to understand and brought in music he thought I would like. Although Ken was someone to talk with, he could do nothing to alter the course of my treatment. He was an outsider, a bit of a freak to the ward staff, who didn't know what to make of him. When he came to see me, the aides would cruelly taunt, "Go see your blind friend, he's here to teach you how to play nice." Later, when I was allowed to go off the ward for activities, I discovered that Ken played several musical instruments and had a beautiful singing voice. Listening to him sing, I could hear and feel the warmth of music coming from a caring heart.

One of the few good memories of my hospital stay was of having Ken lead me through the underground maze of passages back to the ward. Occasionally, he would take me to the cafeteria and buy me a cup of real coffee. Several times I ran into Larry there. Larry's face and demeanor told me that he was struggling with ambivalence about how to relate to me. He always secretly gave me the rest of the pack of cigarettes he had with him. I later learned that his supervisor, Mrs. Brunnell, had forbidden him from seeing me, thinking it was best for all concerned that I did not see Larry. I wondered if Mrs. Brunnell congratulated herself for assessing my hidden pathology during our earlier job interview. Maybe I was an embarrassment to the psychology department, my weakness exposing their vulnerability. My only therapeutic contact with the psychology department consisted of a brief session with a consultant psychologist who said he was assigned to see me for regular therapy. I waited for him to call me back for more sessions, but for some unknown reason, I never saw him again.

I muddled along. They changed my ward several times, and the continuous reorientation to new staff and patients made my adjustment more difficult. I had a different psychiatrist in charge of my case almost every other week, never seeing anyone more than twice.

I had ceased to struggle; the fight, internal strength, or what I view as personal power, was squeezed out of me. I felt depressed, helpless and isolated. I was scared. I didn't know how I could possibly function out of the hospital. The efficiency of performing simple tasks habitually, without conscious direction, was no longer available. I had to pay attention to buttoning my shirt, tying my shoe; just shaving my face could take an hour. In many ways I was in much worse shape than when I had been admitted. However, I was docile and therefore acceptable; no longer did I challenge authority. Righteous indignation, anger and pride were displaced by ennui and apathy. I looked forward to nothing. I planned nothing. I dreamed of nothing. My activities were directed at living hassle-free within my environment. Gone were the illusions, delusions, paranoia and psychopathology. My mind was not strong enough to supply the creative mental energy required for the complex processes involved in being psychotic. I had been bludgeoned into submission.

Four months after I was admitted, lack of choice forced me to accept the only role that was available to me in this hospital drama – that of submissive patient. Once again, I learned to say the right things and do nothing to draw attention to myself. Lacking the energy to behave otherwise, my responses were appropriate. I was self-protective, selfish and only interested in meeting my needs. Throughout, my energy centered on discharge, but now even those requests lacked force. I spoke little, responding only if required. When my parents or Sara visited, I half listened, my requests focusing on material items, cigarettes, money, food. My soul, my *élan vital*, had taken a sabbatical and an empty shell was left to deal with my physical needs. In brief moments of clarity, I panicked at the thought of never having my vitality return.

I "progressed" to the point where days were scheduled with activities: art therapy in the morning, music therapy for the afternoon. My attention span was short and I was easily frustrated by my inability to produce anything of remote value. In art therapy I worked on a project for a short time and then shifted to several other things during the course of a morning. Returning the next day, I would be unable to recognize the previous day's work and started anew, never completing any art project.

Music therapy was no better. I was being taught how to play the guitar, but I could not get the hang of it and lacked the necessary patience to persist. Since I was no longer confined to the ward, a new music therapist replaced Ken. Unfortunately, the new relationship had an impersonal teacher-pupil orientation. The therapist-teacher would sit with me for several minutes and teach some finger movements for the guitar. Afterwards, I would go into a small cubicle to practice. Although I wanted to learn to play, I stopped trying. Still, I continued going to the activity therapies; attending was better than staying on the ward, and I believed it indicated that I was cooperating and showing my readiness for discharge.

Most public mental hospitals were built with a vast below-ground network of interlocking tunnels connecting their buildings. The activities at Overbrook were set up in a series of underground rooms ingeniously squeezed into spaces where every inch was utilized. Perhaps inspiration for their construction was drawn from medieval dungeons, and they were designed to tap into archetypal images of confession and redemption. I wondered if lack of space was solely responsible for the lack of warmth and aesthetics. After breakfast one of the assistant activity therapists would come to the ward with a list of patients who were allowed to participate in activities. The nurse would read off the names as we formed a line. At the ward door, count was checked to make sure no one sneaked out. I futilely tried to get in line many times before I was officially included in the list.

The passageways to the activities were dimly lit and womb-like. I never could master the maze of tunnels to find my way around; I tried to make a mental map and memorize the different routes, but as with other things, I could not retain the information.

The loss of my ability to fight earned me the dubious honor of canteen privileges when escorted by my brother. During one of Sy's visits, I decided to show him the tunnels leading to the activities. We had been talking about my treatment at the hospital, and he was saying that he was pleased that I was participating in so many activities. I wanted him to see what it was really like, that activities actually took place in small, damp, dingy rooms with no windows. We set out but I couldn't find the rooms. Lost in the tunnels, we wandered around for several minutes, randomly trying one tunnel after another until finally, by pure luck, we found our way out. I took a perverse satisfaction from seeing my brother's anxiety build when he realized that we were lost. I may have imagined it, but I felt that he was much more empathic when listening to me, and less taken by the hospital propaganda, after that experience.

Nighttime was definitely the worst time in the hospital. The daytime promised hope and possibility. Maybe some new privilege, or success in convincing someone to advocate on your behalf; just the chance brought anticipation. Night signified the end of another unsuccessful, wasted day. What waited was the TV, and if you were lucky, visitors.

Everything calmed down between six o'clock and eight o'clock visiting hours. The hospital cleaned up and put on its best face. Suddenly the surly staff smiled and became friendly. The patients were also on good behavior. Everyone knew that they would pay dearly if they embarrassed the staff while visitors were there. For two hours every evening, the show went on.

I was considered very fortunate. Both Sara and my parents visited me regularly. As badly as I feel I was treated, I am certain that I would have been far worse off had I been alone with no interested visitors. At the time I was unaware of the significance of that fact. Indeed, my visitors during the first few months triggered my anger and frustration. Almost every time visitors came we argued. No one could appease or comfort me, I would not allow it. "Get me out of here . . . they're killing me." Nothing else mattered. Now I can understand their pain, too. What could they do? They saw my suffering, but also my desperation and irrationality. The hospital personnel told them of the dangers of taking me out too soon. They warned of permanent incapacitation, a vegetable forever. I watched them pass through the heavy metal ward door, the door that set me apart from the world.

Visiting hours were the patients' chance to speak to the outside world. It was our forum to prove that we didn't belong in the hospital, to make our families and friends understand, to get them to believe us and take our side. It was an opportunity to report how badly we were treated. Some of the patients quickly realized that they needed support to make believers of their visitors. Others, like me, who became angry, fulfilled pre-conceived expectations of how mental patients behave; the patients who had not given up persisted in attempting to receive a fair hearing. Before visiting hours, there was always optimism. Some would try to keep their minds focused on what they needed to ask. It was important to remember the date, and the events of the past few days. A big hit seemed to be the showing off of an art or craft project. My pride prevented such a display. I couldn't stand the phony cooing approval over the obviously poor quality work.

Sitting around the tables in the visiting room, the various families got to know each other. The more normal-looking patients were frequently requested by fellow patients to attest to the reliability of something that was being told to a visitor. The substantiation one patient gave to another's story was, of course, highly suspect. But we tried to validate each others' stories and sanity. Our attempts were met with good-natured, knowing smiles. Heads were perpetually nodded in assent, but the lack of affirmative action was evidence of our inability to convince anyone. Yet, every night the visiting game continued. We optimistically psyched ourselves and prepared as enthusiastically as any high school football team before Saturday's big game. But we always lost.

Who knows the extent of pain and damage inflicted through ignorance and good intentions, and whether it outweighs the malicious, intentional hurt? Can anyone distance himself enough to get the perspective required to judge? Who is presumptuous enough to say, "I know what is right?"

High doses of neuroleptic drugs, Thorazine and Stelazine, along with Artane, an anti-Parkinson's medicine, were the hospital's weapons in their war against my psychosis. Eventually, the drugs and confinement drove my emotions underground, blunting my cognition sufficiently for me to be deemed worthy of an off-hospital grounds visit.

The first pass was a trip to the diner with my parents. I felt awkward and embarrassed, uncomfortable being out in public. I was different. Accustomed to the artificial hospital light, I felt the sunlight exposed the inadequacy of my appearance. Everything looked peculiar in the real light of the outside world, light that made me feel dirty and sloppy. I was dull and felt embarrassed by what I had become. I couldn't even feel the glow of my anger to sustain me. I ordered an ice cream soda. I remember how good that strawberry ice cream soda tasted. I longed for the freedom to choose what I ate, to come and go as I pleased, and to sleep in my own bed without a locked door to prevent me from leaving.

During the next month, I was granted increasingly longer leaves to spend time out of the hospital. By the end of the month, I was allowed four days home and three days back at the hospital. It was almost time for discharge, but as I had so painfully learned, it was necessary for the process to proceed in a slow, orderly manner. I wondered why they didn't just let me out. I worried whether they were testing me to see if I could take care of myself. I again began questioning my parents and staff about discharge, but this time I refrained from pressure or challenge. My fawning behavior was directed at not drawing attention to myself. I knew that I had proven I was docile. Had I finally learned the game or did I change? Underneath, fear lurked and sometimes pushed through the drugs and suppression. For years,

I would grieve for the loss of an important part of me. Would it ever be recovered? Somehow, someplace within me, I preserved the seeds of hope and the belief that this was not all I was and ever would be.

It was frustrating spending four days a week home and the remaining three in the hospital. My discharge was delayed by a long waiting list for therapists at the after-care clinic. I was told that when I could obtain an appointment for therapy and medicine supervision, I would be discharged. The possibility of resuming therapy with Mrs. Warner was never presented to me. At least I had finally severed that unproductive relationship. Mrs. Warner never contacted me or my family during that period of time. I wonder if she would have taken me back as a patient.

I waited. For a month I kept going back and forth between the hospital and home. One day, finally, on my return from a leave, the charge nurse asked me what I was doing there. Unprepared for my return, there were no empty beds on the ward. She made some calls to check on my status. Since I had not yet officially come back from leave, I asked if I could return home. She told me that if I had a way of getting home, I would be permitted to go. I told her I would take a bus home. She told me to use my old pass and tell anyone who stopped me to call her. I walked out, expecting someone to stop me but no one did. At each door I waited for a challenge, but I didn't even get a second glance. I could not believe it . . . all the struggles . . . and now, to just walk out. Having no money, I began walking home very quickly. I forced myself to not turn around to see if anyone was coming after me. I never again went back to that hospital.

Why hadn't I just walked out, escaped that very first day? I was blindly waiting for justice, foolishly believing I owed society no act of contrition, and that my innocence would triumph. Again, I stumbled on my unrealistic faith in fairness. I was playing by the rules of a game I did not know how to play. To seize the moment, to step through and act: I had finally learned not to wait for permission, approval, affirmation – to just get myself home.

At last, freedom, but no joy. Relief was more like it, not elation. I did not feel free. My spirit beaten and battered, I could still feel the ropes that bound me. Although they were ripped free from their base and I was mobile, I felt those dense ropes dragging behind me – perhaps like the phantom pain of an amputated limb.

Chapter 8

Turning Points

Self-respect is to the soul as oxygen is to the body. Deprive a person of oxygen and you kill his body; deprive him of self-respect and you kill his spirit.
(Thomas Szasz)

First hello – last goodbye, heralded birth – denied death, we resist the inevitable entrances and exits of life. Enter the hospital, leave the hospital; enter reality . . . sometimes crying, often resigned, and always unprepared. Asleep and dependent, with emotions and intellect blunted, could I resist the life of passive resignation which lay waiting to suck dry what little life force remained?

My parents surprised me by continuing to pay the rent on my apartment while I was hospitalized. What did they tell the superintendent about my not being there for more than half a year? My apartment was unchanged, yet it seemed different. The energy was gone. The outrageous counter-culture posters reminded me of what was, but the apartment was no longer an expression of me.

I felt bored and boring. Nothing excited me. I went through the motions of social interaction but everything I did was directed at pretending that I was normal. Sara tried to pick up the pieces of our relationship. If caring about me was all it took to make me whole, Sara might have succeeded. She tried to stick by me but I was different now and our relationship had changed. Sara had become dominant and deep down I knew that I would never be able to regain her respect.

I always seemed to be outside myself, observing and judging, removed from others and lacking spontaneity. Feeling alone and isolated, the hope for change sustained me. I waited for something to happen. There was a great buried, unavailable part of me that I had to believe would return. Perhaps the fire had been extinguished, but I quietly refused to accept that I would always be this defeated shell that was masquerading as me.

Dr. Tomblin, my new therapist, was a psychologist who worked full-time at a veterans' hospital and part-time at Overbrook's after-care clinic. Trusting him was no small feat, given my suspiciousness of anyone associated with Overbrook. His part-time status helped me to think of him as separate from the rest of the hospital staff and its negative associations. As I told Dr. Tomblin my woebegone story, he seemed to align himself with me. He listened and seemed to understand and empathize. Although I was reluctant to trust him, I felt that he was on my side. He told me who he was, without the secret codes and mystery that had been so much a part of my previous therapy experience, and I appreciated the genuine communication. He helped me break the silences with light talk. We drank coffee and smoked cigarettes together during sessions, and he did not act superior or judgmental. Dr. Tomblin offered me an ear, advice, insight – whatever help was needed. When we discussed therapy, he explained the pragmatism that was at the core of his philosophy of treatment. When I became disheartened, he encouraged me with personal examples from his life. He did what he could and I appreciated it, but what I needed exceeded the limits of what psychotherapy offered. What I did – my actions and reactions outside of the therapy office – were key to the reconstruction of my identity.

Most alarming was my almost complete lack of energy. Part of my lethargy could be attributed to the psychiatric drugs, and some to a hospital-mediated return to "normalcy." I resented having to continue taking drugs, but I obediently continued to follow orders. When I started psychotherapy, the drugs were reduced. The regimen was changed several times during the first six months until I could finally discontinue the pills completely. To try to pull me out of my lethargy, the amount of Thorazine was decreased. Then, I was switched to Mellaril; still there was no increase in energy. Speculation as to possible depression led to the prescription of Sinequan – a pill that I was told would act as both an anti-depressant and tranquilizer. Of course I was depressed, but the anti-depressant didn't help. I had a right to my despair. To not be depressed I would have had to be so high on drugs that I didn't care about anything. I would have to have been completely out of touch with my life circumstances. Finally realizing that the pills were more harmful than useful, I began decreasing them on my own. Later, Dr. Tomblin talked the supervising psychiatrist into letting me try to go drug-free. As had happened before, by that time I had withdrawn from the medication on my own. Unfortunately, I learned that even without the deadening effects of the drugs, I was still depressed, lethargic and feeling defeated. I had hoped the elimination of the medication would allow my mental acuity to return, but apathy and diminished prospects substituted for the drugs in maintaining my sluggish state.

For months I existed in a fog. I had no job and was borrowing money from my parents to live. Much of my remaining hope was attached to the belief that work would be the catalyst to jump-start my recovery. Getting my old job back held promise but also was threatening. To be a psychologist, to resume my dream, was what I wanted and needed. But I had to fight the wish to stay in bed with the covers pulled over my head. Throughout my hospitalization Sara had assured me that Dr. Birjandi was holding my job open for my return. Unfortunately, at the time of my discharge a job freeze had gone into effect at state institutions, making my job temporarily unavailable. For two months I was told, "Any day now, your employment is just around the corner." During weekly phone calls to check my job status, I learned that the hospital was going through yet another reorganization. Every few years, a new reorganization began. The same pieces were reshuffled, reassembled in a different manner, and somehow the maneuver was supposed to enhance patient treatment. If the people are flawed, the rearrangements of the people will only temporarily conceal the harm they will bring to the new structure. Ironically, the once discarded system often becomes the new innovation. The patients, who stand in the middle of the illusory change, are pawns in a reconfigured system that continues to foster dependency, few meaningful choices and an inability to attain dignity and develop self-respect.

When I was officially informed that the job was open, I had to confront my fears. Along with the threatening prospect of a required interview with two Greystone psychiatrists, I needed a letter from my therapist stating that it was okay for me to return to work in a mental hospital. Dr. Tomblin showed me his letter, in which he had written that I was symptom-free, off medication and that my return to work would be beneficial to my mental health. One hurdle had been cleared, but now I would have to present myself for evaluation by the two psychiatrists.

Just prior to my interview, I learned that Dr. Birjandi had resigned from her position as director of the psychology department. Having depended on her help to get my job back, I felt new fears at the absence of her support. The new director, Clarence Terpenning, had interned with me. I remembered my comfort with him at that time, but I worried about how he would react to my hospitalization. I tried to remember what Clarence was like. He was conservative and practical. Would he have any understanding of what I had been through and the challenges facing me? Clarence had worked for most of his career as an industrial psychologist. After turning fifty, he had decided to switch fields to become a clinical psychologist. His choice to take a risk and make a major career change made me hopeful.

Both Clarence and Dr. Birjandi received me warmly when I arrived at the hospital for my interview. They briefed me on the new organizational structure and the whereabouts of former associates and acquaintances. Dr. Birjandi explained that she had become so tired and frustrated by the administrative nonsense that she had resigned her director's position to work exclusively with the geriatric patients at the hospital. I was extremely nervous during the meeting. As long as they did the talking I was fine, but I had nothing of my own to offer to the conversation. Strong feelings of guardedness stifled any possible spontaneity.

They assured me that my interview with the hospital psychiatrists was merely a formality. I wondered if it would be a diagnostic interview – whether the psychiatrists would be looking for evidence of residual psychopathology. I kept wiping my sweaty palms on a handkerchief as I walked down the hall to the meeting. No matter, they would feel the clamminess when we shook hands.

I was surprised by the psychiatrists' friendliness and cordiality. They tried to make it a relaxed interview and their questions were not deeply probing. Somehow I got through it. One question that was asked stuck with me: "How did Overbrook compare to Greystone in terms of patient treatment?"

I stumbled around with the question, focusing on the emphasis Overbrook placed on activities such as art and music therapy. I told them about my music therapy with Ken and talked of its value and meaning for me. Stuck in my throat was the wish to tell them what I really thought of my hospital treatment, but they were not making a request for information nor did they think I could tell them anything they did not already know. Now I have a different, but still unsatisfying, response:

"Doctors, if you only were open to how much you don't know. For the hospitalized psychiatric patient, survival is what it's about, not treatment."

I was glad to return to work. I naively needed to believe that everything would become the way it had been, that I could resume my old life. Unfortunately, nothing came naturally. I felt very strange. I was ill at ease with both staff and patients. The simple requirements of casual conversation seemed impossible to master. In the past, my pride and self-esteem had centered on my perceptiveness. I never was adept at conversation and the subtleties of social interaction, but before, my saving grace was being able to respond intelligently, to make an occasional insightful remark. This avenue of sociability was now blocked and replaced by sluggishness and vacuity. I was doing nothing of interest, so I had no stories to tell and I had difficulty working up enthusiasm for anything. I kept hoping my personality would resurface, but as time passed, I became more discouraged and questioned if anything of value was ever there to recover. I withdrew from social situations. So little of me was there anyway, I preferred being invisible.

Clarence gave me time to acclimate myself to my work. My initial responsibilities centered on doing psychological evaluations and attending clinical staff meetings. I was responsible for administering tests to patients, interpreting the results and then writing psychological reports. I was able to relearn how to conduct the tests, but I was unable to write the reports. The evaluations loomed over my head as insurmountable tasks. Studying the material for hours resulted in nothing productive; the paper stared back at me blank and empty. I tried to draw on my past experience and training, but it was inaccessible, buried too deeply beneath the mental scar tissue. The intellectual processes I had learned to depend upon had deserted me. Despite intense efforts, I was stymied, and I fell behind in my assignments.

Finally, I admitted my inability to do the work and asked Clarence for help. Together we went over test results, but the completed reports were just about dictated to me by Clarence. Steve, a co-worker, also tried to help me with some of the reports. As was the case with Clarence, each report we worked on was beyond my ability. I even met Larry at the public library and he tried to teach me how to do psychological reports. My therapist offered to help me with a report during one of our sessions. All of these people helped somewhat, but the problem of becoming capable of doing the work on my own seemed insurmountable. With their assistance I could complete the required evaluation, but each new psychological report presented a unique situation that would frustrate me and make me aware of my inadequacy. I was unable to assimilate and apply the general concepts from one report to the next. I could not tap into my past experience writing reports, and the self-imposed pressure mounted. Embarrassed and discouraged, I felt more and more like a bloodless, spiritless non-entity.

After three months of work, I saw no progress. I dreaded going in to work each day. I was a fake. I was writing reports that had no meaning and I knew that I was not improving. I would go to the staffing of a patient that I had evaluated and the psychiatrist would ask my opinion. I had no opinion. I imagined that those awkward silences exposed my fraudulent portrayal of a psychologist. Did they all have as low an opinion of me as I had of myself?

Adding to my problems was an inexplicable bureaucratic foul-up that prevented me from getting paid. Payroll operated biweekly with new employees receiving their first pay after three weeks and then being paid every two weeks. My first paycheck did not come until I had worked six months. When I was not paid at the end of three weeks, I met with a member of the Personnel Department. I was told that I would receive two checks after the next two-week pay period. Two more weeks passed: no check. I complained again and was told it would be looked into and remedied. The delay went on for half a year until I was finally paid in one lump sum for the entire period. The only explanation I was ever given for the delay was that I was not officially on record as being rehired. Not being paid during a time when I felt that I was not really working further eroded my feelings of self-worth. I was forced to borrow more money from my parents to pay my rent and cover basic necessities.

The depressed, hopeless feelings were most pronounced during my morning car rides on the way to work. Always I would ask myself why I was bothering to go in to work and continuing such a useless struggle. For the first time, I thought of ending my life and its unsolvable problems. The future loomed dark and empty. Seeing no progress, I didn't want to go on. Severely disappointed in my hope that the job would stimulate my recovery, I was reminded daily, through my inability to do the work, of my failure. When I told my therapist I was going to quit work, it felt like I was leaving a suicide note. I was not ending my life but I was killing the dream – resigning from possibility.

Dr. Tomblin asked, "What will you do?"

I wanted him to talk me out of quitting, but I knew he would not have any convincing arguments.

"I'll go back to work for the welfare department . . . I can do that work. I can't stand working in that hospital any longer. I cannot continue pretending to be what I am not. I give up."

I went to Clarence and told him that I was resigning from my job.

Clarence's response was remarkable. He told me, "If you can continue getting in to work on time, I'll make you my personal assistant. I'll get you an office a few doors down from mine and there will be no pressure to do anything but what you need to do to get your skills back. At your own pace you can reorganize the psychology department's files. You can take as much time as you need. As long as you can stay at work all day, I'll justify your time. It will just be between the two of us."

I don't know what motivated Clarence to give me this gift, but I will never underestimate its importance. Twenty years before the Americans with Disabilities Act was passed, and going far beyond *reasonable accommodations*, Clarence understood the value of developing individualized supports. He gave me a safe place to rest, consolidate my strength and keep alive my hopes for a meaningful career in psychology. I agreed to try.

Meanwhile, the pressure, my inability to handle it, and my wallowing in lethargic apathy pushed Sara and me further apart. Our relationship began disintegrating rapidly. I was self-absorbed and had little to give. She tried to extend herself, but it was an unrewarding, one-sided endeavor. For a while she seemed to believe that I would again become the person I had been before I was hospitalized at Overbrook. The last straw for Sara was when I gave up my apartment after the rent had been raised and I was still waiting for my first paycheck. I knew that my independent living was a farce and I was relieved to let go of the apartment. I felt guilty about the money I was borrowing from my parents. Half-heartedly, I went along with Sara's suggestion that we look for a cheaper apartment and move in together, but in the end I opted to live with my parents and Sara chose to take her first apartment on her own. We were moving in different directions. I was becoming more dependent, and she more independent. We saw each other as lovers for a few more months and parted ways.

Minimally present in my relationship with Sara, I felt alone; after the split, I was alone. In some ways it was easier. Although I felt a deeper sense of loneliness, a significant amount of social pressure was gone. I could withdraw into myself and search for lost inner strength. I had to do things differently. No longer could I look to Sara to meet my needs and then blame her for my unhappiness. But without Sara, there was no diversion or respite from the despair.

My parents were wonderfully supportive during those lowest of times. They just let me be, asked no questions, accepted me. My mother silently suffered as she watched her son giving up. Mom tried to be consoling when I told her Sara and I had broken up. I hated telling her of another failure.

All the immediate surface pressure was gone. I had moved in with my parents, no more need to maintain a declining relationship with Sara, and at work I was able to hide in a safe place. Yet the depression would not lift. Every day after work, I would return home to fall asleep on the couch while watching re-runs of F Troop and McHale's Navy. On weekends, I would take a bus into Manhattan to see a few movies. I told my parents I was going out with friends. In New York I could get lost in the anonymous crowds. But even there, I was alert to the possible embarrassment of seeing a familiar face and being called to justify wandering the streets alone on a Saturday night.

The largest task I faced was the daily decision to get out of bed and go to work. Once there, the struggle with self-hatred commenced. With the removal of my responsibility for doing psychological evaluations, I spent the next month going over old case records. I reviewed reports until they all seemed the same. Guilty and embarrassed at not being able to do the job, each passing minute was a painful test of endurance. Generally I was alone, often staring blankly into space with an open report file on my desk in case anyone wandered by and observed my stupor. But slowly, almost imperceptibly and outside of conscious direction, the awareness gradually developed that most of the reports I was reading were rather unremarkable. Very few reports reflected the standards I had demanded of myself. As I began to consider and then own this insight, my feelings of inadequacy at work began to diminish.

Although my discomfort in social situations remained strong, there were a few non-threatening circumstances in which I could relax. Lunches at work, initially a problem, eventually became a relief and a diversion from the boredom. Eating lunches in the conference room with Steve, I was at ease and did not feel pressured to be socially interactive. Like me a Masters-level staff psychologist, Steve with his quiet, low-key personality suited my needs. We ate lunch together and then played checkers for the remainder of the hour. The checker games were great therapy for me. They were relaxing and helped to focus my concentration. Soon, I began beating Steve regularly. He, in turn, became intent on winning; however, as he improved, I also improved enough to retain a competitive edge. Those silly little checker games did a lot to boost my self-esteem. The rapport we developed while playing even gave me enough confidence to participate in some good-natured teasing.

Small, soft rumblings in my psyche were drawing my attention to how I was beginning to change. My thought processes were beginning to quicken and my concentration was improving. I noticed a growing restlessness and a willingness to take some risks. I tentatively relinquished small elements of security in favor of relieving the tedious boredom. I perceived some faint glimmers of hope pushing their way into my awareness.

It takes considerable time for the deadening effects of psychiatric medication and the trauma of a hospital experience to wear off. I felt a little sharper and a little less timid. I had bottomed out and was ready to start moving up. The foundation was not firm, but the absence of pressure made it the right time. My eyes were beginning to open, to look and see things outside myself. In a process analogous to the Gestalt Therapy technique for stage fright, I reclaimed my eyes. I would not relinquish my right to look at myself and others. I had given my eyes to everyone, they looked at me and I allowed them to judge me. I took my eyes back and saw myself, and in so doing was able to see others. I tried to not be intimidated and frozen immobile in fearful anticipation of a negative evaluation of my performance. I forced myself into making my stage-frightened, life-frightened internal actor look out at all the projected judges whose imagined standards I was incapable of meeting. To finally begin looking out at others helped me begin the climb up.

Since my discharge from the hospital, I had waited for a feeling, a sign, some form of energy to signal the return of me. When you are physically ill, you wait for the fever to subside, for your body and mind to begin feeling the return of healthy energy. My veil of despair lifted; I peeked out at possibilities. The ever-present gnawing fear of irreversible damage to my psyche could finally be challenged. Ready to try, but with trepidation, I edged into Clarence's office and said, "I want to do a psychological."

I was able to perform my work. I became capable of independently writing psychological reports. Hope seeped into my consciousness and I thought of the future. Slowly, my perceptiveness began returning. I began having intuitions and feelings again. I cautiously started interacting with more people.

After a while, my work responsibilities were expanded to include psychotherapy. I knew my limitations but I also realized that the people I saw had no one else but me. I did not pretend to probe deeply into their psyches, but I did not minimize their possibilities to progress. My hospital experiences had taught me how much the little things count. When weather permitted, I conducted therapy sitting outside on a park bench. Walks to the canteen, a cup of coffee or a shared cigarette nurtured the therapeutic bond.

Initially it was difficult to shake off the hospital memories. Easily triggered associations wreaked havoc with my moods. Facing the conflict of closing my eyes or perpetually tilting at hospital windmills caused guilt to flit in and out of my consciousness. As I became stronger, I automatically denied the injustices and coldness of my place of employment and drifted toward identifying with the power of the hospital. But always there was some reminder to snap my experience as a patient back into my awareness. At those times I was glad I could not forget.

There was the time nineteen-year-old Bobby came running up to me, pleading to be taken off the ward for a walk. When we were outside he told me that one of the student nurses was a former high school classmate. Bobby had hidden in his room the last time she was there, but was afraid she would see him during one of her visits. I took him off the ward whenever a nursing class came to the hospital.

Thoughts of my own embarrassment at having to deal with the student nurses unleashed a flood of angry memories. Student nurses with ready notebooks descending on the ward – how I hated their enthusiastic innocence. The assignment was to form a relationship with us, get us talking. At first you are anxious to tell them your story. They look so concerned, so willing to help. At least they listened. But I learned to resent the detached information gathering and false hope for understanding it inspired. I soon began avoiding them. I felt like a guinea pig. I would not make myself available to demonstrate my psychopathology.

I understood and knew the value of the simple things I could do for Bobby and others. I discovered my capacity to listen and empathize. The respectful understanding I had craved, I could give to others. As I became more comfortable with patients, I noticed a developing comfort with myself. The conflict of identifying with the patients or the hospital temporarily worked itself out, but future conflicts would require more active resolutions. Most importantly, I wanted to learn and I was willing to take risks again.

As I became stronger I had new emotional battles to wage. If I got too strong, would I get careless and lose touch with reality? Could I afford to get too strong? Would it happen again? What had I really learned? Was this the road back or a cruel joke temporarily postponing the inevitable repetition of the previous two psychotic episodes? Would I ever have credibility to my family, to myself, or would this ghost haunt me forever?

All around me, I saw the repeaters, the patients with multiple recurring hospitalizations. During the weeks I rearranged files, I came across the file containing my hospital reports. Fair Oaks Hospital in 1966 had diagnosed me with schizophrenia, paranoid type. In 1969, Overbrook had diagnosed me with schizophrenia, chronic type, prognosis: guarded. I questioned Dr. Tomblin about my diagnosis. He pulled his copy of my file and we went over the reports together. We talked of the meaninglessness of diagnosis, of how one is made to fit a category. But am I an incurable schizophrenic, doomed to repeat this pattern? Am I trapped to live out this role all my life? Intellectually, I could deny and logically poke holes in my diagnosis, but emotionally it takes much more to cleanse the psyche of that damning diagnosis.

Give it a name, have something to call it, and the unfamiliar darkness takes on the illusion of light. It is still murky and unknown, but now you feel that it is understood and predictable. If you get others to accept the name, then they too respond accordingly . . . there is validation, but do you have reality?

Chapter 9

Recovery/Transformation: The Opportunity to be Different

Growth and self-transformation cannot be delegated.　　(Lewis Mumford)

In ancient Persia the first healers were priests. Their practice was based on the principle that the devil had created 99,999 diseases, which should be treated by a combination of magic and hygiene. They favored the use of spells on the grounds that although they might not cure the illness, they would not kill the patient – which was more than could be said for many drugs and physical treatments.[17]

Attempts to unlock the mysteries of the disordered mind have attracted, stimulated and frustrated great thinkers throughout our recorded history. Today, modern medicine, through its disease model of illness, has ascended to the position of pre-eminent authority in the understanding, care and treatment of mental illness. With an absolute certainty that in the past was seen only in divinely inspired religious doctrine, organized medicine has promoted unproven dogma as scientific fact.

Diagnosed into being an object, imprisoned with or without walls, cut off from meaningful dialogue, the psychiatric consumer/survivor/ ex-patient (c/s/x)[1] must adapt to that artificial world. When you are diagnosed and treated for a major mental illness, your life's course is deeply affected by how you integrate that experience into your identity.

A question asked to a c/s/x sample in California: *In general, what do you feel is the main source of any psychological or emotional problem you may have?* Thirty percent pointed to the mental health system as the major source of their problems. Interestingly, about 37% of the 110

---

[1]Consumer/survivor/ex-patient is an inclusive generic name for people who have been treated for serious mental illness with a few exceptions in a psychiatric in-patient institution. The variety in terms (hence, c/s/x) reflects the diversity of opinions on mental health treatment issues and allows for self-identification according to one's positions regarding mental illness, treatments, rights, etc.

professionals who were also surveyed said that the mental health system was a major source of the emotional problems of their clients.[18] Repeated consistently in surveys of c/s/x individuals is the complaint that it is more difficult in the long term to recover from the damage of the psychiatric label and the hospital treatment (iatrogenic effects) than from the original precipitating psychological turbulence and crises. Recovery is a complex, time-consuming process in which the iatrogenic effects of treatment, and the crushed dreams and stigma, may be more difficult to overcome than the original condition.

The number of obstacles needing to be overcome after you have been hospitalized and permanently labeled discourages the *recovered* from being open about their experiences and becoming role models that would inspire others. For those occupied with the struggle to stay out of the hospital and survive, the best course may be to distance themselves from their psychiatric history by joining the ranks of the *hidden recovered*. Yet, those who can be open, who can share the successes of their recovery journeys, are invaluable resources. That openness, with its gifts to fellow travelers, provides its own reward, but I had tasks to master before I could self-disclose and use all of my experience.

I faced a somewhat different set of obstacles after my second psychiatric hospitalization. This time, without the treatment-induced memory loss, I could more ably and quickly pretend to fit into most of the role expectations and behavioral requirements of the chronically normal. But now, added to a lifetime of dissatisfaction with who I was, I also had to struggle with a mysterious enemy (madness) which could at any time take control of my life. I was functioning at my job, and although my interactions with people were less than relaxed, I believed that most of the time I did not draw negative attention to myself. Underneath, I fought against resigning myself to living in the misty flat lands of anxious mediocrity. Whereas before I had believed in my future and thought I had the potential to develop into the kind of person I wanted to be, I now concentrated on fitting in and surviving. I was aware of the price exacted by survival. Inaccessible were the gut feelings and intuition that are so integral a part of inspiration or creativity. I was thinking clearly, but seemed to be accessing only the logical part of my brain. Was my intuition irretrievably lost? Always present was the specter of another incarceration. How could I relax my guard when the dormant seeds of madness lay waiting for some cue to wake destructive forces that could wreak havoc on whatever life I had worked to construct? How could I avoid vigilantly scanning for warning signs, those harbingers of a fated process that would always remain out of my control?

My search for answers in psychology books was a fruitless endeavor. It was 1971 and I was uninformed about anything but mainstream approaches to mental illness. The few alternative explanations that I explored, and which at first seemed promising – those of R.D. Laing, Harry Stack Sullivan, Wilham Reich – were too difficult to comprehend and did not connect with my personal needs. At that very same time the c/s/x movement was just beginning in New York and California, but since I was searching for answers from professionals, the birthing of that movement never came to my attention.

Books like *I Never Promised You a Rose Garden*[19] made me long for a therapist with the caring warmth and incisive brilliance attributed to Frieda Fromm-Reichmann, but I knew that my answers would have to be found someplace else. I was not verbal enough, not open enough, not interesting enough to be a suitable candidate for such insight-driven therapy. Plus, my experience with the analytic therapy of my previous therapist had soured me on looking for the magic of an insight-driven breakthrough. My psychotherapy with Dr. Tomblin was tapering off to monthly sessions and I had no desire to find a therapist to do any more than the supportive therapy that he provided.

I knew that my growth and progress would occur and be shaped by what I did in the everyday world, not in a therapist's office. I was twenty-eight years old, living with my parents and too dependent on old friends for my less than satisfying, safe social life. I wished for intimacy but had too many unresolved conflicts to muster up the energy needed to develop a meaningful relationship. My fantasy of someday getting married and having children seemed a pipedream. Was it a sign of health to be satisfied with the safe, half-life I was living? Given my prognosis, was not my maintenance and stabilization the ultimate goal? Or was the safe niche that had enabled me to get back on my feet offering me a stepping-stone to try for more?

Again, I found myself at a plateau which could turn into a developmental crisis. Six years before, stymied and thrown off my career path after earning my Masters degree, I unwittingly had chosen a self-exploration course whose graduation ceremony was commemorated in a psychiatric hospital. Three years after I first became a mental patient, I worked my way back to the point where the road had first detoured, but I continued to be the same adolescent stuck in the doorway to adulthood and facing another confrontation with hospital confinement. Once again, three more years had passed and I still had not become the person I wanted to be. I could not hide from my past. Was it only a matter of time before I faced another, longer, more damaging commitment to a hospital? How many chances would I get? When would hope die?

Do people change? Can they change? Could I change? I had to believe that I was still developing, that real change was possible. I fought the doctors' attempts to change me, but despite my protests, I was angry and frustrated by what I had not become. Most representative of my failure was my inability to get into a doctoral psychology program and become a "real" psychologist. I thought that if I could reach that goal I could use it as evidence to convince myself that genuine change had occurred. A PhD would be my springboard into a new life. The surviving glimmer of possibility sprinkled some color into what had been for the last few years a dreary black and white snapshot.

Ezra Stotland speculated that a person with schizophrenia had lost all hope of goal achievement in the real world and as a result created an imaginary world.[20] Although too simple an explanation for a complex process, it is a recognition of the importance of hope. I fought to nurture the hope within myself, but its sustenance required help and support from others. I had to feel that significant people in my life truly believed in my dreams and potential. I was fortunate that in my lowest, darkest times, my family always expected me to get better, and one good friend never gave up his belief in me.

Researcher Courtenay Harding's longitudinal studies of schizophrenia asked those sturdy old people who had recovered, what really made the difference? After looking down at their feet and shuffling around, they said, "Well, somebody told me I might have a chance to get better. Somebody believed in me and my own persistence, and that gave me hope."[21]

The four Fs – Filth, Food, Fetching and Filing – are the too-familiar job options for those labeled with mental illness. Professionals often encourage the soon-to-be-discharged mental patient to downsize his or her expectations to small, easily attainable, "realistic" goals. Having an advanced graduate degree or other technical skills (carpentry, electronics, engineering) may not preclude job placement in "low stress" jobs.

Stuck in my memory was the complaint expressed by an articulate middle-aged woman at a self-help workshop I was conducting.

"I was discharged with a follow-up plan to attend day treatment. They set up a program for me to learn activities of daily living . . . cooking and taking care of my living space. I know I let everything go when I was depressed, but before that, I took care of a house, cooked, and raised three children. What I need is a job, not learning how to do the dishes and mop the floor. I'm a college graduate."

The absence of meaningful work deflates everyone's self-concept. For those with psychiatric histories it is a solid barrier to making the conversion from being a useless, burdensome object to a person making a contribution to the community. Not having the opportunity to work to the potential that had always been associated with your self-concept, relinquishing your dreams, finding yourself stuck without any prospect of achieving a worthwhile goal, makes you especially vulnerable to the episodic emotional problems arising out of attempts to cope with life's pitfalls.

My work successes signified and validated my progress. Seeing my intellectual acuity return increased my self-esteem and provided receptive ground for future success. Just as failure had paved a spiraling downward stairway, success fed upon itself and propelled me upwards. I became able to take more social risks and as a result developed more social competencies. The positive responses I received at work enabled me to make new friends. I felt a sense of belonging and camaraderie between me and my co-workers. My new colleagues expressed admiration at my ability to relate to patients.

After years of unsuccessful attempts, I once again began applying to doctoral psychology programs. Unlike my approach to previous tries, I researched, planned and organized my applications to maximize my chances. I was accepted into two schools, the counseling program at the University of Southern Mississippi and the new California School of Professional Psychology. When I compared the financial costs, it was clear that Mississippi had to be my choice.

My acceptance into graduate school was my opportunity to make a new beginning, but the fear in my mother's eyes was obvious as she watched me prepare to leave. Twice before, her son had gone out into the world, only to return battered and defeated.

Graduate school in Mississippi allowed me to test myself without the handicap of a familiar environment pushing the buttons of old habits. Being able to draw on unusual, but very relevant life experience, I was ready to profit from the educational opportunity. I was a stranger to the university and to the culture of the south, and that gave me freedom from the usual demands I made on myself and others. I was open to learning all that I could. It was my chance to leave my psychiatric history behind and bury it under newly developed strengths and understanding, never forgetting that foremost and always, the most important goal was to stay out of the hospital. In graduate school I had the opportunity to indulge my needs for self-exploration. My proclivity to disregard safety when enticed by the prospect of new understanding had caused me in the past to wander too far from the beaten path. This time, I plunged into methods and systems of thought and action designed to expand human potential. Looking for ways to grow and become stronger, I read of the Eastern philosophies and religions. I delved into Zen meditation, self-hypnosis, dream analysis, awareness exercises and guided imagery.

Success in my doctoral studies came easily. Free of distractions, and interested in what I was learning, I was able to focus and concentrate on my work. Each success increased my self-confidence. When I expressed opinions that were drawn from my previous work and carefully selected parts of my personal experience, the faculty seemed to be impressed and treated me with an element of respect that was missing from their typical interaction with students. My major professor Brian Kelley, who was only a few years older than I, became a mentor and a friend. Since I was supporting myself with a stipend from my fellowship, it was always helpful when Brian invited me to his home for dinner or when I babysat his children. Although I also became friendly with other faculty and students, I never seriously considered sharing my psychiatric history with anyone. As I became stronger and I closed in on my doctoral degree, I believed I was leaving that disturbing history behind. A few times a month I would dream of being lost in a maze of tunnels or trapped in a locked room where my screams to be let out were ignored. I regarded those nightmares as an attempt to work through the experience and decided to track them in a journal, but not to dwell on them. To be safe, to see myself as normal, I believed that I had to put my psychiatric past in a closed box and keep increasing my distance from that box until it fell completely out of my field of vision, well below the farthest horizon.

In 1974 I earned my doctorate. Almost five years had passed since I had left Overbrook. Self-respect seeped into my consciousness as I began the process of liking and appreciating my value. My diminished intensity combined with increased self-assurance resulted in more positive social interactions. Feeling less anxious with people, I was able to refine my social skills. The future offered possibilities, but I could not help worrying about how long it would be until some haunting questions again demanded attention. Was returning home as a doctor enough to prove my competence and allow me to enter mainstream normalcy? Would I be able to abandon my search for meaning by just chalking it up to an adolescent identity crisis? In order to remain safe, did I have to turn my back on what I had experienced? And what about my obligation to the people who were – and are – going through similar experiences?

I had made the climb out of the abyss. The greater the passage of time, the safer I felt. The longer I stayed out of the hospital, free of medication and treatment, the greater the proof of my stability. Diagnosed a schizophrenic, I was told there is no cure. However, years after I was sentenced to this life-time, progressively degenerating condition, I became aware of long-term longitudinal research studies in countries all over the world showing results that were more congruent with my experience – that there can be complete recovery from schizophrenia.[22]

The Vermont longitudinal study tracked patients for an average of thirty-two years after first admission. Psychologist Courtenay Harding reported that among the bottom one-third diagnosed as schizophrenic and the most "hopeless" of the backward patients, thirty per cent fully recovered. That bottom one-third was described as the worst of the worst – the feces-smearing patients who barely dressed themselves and had forgotten how to tell time. The Vermont study defined full recovery as being symptom-free, holding a job, having a social life and taking no medication.[23] Yet despite the optimistic findings for this supposedly "hopeless" group of people, mainstream psychiatric belief continues to view recovery as rare or impossible. Based on her research, Harding has come to believe that we are not able to predict who will recover and who will not. Amongst her strongest recommendations is to treat everyone as if they have the capability to recover. She advises against triaging patients into different treatment paths based on patient characteristics (age of onset, pre-morbid condition, education) that are supposed to predict who will be able to recover and who will not. During my own struggles to come to grips with my experience and maintain hope, it would have been extremely helpful to have known of this optimistic research. But even now, when I present this research to faculty in graduate clinical psychology programs, I find a general unfamiliarity with these research-generated concepts about recovery.

Bill Anthony of Boston University's pioneering psychosocial rehabilitation program has advocated for a recovery model based on the assumptions that follow:

1. Recovery can occur without professional intervention. The consumer/ survivors rather than professionals are the keys to recovery.

2. Essential is the presence of people who believe in and stand by the person in need of recovery. Of critical importance is a person or persons whom one can trust to be there in times of need.

3. Recovery is not a function of one's theory about the causes of mental illness. And recovery can occur whether one views the condition as biological or not.

4. People who experience intense psychiatric symptoms episodically are able to recover. Growth and setbacks during recovery make it feel like it is not a linear process. Recovery often changes the frequency and duration of symptoms for the better. The process does not feel systematic and planned.

5. Recovery from the consequences of the original condition may be the most difficult part of recovery. The disadvantages, including stigma, loss of rights, discrimination and disempowering treatment services can combine to hinder a person's recovery even if he or she is asymptomatic.

6. *The following recovery assumption confronts a challenge frequently used to diminish the experience of consumer/survivor advocates and as such is reproduced intact.* "Recovery from mental illness does not mean that one was not really mentally ill. At times people who have successfully recovered from severe mental illness have been discounted as not really mentally ill. Their successful recovery is not seen as a model, as a beacon of hope for those beginning the recovery process, but rather as an aberration, or worse yet as a fraud. It is as if we said that someone who has quadriplegia but recovered did not really have a damaged spinal cord! People who have or are recovering from mental illness are sources of knowledge about the recovery process and how people can be helpful to those who are recovering."[24]

I had a client I saw in therapy, an astrophysicist, one of those incredibly bright people who live in a different intellectual domain. Somehow we got to talking about weather prediction and he explained the impossible probabilities of accurately predicting weather for more than a week. He told me that we have sharply decreasing ability to accurately predict after three days and then it gets progressively tougher when the period of time is a week or longer. He argued that even with anticipated futuristic advances in technology, the number, complexity and changing dynamics and interaction of the involved variables make long-range predictability virtually impossible. With the above in mind, are we not being arrogant to assume that we are capable of predicting, many years into the future, the actions, precise development and limits of recovery for an individual? I choose to believe that the human spirit rivals the weather in complexity.

The analytical critical mind revels in its aptitude for constructing questions. I may never find the answers but I am glad that I can continue searching. When I examine what I choose to call my transformation rather than my recovery, I find it extremely difficult to separate and prioritize the significant factors. Even attempts to classify into broad categories, like external/internal, seem contrived and artificial. The attribution of a spiritual, mystical, karmic or divine intervention in the change process is a major component of most of the world's healing traditions. Even devoted practitioners of modern medicine are reluctant to completely shut their minds and hearts to miracles of faith and healing when privately confronting their imperfect science. Until it's personal, those unknown spontaneous recoveries from all sorts of ailments can be lumped together by scientists into what may be medicine's name for hope – placebo.

My ascent from madness to my present state of clarity and self-acceptance was and is a journey whose responsibility always resided within me. However, as I try to describe and share with others what wisdom I acquired, to aid others in their work, I acknowledge one element that I do not understand or take credit for, something that is named or interpreted according to one's unique beliefs and values as luck, fate, karma or God's blessing.

I believe that as long as a person is alive, some seed of hope, some possibility is there waiting to be fertilized. Hope fights the fear, nurtures the courage and inspires the vision and the work required to resist giving up and accepting that your goals are unattainable. Deep in the recesses of our being there are safe sanctuaries, secure hiding places for never fully lost dreams. But sometimes they are hidden so well that we can no longer reach those parts of ourselves. The help we need may come from expected and unexpected sources.

There were multiple, dynamic, interactive factors instrumental in my transformative recovery journey. First I had to return to a place where I could be less fearful, a place where I felt competent enough to negotiate everyday tasks without anxiety and embarrassment. I had to be able to think clearly enough to not feel that every interaction with people was influenced by my humiliation and weakness. *Hope* was nurtured in me by people who cared enough about me to be there in a way that did not diminish me. No matter how low or out of it I was, I seemed to know when someone was connected with me in a way that supported me. I was fortunate to have the personal *natural supports* which enabled me to construct the kind of safe niches that were needed to develop my strengths and consolidate the gains necessary to take the risk for entering a new space.

Living with my parents enabled the redefining of our relationships. Eventually they began to see my progress, but when I was accepted into a doctoral program and was ready to leave for school, they saw the potential risks and dangers. Even returning home a "doctor" was not enough to prove my competence to them. The next few years I fought Mom's final attempts to get me to conform to her values and standards. Eventually, over time, an understanding and mutual respect was reached by Mom and I. During the last years of her life, she enjoyed hearing me read letters of appreciation and thanks from former patients. At first Mom wanted to know if I believed I really helped the patients who came to see me. She did not understand the profession I had chosen and she had seen its faults first-hand. Most of all we discussed compassion and its importance to the healing process. I was never more proud than when she said in Yiddish, "Dein patients dof huben der lieb," (your patients must love you). Mom and I had made our peace with each other.

Dad too, in his own way, was proud of me. I could start enjoying the foibles and eccentricities that in the past had been a source of embarrassment. The understanding between me and my parents freed the energy bound to that conflict and provided a healthy foundation and support for future growth. As I began the process of liking and appreciating my value, self-respect and self-esteem were becoming my friends.

Having always kept my professional and personal life separate, I started drawing from both components and letting them naturally integrate. Although it would still be some time before my experience would be acceptable for a resume, my psychotherapy and hospitalizations were as important in my work as my formal education. Officially diagnosed and permanently stamped a schizophrenic, I found that the labels and experiences that had once defined and explained me were now becoming accessible for positive uses. My struggles made me particularly sensitive to the folly of knowing someone only through a prescribed, agreed upon name. My experience helped me to suspend the judgments, the categorizations, and to be fully present, looking, listening and trying to understand the unique troubled individual who is seeking validation in her struggle to resolve her problems.

There are many way stations on one's life journeys. I do not believe that there is a discrete point or even a fundamental difference between normal and abnormal. What has come to be known as an illness or defect in our mental apparatus may be more constructively approached as a range or continuum of temperaments, skills and learned behavior which are called into play to cope with various forms of stresses and crises. Some of these coping mechanisms when they are ineffective and/or intrude on others' lives result in a search for explanations and interventions which will transform the undesirable into an undisturbing, invisible, harmless state. The objectionable person may be actively noxious or threatening to others or may be passively threatening and unacceptable by his failure to live up to what is expected of him by significant people in his life.

The price of living in a community includes adherence to certain standards of acceptable behavior. Violation of community norms, whether it be purposeful or not, will typically result in incarceration in prison or mental hospital. Alternatively, one may be fortunate enough to access a way station or safe house. We are all familiar with the many "eccentrics" that have established a niche in a job where their peculiarity has become an esteemed skill and the rest of their outrageous behavior is tolerated. For some that safe place may be the street life of homelessness. To provide help for people who have stumbled off course in their journey, who have a "breakdown," hospital repair shops have been ineffective at best, and at their worst have created more serious conditions. Getting back on the road requires real rest stops where people can find assistance that synchronizes with their individual rhythms and needs. To encourage and enhance the developmental process, to reconnect with one's life themes, we need many more varied and flexible safe places.

For progress to occur, physical treatments that can result in permanent damage must be eliminated. I was extremely fortunate to be able to regain most of my memory after undergoing insulin coma therapy. Historically, the desperation to find new miracle treatments has led to a disregard for potential damage. Because we were thought to be hopeless, a "what have they got to lose attitude" has permitted invasive, unproven procedures to be briefly hailed as major advances. Insulin coma treatment, now discredited for its ineffectiveness and danger to the patient, has been replaced with drug treatments. Lobotomies, the ultimate in barbaric treatment, are threatening to make a comeback as a more precise procedure, which is disguised with the less onerous name of "psychosurgery." Of late, the medical profession is reluctantly acknowledging, but still minimizing, the many neurological impairments, cognitive deficits and permanent disfiguring and painful forms of movement disorders that have resulted from the use of psychiatric drugs. It is not too large a leap of logic to look at the documented shorter life span of mental patients and assign some significance to the treatments that they have received. I remain aware always of how close my treatment came to pushing me over the edge to, if not death, brain damage. Had I compliantly continued on a lifetime course of psychiatric drugs, I was a prime candidate for becoming that hospital-dependent shadowy figure who stands rocking back and forth, face distorted, tongue uncontrollably snaking in and out of his mouth while he tries to form words to communicate his thoughts. A lifetime of tardive dyskinesia is a bad gamble.

I have never been completely convinced that I have been free of damage from my treatments. However, as enough time passed and memories and abilities returned, I could once again tap into a belief in myself. Each success put some distance between who I was told I was, what I was told I could become and who I could strive to be. Each new competency I developed, each skill I refined, fed into creating a new conception of myself. Change fueled possibility as each success was my permission to take on more judicious risks and challenges.

A very significant step in my development was my willingness to temporarily set aside my need to actively search for an intellectual understanding of what had happened to me. I was ready to work on myself in other ways and trust that the understanding would come through action and intuition. Starting with Zazen meditation, I sought to rise above my limitations utilizing techniques that were far removed from Western psychiatry. I sat in full lotus posture doing Zazen daily for twenty minutes before breakfast and twenty minutes before dinner. On the surface the effects were minimal. There were no insights that came to me, nor was there any sense of change that I could readily identify. But during that time I began paying attention to the food I ate. No longer would I eat junk food or just about any food that was convenient. During that time I stopped eating meat and that has continued to this day. After a year of practicing Zazen, I realized that this particular meditative path was not suited to my temperament. I thought that at this point in my life I was too restless and would do better with something more active. When I stopped doing Zazen, I felt a sense of accomplishment rather than failure. I had discovered the importance and benefits of training the will through self-discipline. And somehow during that process I had begun to work through the need to rebel against being told what to do. My negative reactions to the injunctions of authority figures had diminished.

Continuing to look into Eastern disciplines, I read of the benefits of Tai Chi Ch'uan and was very impressed with its rationale, a combination of self-defense and meditation which increased health, awareness and sensitivity. By chance I found a teacher from mainland China who came from a long line of masters. This remarkable teacher taught with an exquisite sense of patience and good humor. Grandmaster Kwok instructed his students in the proper postures, movements and breathing techniques. Always emphasizing that you get back what you put into your practice, he imparted his knowledge but made it clear that the rest was up to you. For the first time I could suspend skepticism. I found a teacher who could demonstrate and prove any of the ideas he taught. Seeing his ability to perform what he taught freed me from my usual and automatic response of not trusting teachers.

Grandmaster Kwok would not teach me Tai Chi until I had learned some of the external, hard forms that he believed were necessary foundations to true Tai Chi mastery. So I learned the hard Shao Lin Chuan and then the hard and partially soft Hsing I Chuan until he said I was ready to learn Tai Chi. Each new form I learned gave me a sense of accomplishment as I watched myself getting stronger. Whatever mood I was in when I went for instruction, I was sure to leave the lesson feeling good. Routinely, at the beginning of class, grandmaster Kwok would ask you to demonstrate what you had learned during the previous lesson. Your mistakes were corrected and then something new would be taught. If you had not practiced and had forgotten what you were taught in your last lesson, there was no criticism. Lessons would be repeated as many times as you needed to learn them. Your practice and development were entirely your responsibility. Never would you be compared to another student. In response to my question about progress, he told me to never compare myself to someone else. He patiently explained that some students may initially learn more quickly than others, but practice is life-long with many dips and turns where the quick learners can unpredictably change places with those who were at first slower. He advised, "The only person to measure your progress against is yourself."

I learned the value of focus and commitment. Increased physical strength, greater energy and the attitude of being in charge of my health and mental concentration increased my sense of self-efficacy. An unexpected side effect was the almost complete elimination of the life-long hand tremors that had increased during and after my hospitalizations. My unsteady hands and trembling fingers were a source of embarrassment. Still not steady as a rock, my nervousness is now confined to situations where I am genuinely nervous.

Through my study and practice of Tai Chi I developed new interests and friends. I also had a pursuit that satisfied my need to feel special and interesting to people, a marked contrast to the post-hospital feelings of being dull, sluggish and boring. For more than three decades, I have practiced and continued to develop my Tai Chi.

My attempts to change, to pursue knowledge and to find meaning fit well with my chosen career path. The boost I received from earning my PhD, my union card for entering the field of psychology and the status of being a "doctor," helped me continue the process of redefining myself. I was able to do work that was challenging and in which I could be creative. Being able to draw upon understanding developed from personal experiences as a means of helping others contributed to my sense of competency and made me feel more accepting of myself. Most of all, I felt good about helping people. Helping others promotes one's own recovery. It was an uplifting, surreal feeling to think that I was getting paid for what I felt was the right thing to do. And I was getting positive feedback from my colleagues and the people for whom I was providing services.

Psychotherapy and other forms of assistance I received from mental health professionals played only a small part in my development. Most of my non-drug treatment in the mental health system occurred within the context of one-to-one counseling or individual psychotherapy. I was not a good candidate for individual therapy. However, I benefited from the supportive counseling provided by Dr. Tomblin during the needy time after my second hospital discharge. His therapy validated my thoughts and feelings, permitted me to be confused and yet provided the encouragement to keep going without applying pressure.

I believe my most profound personal therapy experience occurred during a week-long intensive psychodrama training program I participated in at the Moreno Institute in Beacon, New York. At that time, I was working full time in my own independent psychotherapy practice, and I was in the midst of the breakup of a very meaningful intimate relationship. I was facing the heartbreak of losing a loving relationship that had allowed me to be open and feel worthy of being loved. At the seminar, as part of our training, each of our group of twenty was expected to be the protagonist in a psychodrama. The protagonist chose someone to be the director and described and acted out a conflict in his life. The psychodrama took place on a stage with colored spotlights that were used to intensify the mood and emotions of the enacted drama. At my turn as protagonist, I chose the director of training to be my director. I had come to admire and respect her skills during the seminar. I decided to enact a minor issue in my life – my ambivalence about some aspects of my private psychotherapy practice. Surprising myself, shortly after I started to describe my office, I shifted the psychodrama to my experience of being locked in the seclusion room. I could not have predicted that I would reveal my psychiatric history for the first time to a group of professionals I barely knew. The breakup of my relationship had left me emotionally raw and may have overpowered my privacy needs. I tapped into a huge store of suppressed anger. The director asked me to shift the scene to my hospital admission. Almost as soon as I began describing my admission, I was overcome with emotions. I shook with rage. At the Moreno Institute, when you experience rage, you are encouraged to vent it by throwing metal folding chairs at a padded reinforced wall. I learned that throwing chairs will, after a very short time, dissipate the energy in your anger. The afternoon's psychodrama exhausted me but later, I felt a sense of exhilaration. I stayed up most of the night fascinated by an experience I had never had before nor have had since. I sat, with eyes open or closed, watching a string of images with accompanying dialogue that replayed, like a video recording, various scenes in my life. I watched with interest, but felt no emotion other than a mildly pleasant mood. In the early morning when tiredness overtook me I went to bed and slept soundly. When I awoke, the images had ceased. I believe that the psychodrama helped me let go of a major portion of the anger and bitterness I was carrying. Also, the experience of publicly exposing my psychiatric history to a group of colleagues released some of the guilt and shame associated with my secret.

Hope, safe niches, natural supports, reconciliation with family, the absence of irreversible damage from treatment, self-discipline (development of will), belief in myself, successful experiences, meaningful work, psychotherapy, intimate relationships and the passage of time were all significant in my movement out of the mental illness role into becoming a valued member of society. The varied combinations and relative importance of each of the elements were unique to me, yet I believe that the above identified concepts are common to others' transformations. But each of us defies set formulas. For all of us, the timing and options are different. Underlying all of the above is the question of whether a person has the freedom to choose. Without risk, without choice, the whole process is perverted into at best stabilization and maintenance, and at its worst, incarceration.

Of great importance to my growth was the development of the capacity to be part of a full, loving, intimate relationship. To be able to trust enough to let down my guard and defenses, to be open to another and allow myself to give up some of my hard-won independence was an imposing hurdle. Developing the trust, the love and full sharing with my future wife was, I believe, an essential step in separating myself from the specter of a potential collapse into the not-person world of the mental patient.

The passage of time holds critical importance. Staying out of the hospital is essential to the development of self-confidence. It is almost impossible not to measure your success by the increased time you are able to take care of yourself and live in the community. Leaders in the recovery movement accurately point to the non-linear nature of the recovery process, and although I agree with the non-linear premise, each setback, even if short and less intense, becomes another blow to one's fragilely developing sense of self-efficacy and self-esteem. Hospitalization is not a good option and should be avoided. Increasingly greater periods of time when you are free are the ultimate proof of growth and change for a person diagnosed with mental illness.

Chapter 10

Are You a Psychologist?

Good for the body is the work of the body, good for the soul the work of the soul, and good for either the work of the other. (Henry David Thoreau)

Embarrassment, humiliation and dis-ease can be unrelenting stalkers of self-conscious outsiders like me. The ubiquitous Chinese restaurant, with its fast anonymous service and its consistent but soon forgotten food, offers temporary respite.

Catching a quick meal during a break between psychotherapy sessions, I noticed an attractive woman, with two small children, staring at me from the front of the almost empty restaurant. As our eyes locked for a few awkward seconds, I forced a smile and tried to remember if I knew her. She seemed determined to enter my thirty minutes of precious solitude. Her demeanor was baffling – not one of friendly recognition, but quizzical as if she was trying to decide something. Curious, I wondered if I should say something, but what? Something lame like, "Do I know you?"

I ducked my head back into the newspaper I used for comfort when eating alone. Anyone could see I was a busy man who read the news during short meal breaks. When I resumed reading I saw only a meaningless string of words. *Who is she?*

Peeking over the top of the paper, I saw that she had finished her meal. I watched her walk toward me with the kind of self-assurance I wished I possessed, and without the slightest hesitation she said, "I just have to ask you a question. Are you a psychologist?"

I looked at her standing by my booth with her children in tow and realized that she was too striking for me to have forgotten. She was not a long ago, once seen and forgotten therapy client, nor was she a fellow inmate who had shared meals with me at the bin. Funny how a beautiful woman does not have to be tactful.

"Yes," I answered and waited for her to explain.

She apologized for intruding, and immediately began telling me

152

about her friend. "He's a psychologist, too. Maybe you know him, his name is Jerry Wasserman. Anyway, I saw you and I knew that I had to test out one of his funny little pet theories. He told me that if you see a man eating dinner alone in a Chinese restaurant at an off hour, then you can bet he's a psychologist in private practice."

What could I say? I always came up with my bright, witty responses a few minutes too late. I watched her usher her children to the counter to pay the bill. She started to go out the door, hesitated, then turned back to me and said, "By the way, you look a lot like Jerry."

The fortune cookie I sat there absent-mindedly fingering triggered more musings about my past than about the future. I gazed at my reflection in the restaurant window and saw looking back at me a conservatively dressed, middle-class man pensively stroking his beard. My God, had I taken on the habits and the looks? To become chronically normal was not the vision that sustained me during all those years of secrecy and shame. I wondered how I would meet the new role expectations that people were pushing on me.

"Are you really a psychologist? I don't know what to say; you're probably analyzing everything."

"Oh good, you're a psychologist, you can help me make a decision."

"I understand that you are a psychologist. I need some advice about a friend of mine who is thinking of suicide."

"I'm taking Prozac. Do you think it's OK?"

"Are you a psychologist or a psychiatrist? What's the difference anyway?"

1980, ten years since my release from Overbrook. Much changed, but not the feeling of being different; out of step, never quite fitting in. I believed that it was only necessary for me to learn some missing, as yet undiscovered information that would enable me to enter mainstream normalcy. As a psychologist, I believed that I would be able to use my new knowledge and status as a springboard into belonging. My first postdoctoral job as a staff psychologist in a mental health center punctured my fantasy. I was bursting with enthusiasm and new ideas. The Center was a comfortable, conservative agency where policies and practices conformed to the needs of staff rather than of clients. Despite all too regular clashes with the director of the Center, I managed to work there long enough to meet the supervision requirements for attaining a license to practice psychology.

Perhaps if I had been more worldly, more socially skilled, more manipulative or just further along in my own development, I could have continued working in some kind of publicly funded non-profit mental health agency. But now, looking back at the many public agencies and facilities I have seen, and having experienced their dysfunctional, top-down authoritarian, risk-aversive cultures, I believe that deciding to establish my own independent practice was the right choice for me at that time.

My private practice expanded quickly, and I found that I could work as much or little as I wanted. I developed consultation contracts with several local schools that enabled me to maintain a stable and predictable income. I worked well with "difficult" clients and their families. The challenges of working on my own, learning as I went and being creative rather than formulaic, motivated me to dive into the therapy literature and attend as many educational seminars and workshops as I could. I signed on for formal training in family therapy at Rutgers Medical School and used the year-long program to explore my own family dynamics.

The success of my private practice gave me the opportunity to vacation and travel whenever I chose. Yet, I was aware of an unsatisfying, empty feeling. The increasing passage of time without being hospitalized was a confidence-builder, but unresolved questions, isolation and loneliness were ever-present. My contact with other professionals in the community was often disturbing. Their interests, values and beliefs conflicted with mine. I resented their indifference to and objectification of people, their amusing stories about patients and their overuse of psychological jargon. They held themselves apart and above those lumped together as their patients. My professional peers, in turn, might have assessed me as being over-identified with my clients. True, my anger had not yet been reconciled. I wore the uniqueness of my journey through "mental illness" proudly, but secretly. More than a decade would pass before I learned of others, peers who had shared experiences similar to mine.

Knowing that I had to do more than just see people in my private practice, I volunteered to do educational training for the local Mental Health Association. In the late 70s, the National Mental Health Association with its numerous state and local chapters was the oldest and largest organization fighting for the rights of mental patients. Shortly after volunteering I was asked to serve on the Board of Directors. I was apprehensive at the prospect of having to socially interact with people I thought of as successful and respected members of the community. I wondered if my almost compulsive irreverence and social awkwardness would be a source of embarrassment and hinder my credibility. And then there was always the possibility of being exposed as an unstable former mental patient who was only a few inches away from again becoming psychotic. Regardless, it was a necessary step I had to take. It was time to grow, to test myself and to try to make a positive contribution in my community.

To let down your defenses just enough to suppress your fear and take a risk gives you that stepping stone from which to reach up – to grasp a rung on the ladder of possibilities. And if your ascent is successful, when you look down at where you have been, you feel your strength.

Easy acceptance and respect were what I received at my first Board of Directors meeting. As I had hoped, I found that my PhD acted as a shield or a coat of arms that proclaimed instant credibility. Maybe my lack of pretensions was refreshing to Board members who were used to thinking of psychologists as stiff and formal. The willingness to say what was on my mind honestly and directly and the efforts I made for causes I believed in pushed me into a position of leadership. After serving on the Board for three years, I was elected president.

My advocacy work in the community and my ability to learn and adapt to the structure of a large organization became sources of pride. Yet, I was often frustrated when observing the resistance to change and the low quality of services provided by mental health agencies. I worked on advocacy issues, but I became impatient with the committees and task forces our Association was forced to work through.

I was incredulous watching how slowly the various community agencies moved. I am still unable to determine whether it was purposeful foot-dragging, or years of habitual sleep-walking and aversion to risk-taking that made those mental health professionals so rigid. Knowing that many of the leaders of county and state mental health facilities started their careers as therapists, I did not understand how they had drifted so far away from the time when they had encouraged their patients to risk and try new ways of behaving, feeling and ultimately being. Now I realize that the risk-taking professional is the exception rather than the norm. I hated thinking that I might some day begin accommodating myself to contradictions and be unwilling to put my reputation and sense of safety on the line.

At that time, the Mental Health Association's current project involved directing a task force of various county agencies to develop an innovative program for working with a group of people they called young chronics. It was a new term invented for certain people who seemed to have sprung up overnight and were wandering the streets of communities all over the country. As a result of de-institutionalization, people who a few years back would have been permanently locked away in mental hospitals were now right there for everyone to see. The young chronics, who were less passively compliant than their older brethren, were an active irritant to social service agencies because of their resistance to traditional forms of intervention and treatment. I was tense and uncomfortable at the meetings, and when I left, I always felt sleazy and dishonest. Just as rainstorms can make you aware of old injuries, this particular task force picked at the scabs covering my psychic wounds. Here my opinions were thoughtfully considered, but respectful attention was denied to those who needed to be heard. How easily this very group of which I was now a member could classify and dismiss me once learning of the roads I had traveled. I wondered how many they had summarily dismissed without understanding the breadth and scope of their journeys.

By 1981 when my mother died, I had made my peace with her and felt reasonably safe from being locked up in a mental hospital. I intuitively knew that it was time to move out of my safe place, try to make sense out of my experience with madness and attempt to integrate it with my present conception of self. Writing was the vehicle I chose to use as a means to grieve for my mother and to seek new understanding.

The process of writing proved to be more demanding, gratifying and revealing than I had anticipated. Writing became an incisive tool to clarify and sharpen my thinking. New insights were mixed with the revival of old feelings of anger and helplessness. Facing those feelings helped free me from bondage to attitudes and myths shaped by the past but no longer dominant. Writing became an exciting process of discovery, change, and a strengthening of the belief in myself. I also came to believe that I had something important to say that needed to be shared with others. During the time I was writing, I avoided reading any accounts of others' personal experiences of madness. As I recovered some of my lost memories, I tried to guard against confounding my experiences with those written by other people. Years later, when I learned of and became part of the consumer/survivor/ex-patient movement, I realized that I had missed out on information that would have given me an opportunity to join with people like myself who had transformed their mental patient experiences. Ignorant of fellow travelers, I had chosen to study psychology and hoped that the knowledge and understanding I acquired would stabilize and make legitimate my recovery. In so doing, I was absent from the birthing of the c/s/x movement that I so strongly identify with today. I am surprised that even now, psychiatric survivor ideas and literature are virtually absent from the education of most mental health professionals.

During the second year of writing I met my future wife. A recent law school graduate and recently recruited member on the Mental Health Association board, Lindsey aspired to work as a hospital ombudsman, advocating for and protecting patients' rights. Upon first sight I was stunned to see this slender beauty with blue eyes and high cheekbones whose pretty face was set off by long blond hair. I hoped that she was not married. The idealism and compassion I felt coming from her had a familiar resonance for me. We immediately bonded. Attraction and respect turned to a deep abiding love and shared commitment that continues to this day.

As our relationship deepened, I shared my experience and writing with Lindsey. Unlike Sara, her conception of me was not negatively impacted. She offered her insights and encouraged me with her critique of my writing. We both grew from the process. That manuscript was never published, but as my friend and mentor, psychology professor Jim Mancuso told me, "Those who write learn twice."

In 1986 we married. Two years later, our son Jesse was born. Sixteen years had passed since I had been a patient in a psychiatric institution. I was more than a decade and a half removed from psychiatric drugs, psychotherapy, or *symptoms of mental illness*. Years of vegetarian eating, regular practice of Tai Chi and generally healthy living contributed to my energetic optimism. I assumed personal responsibility for actively taking charge of those things which I could control and that helped enhance my physical and emotional health. Successful, competent, middle-class family man, no one would suspect my psychiatric history. Yet, I remained an outsider. On the surface I could look the part and fit in, but my experiences and perceptions said *you are different*.

Our bright-eyed, beautiful baby made a deeply caring, evolving husband-wife relationship into a family. My self-absorbed striving to develop and grow seemed to naturally accommodate to our new family configuration. For once, I found the changes I wanted without trying. Nine months of pregnancy provided some preparation, but not nearly enough to expect the powerful, never before felt, almost agape love which gushed from my heart at Jesse's birth. No longer feeling that I came first, that my needs were the top priority, expanded my being-in-the-world.

For three years Lindsey and I intensely shared the joys of parenthood. We marveled at every nuance of our son's behavior. We planned and discussed and ruminated on how to make everything just right. We worried and wondered how to prepare him for life and protect him from pain. Nothing was more important to us than being the best parents we could be. As Jesse began approaching school age, I began struggling with what I perceived to be a potential problem. While Jesse was a toddler, I could spend the entire morning with him before I went off to work. If I continued my regular work at night with families, then when Jesse entered school full-time, my time with him would shrink. I would miss watching him grow up. Lindsey and I also talked of our increasing dissatisfaction with the materialism and upward striving in the community in which we were living. We dreaded the thought of Jesse someday begging us to buy him $150 sneakers so he could fit in with his status-conscious friends. Both of us knew that we would never share a sense of community with our neighbors. We were not at home there. Change beckoned.

I was ready to begin a new adventure. Though I cared deeply about the people whom I saw in my practice, an element was missing. Since Jesse had been born, I had stopped doing advocacy work and my professional life lacked challenges. I was restless to learn and do more, personally and professionally. And although my therapy work reflected values shaped by my experience as a survivor, I felt cut off from its deep impact on my identity. I began looking at job advertisements in the Monitor, the American Psychological Association's monthly news magazine.

On a sunny Tuesday morning when Lindsey returned from grocery shopping, I asked her how she felt about flying out to South Dakota. She put down the shopping bags and stood waiting for the rest of the story. I reminded her of the job ad we had discussed and the decision to send a resume for the position of Director of Outpatient Services at the Human Services Agency in Watertown, South Dakota. I told her that they wanted to fly us out for an interview and give us a chance to look around.

The following Friday, Lindsey, Jesse and I boarded a plane, curious, eager and excited to contemplate the possibility of setting down roots in our romanticized version of small town life in the "heartland." Once there, we spent a confusing, hectic, soul-searching three days in which I was the object of a surprisingly intense recruiting campaign. All the virtues of small town living, with its inclusive sense of community and family values, were emphasized. Watertown, with its population of about 16,000, was the largest town within 100 miles in any direction. The closest cities were Fargo to the north and Sioux Falls to the south.

A few weeks later I returned to interview again and get another sense of the agency and Watertown. I was lent an agency car and encouraged to explore the area. Immediately, upon driving out of town and experiencing the wide open expanse of the South Dakota plains, I became euphoric. I felt an uplifting sense of joy from being out in a space where you could see land meet sky in all directions. It reminded me of my enchantment with gazing at the ocean. Somehow the affirmation of being small and insignificant paradoxically acted to reassure me of my existential value. Later, when I mentioned my euphoric feeling to a native South Dakotan, I was told that some people were overwhelmed with agoraphobia when they first experienced the plains. I wonder how much my euphoric feeling contributed to our decision to move to South Dakota.

Interested but not sold on such a big move, Lindsey and I discussed our reservations, not the least of which was a too vaguely described job. Also dangled as an incentive was the possibility of running the entire agency upon the imminent retirement of the current president, who was leading the effort to convince me to accept the job. After another visit, a series of interviews, and much thought and discussion we decided to take the chance. We sold our home, I gave up my private practice and our family embarked on our new adventure.

During the next three extremely challenging, often upsetting years in South Dakota, I learned a great deal. Much had been misrepresented or left unsaid during the interviews. The position I thought I was to assume did not exist and was part of a highly-charged, emotional power struggle between two former friends who were in the midst of a serious falling out. The retiring president was intent upon preventing his colleague and one-time ally, the executive director of the mental health center, from becoming the new president of the agency. He had planned for me to become the executive director of the center when his former friend and current nemesis was driven from the agency. After more than two months of working at the center in an ambiguous role and watching the machinations and in-fighting over determining whether the job I had accepted would ever become a reality, I became the new executive director of this comprehensive community mental health center. Without any previous experience and knowing that I had no job security, I set out to learn as quickly as possible all that I could about being an effective mental health center administrator. This trial by fire also involved gaining the trust of a suspicious staff that had mixed loyalties to its former patriarchal leadership. I had to deal with my feelings of anxiety, insecurity and anger over being fooled and manipulated during the recruiting process.

Lindsey had to learn to adapt to mid-western small town life that was untrusting of outsiders – those who did not go back several generations in that particular town – and especially suspicious of city folk from the Northeast. She was more than a bit stunned when our neighbor, who knew that we had lived in Pennsylvania and whose daughter played with Jesse, seriously asked Lindsey if they named Erie, Pennsylvania Erie because the people there were really *eerie*. Then there were the questions we thought at first were jokes, from residents of nearby small towns with populations of a few hundred: "Don't you feel scared when you go to Minneapolis and you see all those people on the street that you never saw before?" Disappointed and isolated, we had no choice but to grow or fail.

A few months after I had become executive director, the directors of all the mental health centers in South Dakota were asked to appear before the Governor's Mental Health Advisory Council to describe the services provided by their agencies for the SPMI, the Seriously and Persistently Mentally Ill. I listened as other directors described the extensive services they developed for taking care of the SPMIs, and I watched and tried to understand the dynamics and inter-relationships of the people who were responding to the presentations. Quite quickly I learned that the chairperson and several other committee members were leaders in the South Dakota Alliance for the Mentally Ill. Later, I would learn of the Alliance's strong political connections in South Dakota and their influence on mental health policy and funding.

An argument erupted in the middle of the meeting. The chairperson was making a point with a member of the committee who self-identified as a c/s/x. In response to a complaint about the unaddressed stigma and discrimination faced by c/s/x, the chairperson responded, "I don't know why you feel that way; I don't think anyone would look at you and think that you were a mental patient. If I didn't know your psychiatric history, I would think that you were normal."

A heated argument over stigma broke out. The chairperson insisted that what she said was not offensive and was meant as a compliment.

I was moved by the heated exchanges, but restrained myself from speaking. My emotions were aligned with the c/s/x. Their arguments resonated with too long unexpressed views of my own. During the discussion, amidst the denials, accusations and counter-accusations, one person, a self-identified psychiatric survivor named Rae Unzicker, expressed her opinion with a clarity and eloquence that elicited my admiration. I wanted to talk with her after the meeting but was unable to get the opportunity before she left. I wrote down her name and address and thought that I would call her at a later time.

Months later I saw a picture of Rae in a psychiatric survivor newsletter, laughing and wearing a T-shirt that declared, "I'm Rae and You're Not." The caption underneath the picture said that she was the president of a group called the National Association of Psychiatric Survivors (NAPS). The articles in the newsletter appealed to me. Still thinking that some day I would contact Rae, I sent in my membership fee and joined NAPS. Although another year would pass before I would get in touch with her, it was becoming apparent to me that I was getting closer to openly using my personal psychiatric experience in my work.

I learned the nuts and bolts of running a mental health center and discovered that I had the facility for providing leadership that cultivated trust and some measure of loyalty in staff. Being valued and respected by staff and mastering the multi-faceted job requirements was another boost to my self-confidence. Along the way, I noticed that my shyness was gradually diminishing and I was developing more social skills. However, I knew that running the Center and living in Watertown, South Dakota was not for me and my family. Although I had some influence on the clinicians' attitudes toward the services they provided, my authority and ability to effect change in the configuration and essence of the services they provided was limited. My position as executive director did not afford me the opportunity to redesign services that were government mandated to reduce risk and care for people who were supposed to be unable to control themselves. The administrative, legal, political and funding constraints were formidable barriers to change.

Exercising one of my job perks, I chose to attend the American Psychological Association's Annual Conference in Toronto with the hope of finding a new job. Like other APA conferences I had attended, the emotional distance between me and the other psychologists stimulated painful memories. Knowing no one, I acutely felt the loneliness of my outsider status. Among the hundreds of presentations, I decided to attend a symposium which offered arguments against psychologists attaining drug prescription privileges. Peter Breggin, a well-known anti-drug, critical psychiatrist was the moderator, and having seen reviews of his book *Toxic Psychiatry*,[25] I was interested in hearing him.

Two psychologists presented research critiques that challenged the efficacy of drug treatments for specified diagnostic conditions, followed by Dr. Breggin's comments on the oppressive, profit-driven, harmful impact of mainstream psychiatric practice. Stimulated by the views and values expressed in the presentations and the ensuing discussion, I was pumped with nervous energy and racing thoughts. I knew I was muzzling too much of me.

One member of the audience, an older bearded man with a warm face and an unassuming manner, asked Dr. Breggin a question about the implications of the newly released book, *Listening to Prozac*.[26] Unfamiliar with the book, and seeming to not understand the question, Dr. Breggin dismissed his first questioner with a humorous quip. I knew about the book, understood the question and shared the questioner's concerns. For the rest of the discussion I was drawn to watching that questioner, a casually dressed man carrying a worn backpack, and whose demeanor and attire made him stand out from my psychologist colleagues.

I approached the man I thought to be a fellow outsider, to talk about the issue he had raised. As we spoke and found a quick rapport, I astonished myself by telling this stranger that years ago I was hospitalized with a diagnosis of schizophrenia. The need to relate and share genuine feelings with someone had become too strong to suppress. Luckily, that someone turned out to be Ken Barney. As we continued our animated conversation and the room began to clear, I was floored when Ken asked me if I wanted to continue our conversation at lunch with Peter and him. It turned out that Ken was a psychiatrist who was a vocal critic of psychiatric practices. He and Peter had studied together under the mentorship of Thomas Szasz.[27]

At lunch, when I mentioned that I worked in South Dakota, Breggin lit up and said, "You must know Rae . . . Rae Unzicker. How's she doing? Tell her I said hello."

Stunned that I didn't know her, he wondered how I could be an ex-patient living in South Dakota and not know his favorite person, the person he playfully called his adoptive mother. He told me that I had to get in touch with her. It was a fortuitous lunch of serendipity. Meaningful talk by passionate, committed people gave me a taste of where my life and work needed to go.

The next day Ken and I met to have lunch and talk. Afterward, we attended a workshop on the formation of a radical psychology group within APA. Again, I introduced my psychiatric experience as a patient into the discussion – this time, for the first time, to a group of psychologists. I felt alive, real and genuine. Ken gave me the name and phone number of Dan Fisher, a psychiatrist in Massachusetts and also an ex-patient who had been labeled and treated for schizophrenia, and was now the Director of the

National Empowerment Center. Some years later, after Dan and I had met and become friends, we were talking about a possible project when I asked him how Ken Barney was doing. He said that he hadn't seen him for awhile and then paused and said kiddingly, "Talking with Ken almost makes me feel guilty about working as a psychiatrist."

I returned to Watertown without any new job prospects, but with the excited and uneasy feeling of knowing that a closed down part of me was opening. Lindsey listened attentively to my description of events at the conference. Both of us recognized that there was no turning back. I could not continue working as a traditional, mainstream psychologist. Even as the director of a mental health center I had to abide by laws and policies and practices that were counter to my beliefs. It had always disturbed me that I could be responsible for someone being committed to a mental hospital against his or her will. I had avoided personally participating in the process, but I knew that even if I didn't do the commitment evaluation and recommendation, as a licensed psychologist, I had accepted the obligation to follow those laws. I knew too much to deceive myself into thinking I could make anything more than minor changes in the system within which I was working. No enlightened leadership could counteract the oppressive requirements of a system which did not value choice and alternatives.

Lindsey and I had to confront some large, practical questions. Would anyone hire an outspoken ex-patient with anti-establishment views? Where could I find paid employment that was consistent with my values and principles? Were we ready as a family to change our lifestyle, reduce our income and live with an unknown, insecure future? Lindsey worried that my professional credibility would be undermined by the disclosure of my psychiatric history. She was afraid that I would get hurt. Despite our reasonable concerns, the chasm had been crossed and possibility took priority over risk. We decided to give ourselves some time to let everything sink in.

A few weeks later, I agreed to participate in a federal mental health block grant planning meeting in St. Louis. Knowing that Rae lived in Sioux Falls and that I would be flying out of that city's airport, I decided to call her to try to arrange a meeting. I did not know what to say other than to introduce myself and ask her if she would talk with me. My voice cracked with emotion when she answered the phone. I explained that I wanted to see her. Without asking me any qualifying questions, she invited me to visit her at her home the night before my flight to St. Louis.

Rae welcomed me into her home with the warmth and openness one offers close family or old friends. She was an effervescent Auntie Mame-like character who made you feel that you and what you were saying were too important for anything less than her complete attention. I blurted out why I had come to see her, but before I finished she reached over and hugged me. Those tears I hid from hospital staff began flowing. On first contact I felt the acceptance and understanding that said, *I've been there and will support and help you.* Our introduction to each other was an emotional embrace more than a discussion. The bond was immediate.

Rae belonged to a community of people who were connected by experiential understanding – an understanding honed in the crucible of painful self-disintegration and abuse, where the anger of the psychiatric survivor still burns but is governed by wisdom and compassion. For the very first time I met a person who truly understood and shared my experience. Before the evening was over, we knew and trusted each other. I came to Rae seeking advice. I found a remarkable, charismatic woman who introduced me to the psychiatric survivor community. I quickly realized that I actually had been a long-time, inactive member. I left her house that night with an armload of books and articles. She gave me the name of a woman survivor to call when I arrived in St. Louis. After meeting Rae, I learned that I could go just about anywhere and find psychiatric survivors, peers in any city, people who by virtue of their psychiatric experiences are loosely networked throughout the United States and other countries.

Whenever I could, I visited with Rae and always left with a new armload of books. Most of the works had never made it into the mainstream publishing market. The "fugitive" books, as she called them, made me aware of many talented, psychiatrically labeled people, my brethren who were fighting to create change in an oppressive, exploitative mental health system. Rae assured me that there would be work for me that could utilize all my training and experience. It was the one thing she said that left me with doubts. I could not imagine what work I could do while being open about my newly forming identity.

Before leaving on a family vacation in the Black Hills, I threw the newly arrived APA Monitor into the front seat of the car to look at job ads during our car ride. We had just crossed the Missouri river into western South Dakota when I saw the blocked-out large advertisement that made me catch my breath and gasp, "I can't believe it. I'm afraid it'll change if I re-read it."

I slowly and deliberately read the ad to Lindsey. We looked at each other in disbelief. Everything was there; even the location, upstate New

York. We longed to get back to our roots in the Northeast. We kept re-reading and repeating the job requirements out loud:

> New York licensed or license eligible psychologist with experience as a recipient of in-patient hospital services. Good writing and group facilitation skills, able to work independently to develop innovative serious mental illness/recovery curricula in graduate psychology programs in New York Universities; Albany based and administered by the New York State Psychological Association and the New York State Office of Mental Health.

On our return drive from the Black Hills, the two of us worked to create the best possible cover letter. We were afraid to get too excited, but we couldn't help ourselves. I called Rae and she told me that she knew people in New York who worked at the Office of Mental Health and they would value the recommendation she offered to write for me. The wait for a response to my application was agonizing. Between the time in April when I responded to the advertisement and the time in early October when I finally interviewed for the job, I could not keep my mind off the possibilities. Optimism being one of my better survival skills, I believed I would get the job. I was right.

* * *

The snow and wind were developing into blizzard conditions when we drove away from Watertown. Although happy to be embarking on a new adventure, I thought of the many relationships I was leaving behind and the expressions of warmth and affection coming from my staff after my resignation. In South Dakota, as during my graduate days in Mississippi, it had been necessary to adapt to the demands of a different culture. Once again, there were risks and opportunities. Towards the end I had struggled with how much to reveal of myself. I had begun disclosing my psychiatric history and sharing survivor ideas and literature with selected staff during the last few months, but drew short of making any public announcements. My career as a mental health center director was at an end, and my life as a rights activist and out-of-the-closet psychiatric survivor was about to begin.

My experiences of living and working in Watertown, South Dakota enabled me to shed old ideas about who I was and begin the construction of a new identity. Longing less to recover what was lost, I began to savor thoughts and daydreams of growth and transformation.

Tomorrow, I would speak truth to power.

Part II

Integrating Knowledge Derived from Living and
Working on Both Sides of the Locked Door

Chapter 11

So Much to Learn About What I Think I Know

The right to speak out is also the duty to speak out. (Vladimir Pozner)

January 1995, twenty-five years after my last psychiatric hospitalization, we arrived in New York. Too rash, perhaps, in taking on this vaguely-defined job, where the more significant half of my credentials was a status achieved from being treated for schizophrenia and recovering. But then again, starting over was a familiar developmental task for me.

Two decades earlier, I was less than three years removed from being hospitalized when I resigned my job at Greystone and left to enter the full-time doctoral program in Mississippi. Then, Mom's eyes were wet with worry about her son taking such a risk. Right up to the time I was about to leave she tried to convince me to stay with my safe and secure job at Greystone. I am grateful no one stopped me from pursuing what was thought to be a bad decision.

Today, I'm grateful for Lindsey's unwavering support, encouragement and belief in me. Moving our budding family from New Jersey to Pennsylvania to South Dakota to New York was accepted with grace and the determination to make each new home warm, welcoming, and also a place for her to pursue her own journey of personal growth.

So, after my years of running to and from my psychiatric patient experiences, vacillating between hiding the experience and needing to broadcast and validate what I had lived through, my new job demanded that I look inside. Angry still, I had much to learn about myself. I had to temper the high of believing my knowledge held a special lofty position. When you are fully conscious of the immense complexity of working with others' emotional pain, arrogance has no place. Too full of innocence and idealism, I arrived for my first day on the job.

"Let your ideology leak out slowly, drop by drop," was the only advice I received from the bureaucrat who had hired me for my new job. The suggestion seemed to make sense, but my new position promised the freedom, even more, the license to express what I had once kept secret. Straining at the bit, I was ready to bolt out of the starting gate like an untrained racehorse with lots of potential but no track record. Did I still have to conceal who I was and what I believed?

I could see the mental health industry from two sides, but I had only worked on one side. I was an "us" who worked as one of "them." Regardless of effective work as a therapist, regardless of any sensitivity I possessed, my knowledge was limited by the distance inherent in my former role as a psychologist. With the professional veil lifted, I intended to redefine how I presented myself and how I worked.

With no role model or mentor, the hybrid role of professional and psychiatric survivor, so highly charged with polarizing tension, was entirely my responsibility. I had to construct the playing field, learn who the key players were, and discover the explicit and implicit rules of the game. I peppered myself with encouraging self-talk:

Stay open, listen to learn. Know your strengths. Let your values keep your ego from interfering and clouding your ability to learn. Respond from your heart. Treat everyone with the dignity and respect of an equal and expect the same of them. You are incredibly lucky. Keep your passion. Stay aware.

Public speaking was a requirement of my new position. I fought to push down the too-familiar fears of speaking in class that had haunted me throughout my education. I worried about the reappearance of sweating, blushing and hand tremors. Would I begin to stammer and freeze? In my heart, I knew that my fleeting wishes for an easier path would never be an option that I would choose.

I had learned to control my anxiety and some of my body's automatic responses in graduate school. Later, in my role as a psychologist, I had overcome some of my public speaking anxiety, but that was usually with small groups. Now, with no experience speaking to large, diverse groups, I had to find a way to share my psychiatric history and communicate what I had learned from those experiences.

I have wondered whether it was growing confidence or merely ignorance propelling me forward. As I often did in the past, instead of putting my toes in the water, then my feet and wading in slowly and gradually, I jumped in all at once. For my first talk, I agreed to be the keynote speaker at the annual meeting and fund-raiser for the Morris County Mental Health Association. There, I had once served as president of the Board of Directors. Rather then peek out of the closet, I would leap out in front of several hundred people who would be compelled to reconstruct their memories of me.

The content of my speech was of less concern to me than my worries about appearing nervous, stumbling over words, keeping on track, or running too long or too short. I agonized over whether I should read my speech, memorize parts or use note cards. Lindsey listened and timed the speech as I experimented with different formats. I knew that I was much better speaking extemporaneously, and at my worst when I read or memorized material. I decided to use note cards, but I wrote too much on the cards. I had too much to say.

People tell me that they admire my courage for speaking out about my experience and doing the work that I do. Usually I don't think of it as courageous; it is simply the right thing to do in acknowledgment of the gifts given to me. However, looking back, I wonder where I got the courage to make that first speech. I was heart-pounding nervous. I forgot my place, I skipped parts that I wanted to cover. Who could miss the nervousness in my voice and demeanor? Yet when I looked at the audience, I saw eyes riveted upon me. Their rapt attention allowed me to pull it together and get through the talk. I listened to the applause and breathed it in. Afterwards, people approached me with questions and shared personal tales of their painful experiences with loved ones. They said I was inspiring. Several asked for contact information to give to a relative who was struggling with mental illness. I left, thinking to myself *I can do this.*

Confronting stigma was the next hurdle. I had to come to grips with feelings about this new identity I had adopted. The public disclosure of my identity as a person once diagnosed and treated for schizophrenia was essential to my job. Would people treat me differently? What would happen to my credibility? No longer would I be in charge of who is privy to this once-private information.

Psychiatrist and ex-patient Dan Fisher describes the disclosure of his psychiatric history:

> Once I completed my residency I felt freer to disclose. I chose a TV show "People are Talking." I invited a former supervisor to join me in a panel on forced medication. On the way into the studio I told him I was going to discuss my psychiatric history. His glib retort infuriated me: "It's now fashionable to have been a psychiatric patient."[28]

In my new role I had less choice in the how, when and where of disclosure. Like Dan, I also was asked if I was looking to capitalize on my psychiatric history. I resisted responding to that insensitivity in the manner it deserved, but it hurt. When I met a new person or colleague, I found it awkward to explain that I did not work as a traditional psychologist. I asked fellow psychiatric survivor Darby Penney whether she felt like she was treated differently by staff at the State Office of Mental Health where she worked. Darby said no, but then she paused for a moment to think, laughed and said:

> Wait . . . there was the time I was sitting in Joel's office talking with him. My chair was against the side wall and Joel was sitting in the other corner where he couldn't be seen by anyone walking past the doorway. A woman I knew and worked with on a number of committees walked by, saw me talking and didn't see anyone else in the room. Jumping too quickly to the conclusion that I was hallucinating, she rushed into the room to ask me if I was OK. After Joel and I got over being startled, we realized what had happened and began laughing – a bittersweet laughter for me.

Emily Hoffman, working on her thesis for a master's degree in social work, went to three schools of social work to interview students like herself who had psychiatric histories. Out of a pool of about 500, only five were willing to talk with her. From that small sample, she found that none felt that they would have been admitted to their programs if they had disclosed their histories on the admission applications. Hoffman's own disclosure came at the end of her master's program. She poignantly describes the emotional conflict she felt as a student: "You sit in class and they talk about your label, and give a list of characteristics on how 'they' behave and what 'they' do. You think, 'Are they talking about me? It doesn't fit.' You want to say, 'That's not right – that's not the way it is.' Instead, you're having to sit on yourself."[29]

My early meetings with academics confirmed how difficult it is to cut through an existing belief structure about mental illness. Their reactions and questions focused on trying to connect the dissonant pieces of information my statements and presence evoked. To some, I was a curiosity. One professor emeritus and psychology department chairman at a major university in New York City was helpful and friendly but made me uncomfortable with his too obvious scrutiny of me. In my new role, I was trying to establish a peer support and advocacy network of psychologists who had been hospitalized and recovered. I asked if he was familiar with any psychologists working at the university or any graduates who had been treated for serious mental illness.

I watched his eyes and face become pensive as he withdrew inward to scan his memory. He told me that he vaguely remembered reading a research paper which claimed that some schizophrenics upon reaching the age of sixty found that their illnesses seemed to "burn out," and they no longer were psychotic. Then the professor thought some more, and said that as far as he knew, no graduate students who had psychotic episodes during their studies at his university were able to return and complete their studies.

I was frustrated that this precise and cautious, most likely decent man was keeping the myths alive. I offered to send him copies of some of the longitudinal research studies that clearly demonstrated full recovery from schizophrenia – with diagnostic assessment and recovery rigorously adhering to the accepted medical model criteria for schizophrenia. I also promised to send him my resume so that he might pass it on to the person who would arrange for my presentation to the graduate students. When we were about to say our goodbyes, he asked me if the next time I was back in New York City, he and his wife could have me over for dinner. "She's a psychiatrist," he explained, "who works with schizophrenics and I'm sure she would be very interested in talking with you."

C'mon doctor, do you really believe I'd want to be the main course for dinner?

I was naive to think that he would know anyone who would risk disclosing her psychiatric history to his biased judgment. I was privileged to have the freedom to be open about my background. If my credibility was challenged, I felt armored by being able to cite my credentials and professional accomplishments. Free of psychotherapy and psychiatric drugs for over two decades, I was reasonably prepared to face stigma and discrimination. With the security buffer of documented productive years, I no longer needed to explain away the gaps in my resume. I had proven that I could pass among the "chronically normal." Unlike my c/s/x peers, I only experienced a tiny amount of the stigma and discrimination they faced daily.

Others had to come to grips with the public disclosure of their psychiatric history. Like me, Frank Cardinal was able to use successful career moves and promotions to distance himself from his psychiatric history. He describes a cold trail that permitted him to keep his past treatment a secret until his teenage son was hospitalized.

> As a parent I impressed upon him that there was nothing to
> be ashamed of – telling him all the "right things" about
> mental illness: It is not something to be embarrassed about;
> it doesn't mean you are a weak person. During one of my
> lectures, he looked at me and said, "What about you, dad?"
> You could have knocked me off my feet. He said, "How
> come you don't talk about it? How come nobody knows
> about you if there's nothing to be embarrassed about?"[30]

Cardinal worked through the issue he had avoided and decided to
set an example for his son. After going public, he realized what a burden his
secrecy had been and felt encouraged by the support of his peers.

I dreaded an inevitable future discussion with my son when he
would someday ask me why I had been locked in a mental hospital. The
hero of his childhood eyes did not fit the stereotype he saw in movies and
children's books. He knew that his father worked as a psychologist to help
people. But his exposure to "crazy" was to see it as bad and scary.

Often cited as the most stigmatized group, individuals labeled as
mentally ill are seen by the general public as dangerous and unpredictable.
Clients surveyed for the Well-Being Project by the California Department of
Mental Health said they preferred their own name or no term when asked
what they would like to be called. They objected to the following terms:
77% insane
76% crazy
74% wacko
70% mad
67% sick
66% flipped out
64% space cadet
61% disturbed
60% psychiatric inmate
58% mentally ill
56% mental patient.[31]

The Well-Being project quantified and documented what c/s/x
know and face daily – that when people are aware that they are dealing with
someone who has a psychiatric history, c/s/x individuals feel they are being
treated like a child (21%), as dangerous (17%), as incapable of caring for

children (19%), as unpredictable (26%), as if they are incapable of holding a job (33%).

Psychiatric survivor and activist Judi Chamberlin[32] recalls the identification of patterns of "mentalism" and "sane chauvinism" during the mobilization of the ex-patients' movement in the 70s. Mentalism is a set of assumptions that people hold about mental patients which label them as incompetent, unable to do things for themselves, constantly in need of supervision, unpredictable and violent. Ironically, many of the mentalist views are held by ex-patients about themselves. Consciousness-raising, the powerful change process used in the women's movement, was adopted by the growing c/s/x movement. They recognized the critical importance of words. The battle to combat the external and internalized oppression of pejorative language has continued to this day and can be seen in the buttons people wear at our conferences.

"We speak for ourselves."
"I'm not a case and I don't need to be managed."
"Label jars, not people."
"Self-determination is for everyone."
"I am not a diagnosis."

When I made the leap from psychologist to psychiatric survivor, Lindsey told me she was worried about inadvertently using the wrong words around our new friends. Knowing that we so often talk casually about *crazy* ideas or exclaim how something or someone is driving us *insane* or *nuts* or *out of our minds*, she wondered whether she would inadvertently offend someone. Both of us disliked the passivity conveyed by *recipient* – the official name for c/s/x used in New York. I bristled at the false assumptions propping up the use of *consumer* – the most commonly used label. A consumer is supposed to have genuine informed choices. The mental health consumer does not have the opportunity to analyze and choose according to cost-benefit ratios. More ironic is the belief that "consumer" is a neutral word – less stigmatizing than "mental patient." The history of the word's use in conjunction with mental patients is not linked to Ralph Nader-like empowerment. "Consumer," when originally applied to those who were mental patients, meant useless eaters – those who consumed resources without themselves producing anything of value.

Lindsey and I laughed about the hot new label that is being pushed – *customer*. Customers shopping for a new TV can compare brands for price and quality and go to another store if they are not satisfied with the choice of products or the level of services provided. I assured Lindsey that the specific words used were less important than their context and intention. For me, "crazy" is fine when the context is right. When a person is humored, treated as if he or she would be overwhelmed by honest dialogue, then no politically correct language is acceptable.

As a psychologist I had always shied away from technical jargon and resisted grouping people into categories. Yet, not until I began identifying myself as a psychiatric survivor and saw that I was more bonded with survivors than psychologists did I grasp the extent of the daily bombardment of demeaning messages. It was some time before I became used to phone calls during which the person calling, expecting to speak to a "mental patient," spoke loudly with very slow and careful articulation. Too many times, c/s/x people find themselves needing to say, "I might be mentally ill, but I'm not stupid."

I admire the humor used by people with diverse disabilities and feel privileged to be privy to some of my fellow travelers' creative responses to communications of bigotry. One of my favorite stories was told to me by a person who repeated a story told to her by a friend who is unable to use his legs because of a spinal cord injury.

The story begins with our storyteller riding in his customized power chair through an indoor shopping mall. While stopped to look in the window of a boutique, he overhears the mother of a seven- or eight-year-old telling her son to stand right at the entrance so she can see him while she's in the store. As he begins to turn his power chair to leave he notices the youngster staring at the chair. Their eyes meet and with natural curiosity, the boy asks him to show what the chair can do. He proudly demonstrates its technological features and the boy fires off questions: how fast can it go, can it back up, does it use gas? The little boy's eyes get very big when he shows him how high he can raise the seat and himself with the push of a button – explaining that few objects are out of his reach. Unknown to the two of them, mother has seen them talking and rushes out of the store. Angrily, she admonishes her son for talking to one of "those people", and for emphasis, points at our astonished chair-rider and warns, "See, I warned you, this is what will happen to you if you keep touching your private parts."

Not one to let her rush away unchallenged, he quickly replies, "Madam, are you sure? Doesn't masturbation make you go blind?"

My sensitivity to negative language became much more acute once I had disclosed my history. Labels (the mentally ill, the SPMIs, the schizophrenics, the borderlines, the chronics, the MPDs, the anorexics, the cutters, the retarded) relied on presumed traits, behaviors or characteristics to put persons in a class or category that would define or explain them at the expense of their individuality. Words like *appropriate, compliance, treatment-resistant, religiosity, therapeutic milieu* and *high functioning,* once eliciting a twinge of discomfort, could now set my stomach churning when I heard them insensitively expressed at policy meetings. When told that "appropriate" is obnoxious to c/s/x, professionals typically express consternation at why this neutral word elicits criticism. If "appropriate" is used as a standard to assess each of your actions and makes you the object of unrelenting judgments, and if those judgments determine the extent of your freedom and what rights you may retain, that word is oppressive. Through my insider experience, I have come to understand the difference between what interferes with recovery and what propels one forward. I continue to hope that professionals will provide more helpful services when they gain a fuller understanding of the mental patient experience.

"To Be A Mental Patient," Rae Unzicker's prose poem, attempts to make that connection:

> To be a mental patient is to be stigmatized, ostracized, socialized, patronized, psychiatrized.

> To be a mental patient is to have everyone controlling your life but you. You're watched by your shrink, your social worker, your friends, your family. And then you're diagnosed as paranoid.

> To be a mental patient is to live with the constant threat and possibility of being locked up at any time, for almost any reason.

> To be a mental patient is to live on $82 a month in food stamps, which won't let you buy Kleenex to dry your tears. And to watch your shrink come back to his office from lunch, driving a Mercedes Benz.

> To be a mental patient is to take drugs that dull your mind, deaden your senses, make you jitter and drool and then you

take more drugs to lessen the "side effects."

To be a mental patient is to apply for jobs and lie about the last few months or years, because you've been in the hospital, and then you don't get the job anyway because you're a mental patient. To be a mental patient is not to matter.

To be a mental patient is never to be taken seriously.

To be a mental patient is to be a resident of a ghetto, surrounded by other mental patients who are as scared and hungry and bored and broke as you are.

To be a mental patient is to watch TV and see how violent and dangerous and dumb and incompetent and crazy you are.

To be a mental patient is to be a statistic.

To be a mental patient is to wear a label, and that label never goes away, a label that says little about what you are and even less about who you are.

To be a mental patient is to never say what you mean, but to sound like you mean what you say.

To be a mental patient is to tell your psychiatrist he's helping you, even if he is not.

To be a mental patient is to act glad when you're sad and calm when you're mad, and to always be "appropriate."

To be a mental patient is to participate in stupid groups that call themselves therapy. Music isn't music, its therapy; volleyball isn't sport, it's therapy; sewing is therapy; washing dishes is therapy. Even the air you breathe is therapy and that's called "the milieu."

To be a mental patient is not to die, even if you want to – and
not cry, and not hurt, and not be scared, and not be angry,
and not be vulnerable, and not to laugh too loud – because,
if you do, you only prove that you are a mental patient even
if you are not.

And so you become a no-thing, in a no-world, and you are
not.[33]

When I broke my silence and began introducing myself as a person
who had been diagnosed and treated for schizophrenia – a psychiatric
survivor – I became an insider in the psychiatric survivor world. As an
insider I discovered the distinct difference in meetings when a group was
composed entirely of c/s/x and when groups contained even one
professional. Genuine expression is inhibited by the presence of
professionals. Many c/s/x have learned the fragility of their freedom and
have learned to be wary of the mental health professional's power. Common
to people who have been treated in the mental health system are personal
stories lamenting the betrayal of trust. The first lie could have been a
family member telling you that you are just going to the doctor's office or
the hospital for a medical check-up, when you are really going to be
evaluated for commitment by a psychiatrist. Or in the hospital when you are
encouraged to reveal your private thoughts of despair to what seems like a
compassionate therapist, and you wind up losing your privileges and being
placed on suicide watch in seclusion. The contradictory and often
inconsistent messages the c/s/x receives from the mental health system
breed skepticism. The patient is taught in assertiveness training groups to
speak out, but the exercise of a choice that challenges a staff decision will
get the behavior charted as resistant or non-compliant.

Reconnecting with parts of long-buried and ignored experiences, I
saw my consciousness being raised. The exclusion of non-patients from the
c/s/x liberation movement was influenced by the black, women's and gay
liberation movements' principles of self-definition and self-determination.
Feelings of anger and lack of power were channeled into demands for
change. As it did for other oppressed groups, "we speak for ourselves"
became a high priority principle. Aware that their own perceptions of
mental illness contrasted sharply with those of most professionals, they
knew that effective services had to reflect core principles and priorities
articulated by c/s/x.

I learned the values and key concepts of the c/s/x movement quite quickly. Amidst the diversity, the contentious issues and the politics, I found much that was congruent with my own beliefs and values. Many of the elements I valued in my own struggles to grow were espoused by psychiatric survivor groups. I was impressed by how much expertise I found there. But I also saw how difficult it would be to get highly trained mental health professionals to value the hard-won experiential wisdom of people who have been branded by their culture as incompetent and of minimal worth.

"Hello, my name is Ron Bassman. Andy Blanch suggested that I call you. I'm in charge of a new project called Collaborative Empowerment . . . the purpose of the project is to create bridges between psychologists and recipients of mental health services. We hope to inform graduate psychology curricula about some of the new ideas and models of recovery. I'm a psychologist and I was twice diagnosed and treated for schizophrenia. Andy said that you were one of the original members of the psychologist-recipient dialogues held last year. You may remember that the proposal to develop a job like mine was discussed at that meeting. Would you be interested in talking about some possibilities for me to speak with faculty and students at your university?"

It was an opening pitch to try and get my foot in the door. When I recognized the strong interest shown towards me by professionals, I overcame my initial apprehension at calling and revealing personal information to strangers. Most of the psychologists I called had not met a person with a major mental illness diagnosis who was symptom-free, off medication, indistinguishable from his co-workers, and a licensed psychologist to boot. As a result, speaking engagements were easy to arrange.

Responses to my presentations at graduate psychology departments were generally favorable, but at one university during my talk to the clinical psychology faculty, I was miffed by the apathy. They were a reserved group who had little interest in what I said. They politely informed me that they were a research-based program with shrinking financial resources and would not be able to accommodate any deviation from their usual curriculum. Following up later in a private conversation with the chairman of the clinical psychology program, I volunteered to bring resource people into the classrooms or arrange other kinds of workshops at no cost to the university. I argued that passion rather than money motivated community activists to spread the word. Even citing what I thought to be the advantages to the psychology department and the individual professors of getting in on the cutting edge of the new recovery research failed to generate any receptivity.

Later in a private meeting with me, the chairman filled me in on the basic facts of life for academics – at least as he knew it.

"Faculty try to develop a special area of expertise that would enable them to bring in grant money to the department."

I countered, "This work is wide open with opportunities for research. Isn't anyone looking to do something new?"

He peeled away another layer of my naiveté when he candidly explained, "The politics of university research requires faculty at the beginning of their careers to build their reputations as experts in a highly defined specialty. To switch your research focus and begin to investigate unrelated phenomena is damaging to your career."

Perhaps responding to my disapproving reaction to his exposition of academic reality and what I would like to think was his own disappointment for his acceptance and years of work in such a restrictive system, he told me, "Our department turns out students that are clones of each other. Our senior faculty probably have not seen a patient with serious mental illness for over twenty years . . . maybe not since an internship at the VA or another public mental hospital. This university has never had a social conscience."

Speaking with groups of graduate students was more encouraging and stimulating. Still shaping their own identities and evaluating where they fit, they were not yet completely invested in closing the lids to the academic boxes that were being constructed around them. But even among students, depending on the emphasis of their particular university or how far along they were in their program, receptivity varied widely. When I lectured to interns who were fulfilling their last academic requirement for a PhD, I could see that if they had had no previous exposure to the lived expertise of the c/s/x experience, there was too great a chasm of cognitive dissonance between the ideas I presented and what they had been taught. Their questions and challenges were similar to the ones typically voiced by seasoned professionals. Almost always, someone asked if I had been misdiagnosed. I could count on someone proposing an extreme hypothetical example of dangerousness to justify the need for involuntary treatment. Safety and the protection of the individual and society were hot buttons. Most difficult to cut through was the students' substitution of labels for understanding. They saw me as an intelligent, high-functioning exception, with an inherent potential for recovery that would not be possible for the majority of "schizophrenics."

Too much learned sorting into categories and labeling of patients, once learned and accepted, progressively narrows the capacity for creative inquiry. It was easy to recognize those who had too much indoctrination to deter them from their "true believer" mainstream course. For those students on the verge of completing demanding educational programs, who were so close to attaining their "doctor" union cards, it would take much more than one presentation. I saw the importance of having c/s/x alternatives presented early and often in the educational programs of future mental health professionals. Despite swimming against the current, I was encouraged by a small minority of incompletely convinced students who usually sought me out for further conversation after class.

On a personal level, I was constantly learning and processing new information. With psychologists I struggled to resist being seduced into engaging in circular intellectual discussions. It was easy to understand why the psychologists' portrayal of themselves as experts is a turn-off to c/s/x. Too often I met a psychologist who was reputed to be progressive, only to be disappointed by a too-quick snap judgment in which I was reduced to a generality. I listened to one well-known psychologist tell me that my value was not in any new ideas I might have, but rather in my willingness to be open about my psychiatric history. Perhaps his absolute statement would have had more merit if it had been offered after that person had taken the time to get to know me and my ideas. An African-American friend told me it reminded him of the time when successful blacks were told that they were a credit to their race. My situation differed in that I was trying to make a mixed marriage within myself work. I had to demonstrate my bona fides with two antagonistic membership groups.

I was invited to present a paper at the 1995 Annual Conference of the American Psychological Association. The Symposium was titled, *Empowering Psychologists Engaged in Public Service.* No longer hiding my schizophrenia label, I believed that at long last I had a credible voice and a forum.

Nervous, uncomfortable and feeling out of place, I also felt a sense of awe as I watched myself register at the Waldorf Astoria. "What do you think this is, the Waldorf Astoria?" was my childhood memory of an often used saying to make you remember your place. The magical name of that hotel reverberated with images of intimidating gentility. I scanned the room, alert and jumpy as a squirrel. The embarrassing faux pas, the half-hidden snickers for violating unknown social graces, were reminders of painful awkwardness. The old feeling of not belonging was a tiny hitchhiker traveling in my jacket pocket. Scientists say that smell, the most primitive of our senses, elicits our most visceral memories. I inhaled the smell of the stately, oh-so-proper elegance, there to confirm the entitled pleasures of the winners. As I played with the irony, I felt my nervousness morph into excitement.

Alone at APA, I brought an outsider's message. I spent the first few days listening to speakers reworking the same old guild-driven issues. Pleas for psychologists to organize, to get in on the ground floor of managed care, to be politically active, to lobby, were the rallying calls. To me, their passion lacked the kinship with desperation they needed for motivating their colleagues.

I was cool to the APA conference's most intense themes. The focus on financial crises and the strategies to combat the possible demise of the psychology profession did not stir me. Hospital privileges, prescription privileges, the privileged fighting to keep and gain more privileges was what I saw. Not my message, but the perceived threats to the security, status and lifestyle of the traditional psychologist were what made me relevant and brought an invitation to speak. The mantra: Total Quality Improvement – the new icon of the business world stood ready to take on the crisis in health care costs. Standing ready to be a valued collaborator, the mental patient was trying on the new role of esteemed customer; it was a shift in status from the "out" to the "in" group.

During workshops, my mind drifted back to earlier that year when I had attended the Alternatives '95 Conference in St. Paul, Minnesota. On the last day of that conference, during a quiet moment waiting for the elevator, I felt a sense of the immense pain contained in that one hotel. Over 500 persons diagnosed with serious mental illness, all survivors of a psychiatric system that had inflicted its will on those whose life journeys veered off acceptable paths. The empathic pain washed over me and turned my thoughts to wondering about the joy, warmth and genuineness I had felt from being part of this group of disenfranchised outcasts. For that brief time while at Alternatives, I had become a member of a sharing, caring community.

I joined in the vitality and enthusiasm of the most denigrated, exploited group of people who reside at the bottom of society's multi-tiered structure. For the psychiatrically labeled, empowerment and freedom are not birth rights that can be automatically claimed. Yet the camaraderie built from sharing our experiences of pain and suffering created community. That

Alternatives, my first, had been an opportunity for me to stop defending myself and hiding from the shame of a schizophrenia label. Here I could be openly proud of being a psychiatric survivor.

I presented two workshops at Alternatives. I learned more than I taught. There was a library full of heart-wrenching stories and it seemed as if each person needed to tell of their struggles. Listening to the stories was the most powerful part of Alternatives. At the last plenary session, to debrief and help everyone get ready to go home, there were two hours of open microphones available for anyone who wanted to speak to the entire group. I was stunned by the creative talent and depth of understanding so beautifully articulated by those people who sometimes look and act kind of funny.

At APA, one listens; at Alternatives, you participate from your gut. What a contrast it is, to see 20,000 psychologists from an affluent organization of over 100,000 who have convinced themselves, and would have you believe, that they are engaged in a desperate struggle to become empowered. At APA, I sit with the formality, apart and unmoved.

My talk at APA went well, but I thought that the compliments and requests for reprints of my paper were not necessarily indicative of understanding. I reflected on how interest, moral indignation, and a stirring of feeling will quickly retreat, and be rationalized and made to fit with other information stored in the intellectual realm. The brief glimpse of drama does not stir the playgoer to action. I viewed the professionals' guild issues and lack of self-awareness as formidable obstacles to meaningful change. I pondered the folly of the typical mental health professional's belief that she understands what is best for the mental patient – too much investment in a helper identity locked onto fixing, protecting and making choices, and ultimately controlling the behavior of her mental patients.

A too-passionate zealot in my new reformer role might be how I would describe myself back then. Battling my unfamiliarity with the terrain, I was a bit too dogmatic in pointing out what I believed was absent from my profession's discourse on mental illness. As time passed and I began collaborating with colleagues at APA whom I found to be dedicated to advancing the profession of psychology and to improving community services, my initial one-dimensional view changed. I developed collegial relationships and formed friendships framed in a mutual respect that allowed us to learn from each other.

But always, with c/s/x I felt more connected. Their curiosity and evaluation of me seemed to be more here-and-now centered and determined by their relationship with me. C/s/x related to me with a candor and directness that was extremely appealing. It did not take long for me to feel accepted and know where I stood. Unlike my early experience with my fellow psychologists, with peer survivors I shared deep knowledge of the pain and anguish one feels from the ravages of a disordered state of consciousness. We also shared a profound awareness of the inadequacy of "help" offered to us by state sanctioned *Godfathers* who made the offer you can't refuse – drugs. Those of us who have had varying degrees of success overcoming our emotional demons know what can be helpful in such times of extreme vulnerability, and what is damaging.

Soon after I arrived in New York, the state began to make the transition from twelve years of Democratic party leadership by Governor Mario Cuomo to Republican party governance by George Pataki. As in other state offices, the personnel of the Office of Mental Health tensed and waited to see how the changes would affect them. Those in governor-appointed management positions polished their resumes and prepared to leave as soon as they could find jobs; they knew that the new political power brokers would be hungrily viewing their jobs as ways to dispense patronage perks. When those who had designed my position and recruited me left, the grant contracted to fund my work was eliminated. The Collaborative Empowerment Project lasted a little more than one year, just long enough for me to get a basic education in how the shifts in political power influence mental health policy decisions. With the changes, I wondered if I would be able to continue doing work as a survivor psychologist or be forced to return to working as a conventional psychologist.

Fortunately, my participation on a number of planning committees had made enough of a positive impression to get a new position created for me. In my new job, I would be responsible for developing self-help and empowerment projects in the eighteen NY state-operated outpatient facilities, providing technical assistance to c/s/x for their self-help projects, and educating staff as to how to support new self-help initiatives. My title was Director of Self-help and Empowerment Projects and my supervisor was Darby Penney, Director of the Office of Recipient Affairs. She was a psychiatric survivor, a peer. Not only was I relieved to be able to continue the work I wanted to do, but I found in my new boss a kindred spirit who shared my values and allowed me the latitude to be creative in implementing new ideas and projects.

Chapter 12

Empowering Ourselves

Only those who have helped themselves know how to help others, and to respect their right to help themselves. (George Bernard Shaw)

In his 1957 acceptance speech, Nobel prize-winning author Albert Camus said, "The nobility of our calling will always be rooted in two commitments difficult to observe: Refusal to lie about what we know, and resistance to oppression."

I like to think that my peers and I have the privilege and obligation to adhere to the same standard accorded to the artist. Our experience-based wisdom demands that we provide our fellow travelers with the opportunity to tell their stories. By sharing those personal narratives in a supportive setting, c/s/x can be inspired to find new meaning and reconstruct the negative self-concepts attached to the role of helpless and dependent mental patient.

Our current treatments of mental illness are woefully inadequate. Clinicians and policy-makers need to consider other possibilities. What is defined as behavior arising out of poor functioning can be recast as stemming from a social structure which deprives certain people of the opportunity and resources to allow their genuine abilities to manifest. An episodic crisis may be reflective of developmental issues and can contain potential for growth when evaluated within the whole and unique context of that individual's life. Can we be so sure that we know a person's limits – the beginning and ending of a unique life story?

The assumptions driving research and clinical work with serious mental illness rest too comfortably on an almost a priori foundation:
- Mental illness is a biochemical disease.
- A diagnosis is essential to the development of effective treatment plans.
- Treatment for serious mental illness must begin with medication.
- The mentally ill need to accept the fact that they are

mentally ill.
- Clinicians know what is best for people who are mentally ill.
- The mentally ill must accept their limitations.
- The mentally ill must down-size their expectations.
- The mentally ill should work at low stress jobs.
- Thinking and behavior that deviates from societal standards is pathological.
- The mentally ill cannot make good decisions for themselves.
- Progress can begin only after symptoms are under control.
- Psychotherapy is useless for schizophrenia.
- Counseling must focus on maintenance and stabilization rather than personal growth.
- The mentally ill refuse medication because they don't believe that they are mentally ill.
- If the mentally ill refuse treatment, forced treatment is appropriate and necessary.
- Mental illness is life-long and irreversible.
- Complete recovery is rare or non-existent.

* * *

The Managed Care industry has created an image of itself that promises much. It purports to possess the capability of controlling upward spiraling costs while providing more quality by being more efficient. The tools of business are supposed to weed out excessive wasteful costs, determine the real wants and needs of its customers, measure outcomes and improve the quality of services. The rallying slogan: *No more of those costly ineffective plans created by good-intentioned bloated public sector bureaucrats.* If believed, big business will create a new, lean, customer-friendly, efficient and profitable industry to take care of the "mentally ill."

Mental Health Managed Care, whether it elicits fear or tugs on the would-be entrepreneur's heart, is playing a major role in reshaping the mental health system. By forcing mental health professionals, program administrators and bureaucrats to examine their methods and practices, Managed Care may have cracked open a window of possibilities for c/s/x.

Mental health professionals typically see managed care as a major threat to their ability to maintain not only their professional independence and integrity, but also their status and income. They are smarting from attacks on the value of the services they provide and even their claims of broad and specific expertise. New mandates to evaluate the quality and value of services have made the c/s/x a sought-after collaborator. The emerging roles have demanded a different kind of listening, with more respect for experiential wisdom – a necessary but uneasy collaboration between the professionals and the c/s/x that requires new openness, risk-taking and much hard work by both sides. It is important to remember that Managed Care is an administrative method, not a paradigm shift nor a sea change, but as such it can be a major catalyst in opening up a formerly closed mental health system.

The state of New York confronted the massive task of changing its mental health care delivery system. I was one of four c/s/x among the twenty-six members appointed to the governor's Mental Health Subcommittee on Managed Care. I began to learn about the attitudes and feelings held toward the c/s/x I represented. The subcommittee, co-chaired by a physician and a c/s/x, was charged with coordinating, reviewing and approving the recommendations of four task forces that were responsible for designing a carve-out Special Needs Plan (SNP) for the "severely and chronically mentally ill" within the New York state Medicaid system.

SNPs were being designed to serve the approximately 60,000 people with serious mental illness in the New York state mental health system who received Medicaid and were high users of mental health services. Recognizing that these people could not be served in a basic managed care plan that is configured to provide only a limited number of counseling sessions and a fixed number of psychiatric inpatient days, the statewide SNP system would be designed to provide a large and varied array of intensive services. The Mental Health Subcommittee provided oversight to the four tasks forces (Admission/Discharge, System Design, Clinical Linkages and Quality Assurance/Performance Measurement) which totaled more than 200 members, including forty c/s/x. The remainder were providers, administrators, clinicians and family members. The primary goal was to create a plan that would enable the state to obtain a 1915b waiver from the federal government that would permit the state to implement mandatory mental-health managed Medicaid enrollment throughout New York. Of course, cost savings was the driving force.

I was also a member of the Admissions/Discharge team where I participated in a task force struggling to define who would be eligible for a Special Needs Plan. All the of the various stakeholders on our task force, with the exception of the c/s/x, wanted to use diagnostic tests and assessment instruments based on symptoms and psychopathology. C/s/x wanted admission and discharges to be based on needs and functional assessments. My peers and I pointed to the lack of information conveyed by diagnosis when assessing current needs for services. A person can fit the criteria for the diagnosis of schizophrenia and be actively hallucinating, yet not be in need of intensive services until, perhaps, she has lost her home, job or friend – any one of which may have been crucial to her support system. We argued that a specific problem and its rippling impact trigger the need for help, not the nature or frequency of the hallucinations or the longstanding diagnosis.

Along with the almost universal concern about Managed Care's bottom-line agenda of cutting costs by limiting access to services, c/s/x see the push to develop standardized practice guidelines as a dangerous trend. Treating a person by consulting a decision tree designed by expert consensus stands in polar opposition to the c/s/x's demand for people to be regarded as individuals rather than as representatives of an interchangeable class of objects. Clinical pathways ignore the totality of the individual in favor of expert conjectures being passed off as scientifically researched best probabilities. It would scare me to be subjected to a prescriptive treatment that said something like *When a person meets the diagnostic criteria for bipolar disorder start on X mg of lithium; if not responsive in four weeks, increase to Y mg of lithium; still lacking positive response, then switch to X mg of Depakote.*

The power and attributed legitimacy of practice guidelines rests uneasily upon its assumed derivation from a sound scientific knowledge base. An examination of the literature and research on practice guidelines points to complex incentives and competing motivations influencing the increased demand for the development and utilization of guidelines.

Ignoring complex issues of mind, self, soul, spirit, perception and other ontological mysteries, the mental health industry is leaping with both feet into the unknown. Practice principles based on a disease model of mental illness are diametrically opposed to the person-centered values that c/s/x want to see in publicly funded mental health services. The American Managed Behavioral Healthcare Association (AMBHA) represents most of the large behavioral healthcare organizations in the United States. AMBHA recognizes the importance of c/s/x to the process of negotiating government contracts and recommends that its members demonstrate substantial c/s/x involvement. Managed care companies are also aware of the potential for self-help and empowerment services to decrease utilization of costly inpatient hospital treatment. C/s/x advocates are encouraged by but also wary of the alliances with pharmaceutical companies and the bottom-line profit motive that drives managed care companies. The AMBHA website points to the influence of companies promoting their drugs for mental illness (http://www.abhw.org/vendoradvisor/index.htm):

> Specifically, consultants, pharmaceutical companies, and other suppliers to MBHOs [managed behavioral healthcare organizations] may financially contribute to AMBHA. Such contributors would receive all AMBHA executive director's reports, all AMBHA state tracking reports and they would meet with the AMBHA board of directors, in special session, at least twice a year.

Members of the AMBHA Supplier Advisory Panel
    (December 6, 2006):
    Bristol-Myers Squibb Company
    Eli Lilly and Company
    Pfizer Inc.
    Smithkline Beecham Pharmaceuticals
    Wyeth-Ayerst Laboratories
<http://www.lilly.comhttp://www.depression-info.comhttp://www.sb.com>

Too often, at the managed care meetings I attended I was left scratching my head in wonder about some nonsensical turn of words that popped out to justify a breach of integrity or to bypass the spirit of a law or regulation. At one such meeting, in disbelief I wrote down one of the more outrageous phrases I heard a psychiatrist say: "We can get *retroactive pre-approval*."

In contrast to the formulaic treatment protocols of managed care entities that adhere to the medical model – diagnose pathology, then plug in treatment for that diagnosis – self-help asserts other values. The following definition and principles come from the unpublished findings of a work group of c/s/x that I facilitated at the New York State Office of Mental Health in 2002:

Definition: Self-help is the process in which a person
actively chooses to work toward improving some aspect(s)
of his or her life and takes responsibility for the results.

Principles:
1. Self-help can be an individual or group activity.
2. Persons engaged in self-help pay attention to developing
meaningful structures or activities that will enhance their
lives.
3. The different forms that self-help can take and the
direction of a person's self-help activities are not something
imposed from the outside but are self-generated.
4. For self-help to achieve positive results, hard work and
commitment are essential.

Today, self-help is a well-known adjunct to treatment in most areas
of health care. Self-help groups assemble around issues of well-being,
personal growth, gender, racial and community concerns. Self-help referral
services and clearinghouses keep extensive lists of existing services which
are easily accessible by toll-free 800 numbers throughout the United States.
Many forms of self-help are supportive of and secondary to "expert"
professional opinions. Until recently, in health areas other than "psychiatric
disorders," there has been little challenge to the primacy of experts.
Theorists and researchers are drawing attention to conflicts in the health
care domain: "The pervasive belief that experts should solve all of our
problems in living has created a social and cultural iatrogenesis which
extends the sense of alienation and loss of ability to control life even to
one's own body."[34]

Historical precedent for the emerging c/s/x activism may go back to
The Petition of the Poor Distracted People in the House of Bedlam, a
pamphlet published in 1620.[35] The prototype of today's c/s/x self-help
groups was the Alleged Lunatics' Friend Society – in which obtaining the
cure constituted an act of resistance to the system. The British newspaper
The Times on March 27, 1846 ridiculed the efforts of these ex-patients:

Some of the names we have seen announced suggest to us the
possibility that promoters of this scheme are not altogether
free from motives of self-preservation . . . we think the
should be satisfied to take care of themselves, without

tendering their services to all who happen to be in the same position.[36]

In 1838, Richard Paternoster was released from the madhouse after being confined there for forty-one days. His commitment had followed a disagreement with his father over money. After he was discharged, he advertised in a newspaper for fellow sufferers to join him in a campaign to redress abuses suffered by mental patients. Initially, he was joined by four men, the most important being John Perceval, son of the assassinated prime minister. The self-help group of Paternoster and Perceval was joined by William Bailey, an inventor who had spent five years in madhouses, and Dr. John Parkin, another ex-patient. The four men named their self-help group the Alleged Lunatics' Friend Society. The objectives of the Society were: to reduce the likelihood of illegal incarceration and improve the condition of asylums; to offer help to discharged patients; and to convert the public to an enlarged view of Christian duties and sympathies.[37]

Self-help has been with us for a long time. The desire to join together in groups for purposes of survival and gratification of social needs is evident through surveying the history of common interest associations like hunters, merchants and storytellers. Self-help appears most often at times of rapid change in complex societies, and in slowly developing pre-industrial countries.[38]

One of the earliest United States groups organized specifically as a self-help group was formed in the early 1800s. The group was called the Washingtonians and while its existence was brief, it may be considered a prototype for Alcoholics Anonymous (AA). The Washingtonians was started by six drinkers who pledged to stop drinking and to recruit other drinkers in order to reform them.

It was with the formation of Alcoholics Anonymous that we first see self-help develop muscles and staying power. AA was founded in 1935 when two "hopeless" alcoholics, Bill W., a stockbroker and Dr. Bob, a surgeon, met in Akron, Ohio. In 1939 the AA textbook, *Alcoholics Anonymous* was published to explain AA's philosophy, methods and its core twelve-step strategy for recovery. AA has grown to include 105,294 groups with 2,082,980 members world-wide. In the United States, AA has 1,190,637 members participating in 52,652 groups.[39] The Alcoholics Anonymous twelve-step program has served as a model for a large number of other addiction-based or compulsive behavior self-help groups, such as Al Anon, Narcotics Anonymous, Gamblers Anonymous and Overeaters

Anonymous.

The 1960s served as the incubator for groups of people who banded together to focus on making major societal changes. The civil rights movement was fighting to end discrimination against blacks; the women's movement, the anti-Vietnam War movement and people with disabilities were some of the groups who were challenging legal barriers and institutional practices. These social movements and self-help groups had several common themes centered around a critical attitude toward authority and the bureaucratic organizations that controlled rights, policies and services. It was during this era of critics and dissenters that psychiatric ex-patients began to speak out and organize against what they felt were damaging treatments, unnecessary confinement under harsh conditions, and the inability of the existing mental health system to meet their needs.

In the United States during the 1960s and 1970s, the organizing efforts of former psychiatric patients are identified as the birthing for the current c/s/x movement. For the first time in American history, formerly hospitalized mental patients created and ran their own organizations. People who were lumped together as mental patients rejected the inevitability of their heretofore powerless place in the world. After first co-opting their own pejorative labels to draw attention to their new activism, they used the names to self-identify their relationship to the mental health system. Early names like "mental patient" and "client" were closely tied to the mental health system, whereas "consumer" represented persons who desired more choice and better mental health services. "Ex-patient" implied moderate criticism of the public mental health system coupled with the desire to leave behind the role of once being a mental patient. "Ex-inmate" and "psychiatric survivor" became the names favored by those who rejected the medical model of mental illness and its legal mandate to provide forced treatments. I chose to identify myself as a psychiatric survivor, the name that was closest to reflecting my values and attitude.

The earliest groups formed spontaneously in Oregon, California, New York, Massachusetts, Pennsylvania and Kansas. The first formally organized group was the Insane Liberation Front, founded in Portland, Oregon in 1970. A year later, the Mental Patients' Liberation Project was founded in New York, and the Mental Patients' Liberation Front was organized in Boston. In 1972, the Network Against Psychiatric Assault was established in San Francisco. Other groups formed in the early 1970s included Project Release, in New York, and The Alliance for the Liberation of Mental Patients, in Philadelphia.[40]

The strongest critics of mental health treatments have always been former mental hospital patients. The ex-patient groups openly expressed their pain and outrage, and said that the therapies forced upon them were not effective. Members of these groups asserted that they were best qualified to judge how they needed to be treated. A number of groups sought to establish their own support programs as alternatives to hospitals. Activities of the emerging ex-patient movement included: organizing support groups, advocating for patient rights, lobbying for changes in laws, identifying themselves as former mental patients when speaking out in public, and publishing articles and books about their experiences. The experiences they shared with peers had taught them that the treatments of people diagnosed with mental illness were rife with physical and emotional abuses, and were often insults to the basic dignity and integrity of the individual.

The appeal of self-help to those who resist participating in conventional treatment services lies in the honoring of personal responsibility. Their experiences told them that being confined to a mental hospital and taking psychiatric drugs did not improve their lives. Mental health professionals told them that they were doing well as long as they were passive, stayed out of trouble and didn't bother anyone. Psychiatric survivors refused to accept the mandate to live lives of flattened emotions with an absence of joy or sadness. We know that anger and pain at least remind us that we are alive and have possibilities.

Sociology professor Robert Emerick looks at self-help and mutual aid groups as part of a social movement he calls "mad liberation." Building a structure for his social movement hypothesis, he cites what he believes is a good definition of empowerment: "The degree to which individuals, groups, or the environment are changed so that individuals gain more control over the environment." Emerick's research sample of 346 self-help groups indicates that only a minority of mental patient self-help groups fit the category of individual-change-oriented, alternative therapy groups that are considered complementary to traditional treatment services. He suggests that the majority of enduring self-help groups qualify as social-change-oriented survivor groups and "[t]he failure to detect the mad liberation movement is due, in large part, to the psychologistic theoretical and methodological biases of most of the researchers who, nonetheless, acknowledge the growth of the self-help phenomenon."[41]

Comparing the typical self-help group to a miniature democracy illuminates some common characteristics: self-governance, equal rights within the group process, leadership serving at the pleasure of the group, similarity of member concerns, reliance on the collective experiential knowledge of the members, and non-profit focus.

Today's medical model too often blames the victim and artificially separates the *subject* from the *objective* social world. The medical model has minimized the multiple conditions that contribute to an individual's specific situation. In the self-help model, the personal and the political are irreversibly enmeshed. Empowerment becomes the transformation of the passive objects called mental patients to historical subjects fully capable of acting to transform the conditions that forced them into lives of passivity.[42]

In self-help groups and other peer-run alternatives, there is an awakening of the ability to trust yourself and others. For many, it is the long absent, genuine invitation to be real in a place of safety and hope, where the exercise of control is an individual responsibility, and you are able to rethink your professionally adjudicated label of incompetence. With everyone being equal, compliance and passive dependency are less valued than in therapy systems with designated experts and the associated power imbalances. Inspired by the success stories of their peers, group members see the possibility of working to achieve goals that they had been told were beyond their reach. In a mutual-help alternative, each participant is valued for what he or she has to offer. Being involved in self-help initiatives is being in the position to help others feel good, which in turn feeds your own self-esteem. With peers you do not have to bury your anger, but instead you have the opportunity to give it positive expression in advocacy efforts. Most importantly, the self-help process allows people to redefine their experience by giving voice to their own unique stories. Physician and medical ethicist Howard Brody asserts that the meaning we attach to our particular stories is the primary way that suffering is produced or alleviated. He argues that the placebo effect or healing by symbolic means occurs best when the meaning of the illness experience is changed in a positive direction.[43]

Activists see few boundaries to the self-help phenomenon, and view the possibilities as only limited by the imagination and creativity of participants. Peer-operated alternatives take many forms. Peer-run telephone *warm lines* provide a service that professionally staffed or professionally backed-up crisis (hot) lines cannot. When calling in crisis, the person may unhappily discover that hotlines can function as entry points into forced interventions. Hotlines typically operate as last-resort places to call when one is teetering on the edge and about to lose control. If someone is anxious, lonely, frightened or desperate, and calls a hotline staffed by a person who is required to exercise legal responsibility – a counselor who is instructed to reduce all risks, who is sensitized to any expressions of anger or sadness and its "automatic" potential for triggering violence or suicide – then safety is paramount and heroic interventions are standard policy. By contrast, warm lines offer the support of a peer who listens with the mind-set of someone who may have been in a similar state, a peer who has not been trained to maintain emotional distance, a peer who can identify alternative resources and who is not mandated to always be safe rather than sorry. People who work on warm lines have told me that most of the people who call do so because of a need to talk with someone who is patient and willing to listen on a lonely night.

Peer-operated clubhouses and drop-in centers are proving their value in cities and towns throughout the world. Their emphasis on personal responsibility, camaraderie and freedom to choose one's own level of participation is appealing to people who have lost trust in coercive programs. Clubhouses and drop-in centers are becoming places where the seeds of advocacy and empowerment are nurtured among members.

C/s/x have formed organizations to develop a variety of housing options. C/s/x have developed crisis response alternatives, such as "crisis hostels" and in-home support. Peers have developed formal and informal outreach networks to people who they know are in distress and have isolated themselves. C/s/x are helping their peers navigate the maze of social security disability requirements. Peers are sharing information about medication, coping techniques and educating each other as to their rights.

In New York, creative programs like *Incube* and *Share Your Bounty* were started by c/s/x who saw needs that were not being met. Peer initiated and operated, Incube provided technical assistance and support for aspiring entrepreneurs. Incube is a business incubator helping peers start and run their own businesses. Share Your Bounty was conceived and developed by inpatients at Bronx State Psychiatric Hospital. Lenox, a patient, saw large amounts of food being wasted at the hospital; he suggested that the food could be delivered to people living on the streets in New York City. With the acceptance of staff and the participation of other peers, a weekly food-run to the Bowery was begun. The functions of this small core group grew more complex and evolved into an organization that distributed food to multiple sites: Grand Central Station, Port Authority Bus Terminal, Central Park and a number of soup kitchens in Manhattan and the Bronx. After existing informally for more than three years, Share Your Bounty applied for and received a three-year $350,000 National Institute of Mental Health grant.[44] The success of Share Your Bounty challenges the commonly-held myth that in-patients at a psychiatric hospital are incompetent and incapable.

Today, c/s/x find themselves somewhat in demand. The federal government's report by the New Freedom Commission for Mental Health[45] recommends that all services should be consumer and family centered. Managed Care's competition for state Medicaid contracts, with its emphasis on outcome and satisfaction, has brought us to the policy table. Ironically, the most important "stakeholder" is now, at last, being officially acknowledged as a stakeholder. In this new environment, the key issues are:

- Making sure that we are significantly involved in the governance, design, implementation, administration, provision of services, evaluation and management of any new managed system;
- Having access to a wide-range of peer-run self-help and empowerment services;
- Crisis support and hospital-admission diversion services;
- A recovery-based model focusing on the unique needs of the individual;
- Real choice;
- For the individual to be central to the planning of treatment and support services;
- Confidentiality and access to one's own records, and the ability to correct inaccuracies;
- Recognizing that forced treatment is the failure to offer an acceptable alternative.

The new activists share a belief in the need to have their rights restored and protected. Quality alternatives to forced treatment are a priority. No issue is more powerfully charged than *forced treatment*. The value of self-help begins with the free and non-coercive choice exercised by participants. The denial of freedom in all its involuntary treatment forms cannot be over-estimated in its implicit and explicit consequences. When you are no longer permitted to assume responsibility for your own health and actions, you are profoundly affected. Even those consumers who are grateful for having been forced to undergo what they construe as a life-saving intervention face the prodigious task of disengaging from their journey down the narrow, high-walled, regimented path of passive dependency. Many who have been forced into a hospital avoid mental health treatment even at the cost of a homeless life on the streets.

In a research study supported by the California Department of Mental Health and conducted by c/s/x researchers, 55% of the people who had been involuntarily hospitalized reported that they would avoid treatment out of fear of involuntary commitment.[46] The authors reported that 93% of 234 clients felt that their human rights had been violated. Among the freedoms taken away were:

- The right to refuse treatment;
- The right to make choices;
- The right to have basic needs met outside of institutions;
- Self-determination;
- Freedom from incarceration when no crime has been committed;
- Freedom from restraints and forced drugging;
- The right to communication;
- The right to due process;
- The right to be fully informed about the treatment and its side-effects.

When c/s/x talk about what helped them, they generally credit some person who believed in them, who respected them – someone who made a genuine person-to-person connection. Often cited as a barrier to recovery is the loss of the ability to trust when deprived of one's freedom of choice.

Psychiatrist and researcher Loren Mosher, founder of the Soteria Project, laments the gross irony attendant upon the branch of medicine that is supposed to be the most expert in the use of the patient-doctor relationship:

> Psychiatry's current biologic zeitgeist supports the position that it is not possible to have a therapeutic relationship with a person with a "diseased brain"; hence, coercion is justified. This rationalization flies in the face of decades of clinical experience and research indicating that while often more difficult, it is usually possible to establish a collaborative relationship with even the most disturbed and disturbing persons. When this is not possible, it is usually the result of multiple experiences of betrayed trust, which are then reinforced by involuntary hospitalization.[47]

For many, a first admission into a psychiatric facility is made with an expectation to find help and relief. From my friend Rae Unzicker:

> I go with my eyes blazing inwards with hope. The eyes I allow the world to see are empty now. Yes, a hospital. Kindness. A doctor who understands suffering. Rest. I believe. I must believe. I am sick. I need help. The hospital will help.

> And then the final fraud, deception, treachery, betrayal. Tennyson wrote, "A lie that is half a truth is ever the blackest of lies."

> I have finally discovered the lie, the fraud that is "help" in a hospital.[48]

Dissatisfaction with the existing mental health system is not a denial of the need for help, but rather a criticism of what is passing for help. The cruel joke well-known to c/s/x: You are put in a mental hospital for acting like you are crazy, but once you are in the hospital, you are punished if you do not act normal in an environment that is abnormal. The need to find explanations, understanding and above all, a safe haven, is rarely honored.

In recent years, c/s/x have struggled to continue their independent grassroots efforts while resisting co-optation. Funders have recognized the importance of c/s/x in establishing better methods to assess, monitor, regulate and control services. The new flow of government money to c/s/x leaders has placed them in unfamiliar roles as players with power. The difficulty of advocating against a system that pays you is at the top of the list of newly emerging problems. For those working within the mental health system, "reasonable accommodation" often needs clarification. Many states have established offices of consumer affairs within their departments of mental health. With consumer directors in charge of departments employing consumers, new and extremely difficult accommodation issues are emerging. How does a peer/director deal with an employee/peer who is too depressed to get out of bed and do the required work? To what extent should norm-defying behavior be tolerated on the job? What if one of your workers is involuntarily hospitalized and you successfully advocate for that person's release: do you let him come back to work in an obviously disruptive condition? Do you recommend treatment, medication, peer support as a condition of employment?

When I consider the special accommodations made to me that allowed me to work when I was unable to adequately perform my job duties, I am convinced of this approach's value. Critical to my recovery was the gift of time, the time to throw off the effects of my treatments – memory loss, shame, passivity, and the deficits in energy, confidence and hope. Yet how far can accommodations be extended and where do these change into being unproductive crutches? Again, we are faced with difficult decisions that require creative, flexible, individually determined plans.

Despite the potential problems, the opportunities for c/s/x to have genuine voices within and outside the system are encouraging signs of progress. Exposing clinicians and policy-makers to the ideas and experiences of people who were seen before only as members of a class sharing similar pathologies can be an eye-opening educational experience. Rappaport recommends that experts turn to non-experts to discover the multitude of different, paradoxical and sometimes contradictory ways that people gain control, find meaning, and empower their lives.[49]

When I attended taskforce or workgroup meetings I was surprised by the inability of many professionals to see what is fundamental and extremely obvious to anyone who has been diagnosed and treated for serious mental illness. However, working on problems with professionals and administrators, even being on opposite sides of an issue, permits policy makers and c/s/x to get to know what they like or dislike about a specific person, rather than what that person represents.

When c/s/x no longer own the dubious privilege of having obnoxious behavior excused or rationalized, and when accountability is expected, a major "all people who . . ." myth is debunked. When professionals are required to move out of their caretaker roles and look at the whole person, it becomes much more difficult to remain unaware of the oppression that particular people face daily in their particular lives. Stigma, discrimination and patronizing attitudes may be best undermined when people are working shoulder to shoulder, or even shoulder against shoulder as respected adversaries.

Chapter 13

The Epistemology of Hubris: Theories and Myths Used as Laws

Man has to awaken to wonder – and so perhaps do people. Science is a way of sending him to sleep again.   (Ludwig Wittgenstein)

Early in my childhood education I was taught to believe that with enough knowledge, our enemies (disease, poverty, war, nature) could be defeated and we would be able to control our destiny. Exorcizing superstitions and replacing them with science was the key to living the good, safe life. At that very same time, during periodic air raid drills, we would huddle in fetal positions underneath our little desks. Some of us accepted the belief that those insubstantial wooden desks were adequate shields. But even then I began to wonder whether it was knowledge or faith that promised safety.

Sociologist Ernest Becker in his Pulitzer Prize winning book *The Denial of Death* wrote, "the only secure truth men have is that which they themselves create and dramatize; to live is to play at the meaning of life."[50] He asks us to consider what might be the best illusion we can use to guide our lives. Or, in other words, how do we legitimatize foolishness? Perhaps we can find a way to evaluate the worth of an illusion by measuring how much freedom, dignity and hope a given illusion generates. When you live outside the agreed-upon illusions you are putting yourself in harm's way.

Even now, it is too easy for me to identify with the feelings of hospitalized mental patients. I remember being only a few years removed from my own foray into madness and doing a patient assessment as part of my internship, when an answer given to a sentence-completion item grabbed my attention. The stem sentence, *Wouldn't it be funny if* was completed by this patient as, "Wouldn't it be funny if *all of us in this here hospital were sane, and all of you out there were the crazy ones.*" Not a novel idea, but for me it opened a gateway into memories of the fragile reality membrane that I too had once stepped through. It was a poignant reminder of my ongoing struggle to fit in and appear normal. Did being normal mean I had to block out empathy and forgo further exploration of who I was and what I wanted to become? Must I forget?

Those officially designated as "mad" pay a high price for their inability or unwillingness to deny what they intuitively sense. Becker goes on to say that society pays another kind of steep price for its accommodation to a different kind of pretense: "the briefest explanation of all the evil that men have wreaked upon themselves and upon their world since the beginnings of time right up until tomorrow . . . it would simply be in the toll that his pretense of sanity takes, as he tries to deny his true condition."[51]

Was my madness manifested because of my failure to build sturdy and dependable ego defenses capable of filtering competing interpretations of reality? A few who possess societally admired talents may be permitted to wear the cloak of madness and remove it when they choose, but it is a dangerous dance even for the revered artist.

The construct *madness*, like *love* and *war* and *jealousy*, is a well-worked theme of literature. From the romantic and sublime to the titillating horrors of mythic monsters, the mysteries fascinate us. Seeing the madness of others can force us to confront our denied fears and mourn once-longed-for but now rejected possibilities. The medical model of mental illness shields us from seeing persons who can stimulate disturbing, soul-searching thoughts – questions that force us to think about our physical and psychic fragility. Those mad, unpredictable characters are transformed into pitiful victims who inspire little fear or awe when seen in their drugged stupors. Must we continue to desperately pursue and honor the twin apparitions of predictability and control to soothe our existential angst at the expense of truth-seeking?

If you are a c/s/x you have experienced the medical model of mental illness first-hand. Many have been "psychoeducated," or coerced into believing that they have a brain disease – a neurobiological disorder (NBD). A friend of mine recalls with humor and a bit of bitterness what she and some other mental patients on her hospital ward would say among themselves when they were called to participate in the psychoeducation group: "We don't need to be educated on how to be psycho, we already know – isn't that why we're in the bin?"

Considerable effort is directed at promoting the benefits of looking at mental disorders as real diseases, and seeking insurance parity with the other physical diseases. A frequent comparison to diabetes is made and the obvious logical conclusions are drawn: neither patient nor family is responsible, therefore no shame or blame for anyone. When one is diagnosed with diabetes, the distress of realizing that you have diabetes, and the shock of recognizing that you have a life-long incurable condition, are tempered by the knowledge that your mysterious and troubling symptoms are responsive to treatment.

Diagnosing and giving a name to confusing thoughts, emotions and behavior is at first comforting to the identified patient and family who are seeking answers from the medical expert. With the name comes the hope of cure, or at least the belief that the best treatment will then be known and administered. Unfortunately, the relief is short for the complex conditions we designate as diseases of the mind. The person is taught how his feelings and behaviors are symptoms that fit together into a diagnosis. But after the diagnosis comes the self-fulfilling prophesy – that is when the individual learns that he is his diagnosis, and he acts out his part. The treatment outcome is considered to be positive. Once he was mad and uncontrollable, now he is passive and dependent, harmless.

Anyone with mental illness experience, as either a patient or a worker, has been exposed to stories trumpeting the value of psychiatric drugs. There was the early Thorazine "miracle" that was supposed to have cleared out the back wards and enabled those former inhabitants of the "snake pit" to return to their communities. We are told of the remarkable, almost miraculous benefits of Clozaril and the new atypical psychiatric drugs. Advance promotions from the pharmaceutical industry announce the introduction of better drugs without the side-effects of the older drugs that up until the arrival of the newly promoted breakthrough drugs were barely mentioned. If you are involved with "psychiatric illness" you have heard the personal stories of lives changed or saved by medication. I am aware of too many of the untold stories.

Outpatient day treatment, group homes and psychiatric drugs share their patients in a cozy, mutually supportive arrangement. The typical resident/patient has a documented history of multiple changing diagnoses, a variety of drug regimens, and confinement in numerous psychiatric facilities. For patients to maintain the privilege of living in their group homes, they must comply with their service plans. With minor variations, the service plans require these indentured residents to take their psychiatric drugs and be out of the residence during the day. Each morning they are bussed to the day treatment facility, where they stay until they are returned to the group home for their evening meals.

The day treatment programs invariably provide social skills, personal hygiene, support and current events groups. Some individuals amiably attend groups. In those groups, regardless of theme or activity, hints of vitality can only be glimpsed at the end of the group activity when the cookies and coffee arrive. Then one can observe patients begin the slow procession out to the gazebo to smoke. There is little difference between day treatment sites. At almost any site, a visitor is sure to see people alternate between pacing, sleeping in chairs and shuffling outside to the smoking area. The day treatment centers are predictable and safe; one day or week or month is indistinguishable from another. The glazed eyes, the missing teeth, trembling hands, distended stomachs, slurred speech and other drug-related side effects will not be remarkable there. I look and see squelched dreams and resignation. I wonder what their lives were like and what could have been. Before they became mental patients, how did they envision their futures? Can we say that psychiatric drugs improved their lives? Were there no other possibilities?

Other models of madness exist, but receive little exposure. For those lacking a background in psychology, sociology or philosophy, such explanations tend to be too obscure or academic for those who could benefit from framing their problems differently. In the book *Reaching Across: Mental Health Clients Helping Each Other*, the three psychiatric survivor editors provide information and advice designed to help their fellow travelers. Howie The Harp's chapter gives a clear and useful introduction to some other explanations and interventions for mental illness. The late Howie the Harp, revered for his leadership and activism in the c/s/x movement, spent most of his adolescence as an inpatient in a psychiatric hospital. There, a kindly attendant taught him how to play the mouth harp – thus, his adopted name. Howie learned that if he played the harmonica, it would keep him from crying and suffering the consequences for letting his feelings show in a psychiatric hospital.

The five models Howie described are: 1. Medical; 2. Social/Economic/Political; 3. Disability; 4. Nutritional/Orthomolecular; 5. Spiritual.[52]

The medical model views the "mentally ill" as having diseases of the mind, with treatment usually taking place in a hospital and highly influenced by the use of drugs and medical procedures. The "sick mind concept" makes it possible for a person designated as mentally ill to be considered incompetent, and for that incompetence to be regarded as global and extended to all areas of that person's life. Inherent in the concept of incompetence is the inability to make good decisions. Here stands the legal basis for taking away the rights of mental patients and opening the door to forced treatment. Howie the Harp writes that people in self-help groups find the "medical model to be the major contributing factor to psychiatric oppression, as well as the loss of human rights and dignity."[53]

Believers in the *social/economic/political* model view people's problems as essentially determined by the environment that existed when they were raised, along with how current conditions affect where and how they are living. Oppression, injustice, bigotry, discrimination and poverty keep groups of stigmatized people – ethnic minorities, people of color, people with different sexual orientations, elderly – locked into the status of lesser citizens. This model is popular among self-help and advocacy groups. The realization that all problems are not necessarily your fault and that you are not a bad or sick person can be quite helpful. Rejecting an identity that says they are flawed and damaged, people can begin devising practical solutions to change the conditions that caused and continue to sustain their problems.

The *disability model,* which is an outgrowth of the disability rights movement, demands that certain accommodations be made that allow people to function as they themselves want to function. The examples Harp offers to illustrate the accommodation process are: A blind person can use Braille to read as well as a sighted person; if curbs, narrow doorways and other obstacles are accommodated for, a person who cannot use her legs can, with the aid of a wheelchair, be mobile. People who adhere to a disability model do not choose to view their disability as an illness or a negative condition. Harp writes,

> A 'healthy' disabled person is not a contradiction in terms. Similarly, a person with a psychiatric or mental disability is not 'mentally ill.' Mental disability does not mean that someone's mind isn't working or is, in any way, inferior. While everyone can do some tasks better than other people, everyone also has some limitations. With the disability model, an emotional problem or limitation can be resolved by accommodating it.[54]

The *nutritional/orthomolecular model* may be looked at as similar to the medical model, but without the oppression associated with medicine's legal mandates. However, this model also assumes the primacy of an abnormal body chemistry or other physiological conditions. Megadoses of vitamins or special diets are used to treat and correct imbalances. Related approaches to dealing with imbalance are some of the newly popular healing arts (reflexology, acupuncture, aromatherapy, therapeutic touch), which have borrowed heavily from ancient cultures and traditions. In practice, the nutritional/orthomolecular model differs from the medical model in the absence of the use of force. People are not routinely court-ordered to take megavitamins.

The *spiritual model* looks at altered states of consciousness as part of a natural spiritual process. The paranormal and psychic processes are viewed as one's spiritual journey through higher levels of consciousness, rather than pathological delusions or hallucinations. The religious traditions of the past and present are full of examples of mind states and beliefs whose meanings are derived from the life circumstances from which they are interpreted. Within the spiritual model, one looks at the person's confusion, struggles and disordered life as an attempt to establish meaning and develop personal identity. The person has embarked upon a quest to attain a higher state of consciousness. If it is part of the tradition of his culture, upon return and resolution of his spirit quest he may be revered as a shaman.

Today, alternatives to the medical model make up a minuscule percentage of the services available to people struggling with diagnoses of serious mental illness. Because the medical model dwarfs all other models, the remainder of this chapter will examine the brain disease medical model and its impact.

* * *

I listened attentively to psychologist Ty Colbert's keynote address at the 1996 National Association for Rights Protection and Advocacy (NARPA) annual meeting. Drawing from his book *Broken Brains or Wounded Healers*, he examined the soft, quasi-scientific foundation of the medical model of mental illness. In his book, Colbert cites Ken Barney's assertion, "The idea that 'schizophrenia' is a hidden disease entity, with a soon-to-be discovered biogenetic 'cause' has been thoroughly debunked."[55] Barney lists seventeen references to support his declaration.[56] Starting with Thomas Szasz's pioneering book *The Myth of Mental Illness*,[57] the unproven premises of the medical model are challenged. Yet as Barney laments, there is a socio-political environment that feeds this booming multi-billion-dollar growth industry, despite the absence of legitimate scientific credibility supporting the medical model of mental illness.

Colbert's use of the metaphor "four false pillars of biopsychiatry" was of particular interest to me because it offered a clear, succinct and easy to follow critique of psychiatry's love affair with the biology of mental illness. Colbert argues that the medical model platform is flimsily supported by its false pillars:

1. Chemical Imbalance Pillar – Medication works by correcting a chemical imbalance.
2. Inheritance Pillar – Mental illness runs in families, therefore it must be inherited.
3. Defective Gene Pillar – Gene markers will eventually lead to the identification of genetic causes.
4. Brain Scan Pillar – Evidence of diseased brains can be seen through brain imaging.

At the core, the *chemical imbalance pillar* relies upon the dopamine hypothesis: If drugs that reduce dopamine transfer decrease the symptoms of schizophrenia, then this disease must be caused by too much dopamine activity. Actually, when dopamine transfer is inhibited, there are inconsistent general and specific effects. One specific effect is the decrease of reported hallucinations; another is the blunting of affect. The decrease in hallucinations does not occur all the time; however, the sedation and dulling of emotions (negative symptoms) occur with regularity. The obvious hole in the dopamine theory was easily grasped by a psychiatric survivor in the audience who was listening to Ty Colbert's lecture. In reaction to this leap in logic, he called out, "I get it; it's just like headaches are caused by an aspirin deficiency."

To justify the *inheritance pillar*, twin studies and adoption studies are cited. Depending upon methodology and the interpretation of the information, concordance rates vary greatly across studies.[58] The numbers may in fact point to a stronger argument for environmental factors than for inheritance. It is important to remember that we are dealing with unproven hypotheses that are not supported by consistent evidence from twins and adoption studies.

To challenge the *defective gene pillar* Colbert offers an analogy:

Although it's a political outlook, not a mental disorder, Republicanism can run in families. If we were to line up all the members of a kindred who have registered as

Republicans, and begin looking for a marker that correlated with that characteristic, there is a good chance that we would find one. This would not necessarily be because all Republicans carry a particular gene, but because all the people in the study are related and have many genetic similarities . . . . Actually, there could be some validity to the idea that such a gene exists. There could be a gene for a certain type of personality trait that would result in a higher percentage of individuals who carried it choosing to be Republican, just as a gene for extra emotional sensitivity could be associated with schizophrenia or depression. But that does not imply that the gene in question is defective or that it results in a chemical imbalance that forces a person to choose to be a Republican.[59]

Readers of weekly news magazines like *Time* or *Newsweek* could search their old issues and see the many times the magazine covers have hailed the discovery of gene markers. The new breakthrough research studies were sure to lead to the cure and prevention of diseases like schizophrenia and bipolar disorder. Richard Lewontin, Alexander Agassiz Professor of Zoology and professor of biology at Harvard University, writes:

The concentration on the genes implicated in cancer is only a special case of a general genomania that surfaces in the form of weekly announcements in *The New York Times* of the location of yet another gene for another disease. The revealing rhetoric of this publicity is always the same; only the blanks need to filled in: 'It was announced today by scientists at [Harvard, Vanderbilt, Stanford] Medical School that a gene responsible for [some, many, a common form of] [schizophrenia, Alzheimer's arteriosclerosis, prostate cancer] has been located and its DNA sequence determined. This exciting research, say scientists, is the first step in what may eventually turn out to be possible cure for this disease.'[60]

Lewontin further explains that skeptics have pointed out that we do not have a single case of prevention or cure arising from our knowledge of DNA structure. He asserts, "The prevention or cure of metabolic and developmental disorders depends on a detailed knowledge of the mechanisms operating in cells and tissues above the level of genes, and there is no relevant information about those mechanisms in DNA sequences."[61]

The fourth false pillar of biopsychiatry – *evidence derived from brain scans* – also does not support hypotheses of brain abnormalities for people diagnosed with schizophrenia. All that has been shown with any degree of consistency are small differences in areas of the brain. These differences fall well within the normal range of human brain anatomy and may be due to a number of other factors, i.e., stress, diet, drugs.

Although admittedly the above critique of the biochemical basis for the medical model of mental illness is far from a comprehensive or balanced presentation, I offer it as a starting point for people to begin their own examination of what they have come to accept as fact. The medical model, although as yet to be proven, remains at the center of the education and training of mental health professionals.

Psychiatrist Ron Leifer looks at the medical model as an ideology that is used to redefine deviance as mental illness. The medical model asserts that a person's actions are determined by biochemical, social, psychological or historical causes. The moral model, by contrast, assumes that people are capable of free choice and are responsible and accountable for their actions. When the medical model declares that the mind is a part of the body, it becomes particularly useful for social control, "For the model makes it appear not only that the individual is not acting freely and intelligibly by holding certain values and pursuing certain goals, but that the individual may be actually incapable of free and responsible action. This belief is then used to justify depriving people of their rights and confining them against their will."[62]

When I heard Leifer say at a workshop that mental illness was the only disease that you could catch by word of mouth, I laughed along with the rest of the audience.

Leifer traces psychiatry's embrace of the medical model to the practical need to resolve its own identity crisis. Psychiatry found itself torn between its psychoanalytically oriented adherents and the hospital-based psychiatrists who were becoming enamored of the new drugs and their heralded potential for the cure of mental illness. Promoting psychiatry as a medical science would give psychiatrists distinct advantages in their competition with non-medical practitioners, and help overcome their perceived designation within the medical community as second-class doctors. The medical model won.

Since the 1960s, organized psychiatry and the pharmaceutical industry have waged a successful campaign to convince the public that mental illness is a disease and that medical science is on the verge of finding the physiological causes and cures. The success of this campaign is verified by the popularity of the belief that mental illnesses "are biological entities which exist independently of human perceptions and labeling strategies."[63] Critics of the medical model remain a tiny minority, relegated to the fringe. Their challenges to the prevailing mental illness doctrine are David versus Goliath confrontations in which truth has yet to become a potent slingshot.

The therapeutic state and its medicalization of life has intruded itself on all aspects of social life. "It constitutes one of the most encompassing projects in socio-political history, and its ideology – the medical model – now reigns supreme in the post-industrial world, explaining the innermost thoughts of individuals and shaping the social policies of nations."[64]

Central to the medical model is diagnosis. Sociologist Phil Brown has argued for the need to examine and understand the bias and social control factors so important in the creation and use of diagnoses. Benjamin Rush, one of the signers of the Declaration of Independence and considered the father of American psychiatry, thought up the diagnosis anarchia. Rush declared anarchia to be a mental illness which afflicted people who were unhappy with the new political structure of the United States and wanted it to be more democratic. People who wanted to expand voting rights beyond white male property owners could be considered by this definition to have a form of mental illness. Rush, whose cameo appears as a logo on the American Psychiatric Association's publications, invented the "tranquilizer chair" in which patients had a cage placed over their heads and were tightly bound by straps to prevent all movement.[65]

Ken Barney cites a large number of credible critiques of psychiatric diagnosis.[66] He is disappointed by the ineffectiveness and lack of results generated from the intellectual dismantling and debunking of the medical model of mental illness. Decades of critique and rights advocacy have failed to make a significant difference in the mental health system. Barney calls for expanding the advocates' perspective to include the larger socio-political dimensions of experience and mental distress. "The culture of late capitalism – with its fragmentation and dissolution of community and general deterioration in the conditions of existence – plays a crucial role in the production of constricted existence, insecurity, and powerlessness, creating and aggravating individual and family suffering and disorder."[67]

The Myth of Mental Illness, written by psychiatrist Thomas Szasz, was published in 1961. His challenge to the concept of mental illness made him an instant celebrity and he became the center of heated debate among both the public and mental health professionals. He was a sought after guest appearing on Johnny Carson and many other TV talk shows. Szasz, a prodigious writer, continued throughout his professional career to write books and articles. With impeccable logic he attacked the validity of mental illness as defined by psychiatry. Among Szasz's students and disciples were previously cited dissident psychiatrists Ken Barney, Peter Breggin and Ron Leifer. It is notable that Thomas Szasz, although continuing to write to this day, is rarely taught or acknowledged during the education of mental health professionals. I had the honor and privilege of meeting with him at his home and finding his warmth, curiosity and sharp mind refreshing. At lunch, he told me that only a few small publishers are interested in his latest work. Dismayed, but not surprised, I became aware of the extent of his banishment from discourses on psychiatry while I was teaching a graduate psychology course in Community Mental Health. Beginning a discussion of Szasz's ideas, I gazed at the puzzled looks of students when I asked if anyone was familiar with the work of Thomas Szasz. Now, after more than a dozen times teaching such a class, I am no longer surprised at the students' lack of exposure.

Mental health professionals throughout the world have bought American psychiatry's official nosology. Based on psychiatry's diagnostic model, epidemiological studies report that, in the United States, one in five people live with mental disorders. It is not philosophy, statistics or brilliant logical arguments that convince me that the medical model of mental illness is dangerous. Those of us who were able to resist the brainwashing saw no salvation in accepting our "illness," or accepting the need for a lifetime regimen of noxious drugs. Those of us who were able to come out on the other side of our ordeal know that the medical model crushes the spirit and attacks our humanity. We were betrayed by a branch of medicine that blatantly violates its most important principle: *First do no harm*.

I met Sonja Kjaer at the 1996 NARPA annual conference in Seattle. For three decades, she had been an advocate for people who live with the ravages of Tardive Dyskinesia. The American Psychiatric Association Task Force Report *Tardive Dyskinesia*[68] described TD as a serious, usually irreversible, untreatable condition resulting from the use of neuroleptic drugs.

Sonja was introduced to the audience as the winner of the "Giraffe Award" – yes, she was a woman who stuck her neck out. From the moment Sonja struggled to rise from her wheelchair to stand before the microphone, I was transfixed. She leaned against the podium for support. There was no missing the focused single-mindedness of purpose and the strength of will she had summoned to command her mind and body to perform.

Sonja challenged the audience to look around at our conferences and our local advocacy groups and to remember the missing – the hidden people suffering from the disfiguring, painful, embarrassing, irreversible afflictions caused by psychiatric drugs. She spoke of the times she was too ashamed to be seen in public. I listened with wet eyes and felt ashamed – ashamed of my own denial and failure to notice and pay attention to people coping with tardive dyskinesia. Sonja implored all of us to reach out to people in our local communities who are usually too embarrassed by their conditions to attend our self-help groups. We were reminded of the grace we were granted and with it an obligation to not forget our least powerful brethren. I listened to her talk of the numbers, the different kinds of involuntary movement disorders, the callous disregard and under-reporting, and most of all her personal account of what it's like to live with a body that responds not to your requests but to its own unfathomable rhythms. I also realized how easily this could have happened to me.

Since 1988, when Sonja co-founded the Tardive Dyskinesia/Tardive Dystonia National Association (TD/TDNA), she has received thousands of letters and inquiries. During her lecture, she distributed a list of questions and comments from some of the survivors who contacted TD/TDNA:

"Please stop this pain. I've been sick since age thirteen and am now thirty-three. I feel like giving up life! Can someone help me? You're my last chance. No one will accept me this way."

– T.D. Survivor, Louisiana

"The worst thing for me is people looking at me on the bus, laughing and pointing."

– T.D. Survivor, Washington

"The twitch machine has a clear message. Psychiatric drugs can cause unending pain."

– T.D. Survivor, Washington

"Why wasn't I told about the risk before?" (This is the most frequently asked question to TD/TDNA.) "Though the new medicine has given me emotional peace, it has left me with a maimed and disfigured body."

– T.D. Survivor, New Mexico

"Tremors and spasms make my arms do a sort of jitterbug. Spasms in my neck pull my head to the side. My tongue sticks out as often as every thirty seconds."

– T.D. Survivor, Washington, DC

"Though well qualified, employers tell me I'm too great a distraction, few volunteer agencies accept me."

– T.D. Survivor, Louisiana

"Having TD is being unable to control my arms, fingers and sometimes my facial muscles; having a spastic digestive tract and trouble breathing. Getting food from my plate to my mouth and chewing it once there can be a real chore. I've bitten my tongue so severely it's scarred. I often bite it hard enough to bleed into the food I'm trying to eat. I no longer drink liquids without drooling."

– T.D. Survivor, New York

"TD means I have difficulty doing simple tasks requiring manual dexterity such as shuffling cards, dialing, using a push button phone or writing."

– T.D. Survivor, New York

"The TD in my back and arms makes it almost impossible for me to sit even for a short length of time."

– T.D. Survivor, Oregon

"Embarrassing as it is, I often delay using the bathroom because it is so difficult to wipe myself."

– T.D. Survivor, New York

"I've always tried to feel better and I felt how could any prescribed medicine meant to help me, do more damage than the illness itself."

– T.D. Survivor, Louisiana

"At five feet six, the constant motion left me flesh and bones and 79 lb. even though I ate six meals a day. My once poised body was often distorted and usually disfigured. My friends and colleagues found it easier to dismiss the tragedy so vivid to them. Few stayed loyal; though I was the same person they'd respected, my body frightened most away . . . and I was alone."

– T.D. Survivor, Washington

"I've been injured, humiliated, controlled and ignored in the twenty-one years I've had TD. My spirit has risen to abet and assist the innocent, helpless, and unwary. God help me to relax and live in peace until my work is done."

– T.D. Survivor, Oregon

"I fear places where strangers will see my peculiar and uncontrollable movements."

– T.D. Survivor, Oregon

"An unending search for answers and alternatives began over twenty-five years after my godchild looked up at me and with sincerity said, 'Auntie, why do you make such funny faces and walk like a galloping horse?'"

– T.D. Survivor, Washington

"How many times have you heard a CAT or PET scan technologist tell a person with TD, to stay perfectly quiet and not move? Absurd!"

– T.D. Survivor, Washington

Although it is difficult to determine the total number of TD sufferers, estimates have ranged from 400,000 to several million.[69] Despite the known and established risks of these psychiatric drugs, psychiatrists continue to prescribe them to vulnerable people who are minimally informed about the risks. The organized pushing of the need for lifelong maintenance treatment with neuroleptic drugs has triggered a wide-spread epidemic of neurological movement disorders.

Drug side effects are problems that psychiatry is finding increasingly more difficult to ignore. Anti-drug activists say that the side effects, like sedation, are really the main "therapeutic" effect of the drugs. Adverse reactions are common to all takers of psychiatric drugs and range through sedation, dry mouth, drooling, loss of sexual desire, weight gain, lethargy, depression, disruptions in memory, cognitive deficits, diabetes, drug-induced psychoses, neuromalignant syndrome and death. Now we are witnessing the introduction of new "atypical antipsychotic drugs" and again seeing "[t]his pharmaceutically fueled faith, not any valid new or improved understanding of the nature of schizophrenia . . . as the driving force in the field today."[70] And once again, the absence of rigorous research studies does not prevent the trumpeting of poorly substantiated claims without drawing attention to the potentially toxic effects.

> Forty years after the discovery of chlorpromazine finds us with the enthusiasm of the introduction of clozapine. At the same time, however, it is sobering to reflect on how little we have learned of the aetiology of the functional psychoses, despite the fervor generated by the excitement of the psychopharmacological discoveries of the 1950s.[71]

Beyond the excitement and fanfare generated by their introduction, chlorpromazine and clozapine share other parallels: exaggerated therapeutic claims; highly publicized personal accounts of miraculous recoveries; selective denial and misperception of obvious side effects; and avoidance of the public health consequences of the iatrogenic effects of previously acclaimed miracle treatments.

Psychiatric drug critic and researcher David Cohen concludes:

> 1. We do not know what the minimal or optimally effective doses are for the neuroleptic drugs.
> 2. The non-response rate to neuroleptic treatment by patients with schizophrenia is probably in the 45-70% range, as opposed to the previously stated 5-25% range.
> 3. Clinicians routinely fail to recognize extrapyramidal symptoms.
> 4. Contrary to recommendations from the research studies and from official guidelines, psychiatrists have continued to increase doses over time.
> 5. Evidence suggests that clozapine is not as "remarkably free" of side effects as claimed in unequivocal statements by renowned psycho-pharmacologists.
> 6. Violation of the double-blind in studies measuring drug effectiveness in comparison to placebo makes the results questionable.

Keeping the above points in mind, Cohen asks whether any field of applied science other than psychiatry could avoid being judged to be in a state of crisis that cried out for a major paradigmatic change.[72]

The appeal of psychiatric drugs is their ability to control undesirable behavior and to quiet down very excited people without inducing sleep. The use of drugs as a substitute for services and to provide cheap social control is clearly demonstrated by their massive use with the elderly in nursing homes and for persons with developmental disabilities. When these drugs are prescribed for such populations, can anyone legitimately say they are antipsychotics? In fact, what they are called in institutions for developmental disabilities is not neuroleptics or antipsychotics but "behavior modifiers." It is illuminating to look at how the names for classes of drugs change to become what manufacturers and prescribers tell us they do for people. The drugs directed at controlling hospitalized mental patients were first identified as major tranquilizers, then those types of drugs were called neuroleptics, and when politically and financially expedient, the drugs' control function morphed into "treatment" for psychosis – thus to be marketed as antipsychotics. After the major debilitating side effects of the drugs were documented, pharmaceutical companies began touting their latest creations as "new atypical antipsychotics." These powerful, mind-numbing, incapacitating drugs are called psychiatric medications, and when they are colloquially shortened to "meds" they sound almost warm and fuzzy.

For too long, mental health professionals have been trained to look at psychiatric drugs as the primary treatment for psychoses. Even non-medical clinicians defer to the primacy of drug treatments when confronted with illogical, disordered thinking and behavior that demands a severe diagnosis. Although there exists a small cadre of dissident voices speaking out against the established drug and illness ideology, mental health students are seldom exposed to those opinions. Instead, future mental health professionals must study diagnostic and treatment models that present such hypotheses as indisputable facts. Despite credible arguments and research evidence supporting the dismantling of the dogmatic premises of the disease model of mental illness, critics have seen their work and ideas cavalierly dismissed (see the work of Thomas Szasz, Ron Leifer, Ted Sarbin, Jim Mancuso, Peter Breggin, David Cohen, R.D. Laing, George Albee, Lee Coleman, Joel Kovel, Loren Mosher, John Perry, David Richman, Isaac Prilleltensky, Tom Scheff, Erving Goffman, Stuart Kirk, Herb Kutchins).

I am glad to finally see a study – Clinical Antipsychotic Trials in Intervention Effectiveness (CATIE) – confirming what we, psychiatric survivors, painfully learned first hand. The validating results of this study draw from the experience of 1,500 patients and are published in the *New England Journal of Medicine*.[73]

> This sixty-seven-million-dollar federally funded study. . . paints a sobering picture of the state of treatment of schizophrenia, a disabling illness that afflicts about 3.2 million Americans with symptoms such as delusions, hallucinations and disordered thinking: Every drug, old and new, caused serious side effects, and the vast majority of patients stopped taking each of them. 'The study has vital public health implications,' said Thomas Insel, director of the National Institute of Mental Health, which funded the study. 'It is the largest, longest and most comprehensive, in-dependent trial ever done to examine existing therapies for this disease.'

The article in the *Washington Post* goes on to say:

> The study is likely to stoke one of the most contentious debates in psychiatry – whether drug treatment ought to be forced on unwilling patients. The fact that three-quarters of patients discontinued treatment because of side effects or a lack of benefit showed that patients 'trying to say no to forced neuroleptics [drugs] have had a better grip on reality than the medical community,' said David Oaks, a patient advocate who has himself been given five antipsychotic drugs at various times for a range of diagnoses, including schizophrenia.[74]

Some people who have been diagnosed and treated for serious mental illness have successfully reintegrated into their communities, and continue to use psychiatric drugs. I believe that unrecognized and under-reported are the individuals who have transformed or recovered from their experiences and do not take any psychiatric drugs. They are the "hidden recovered," a group of which I was a member for a long time. Public c/s/x are very familiar with a phenomenon that occurs with regularity after our work, ideas and stories are shared at workshops and presentations. Always present in the audience is someone who waits for a private moment to identify himself as a former mental patient and to thank you for validating his experience. Also frequently present is a parent whose hope for her "adult child" is re-kindled and asks if you would talk with her. But also present are the true believers who cannot accept that you were one of the "real mentally ill."

While working at the New York State Office of Mental Health, I asked a division director to intervene to stop an inpatient in a hospital on Long Island from being forced by the court to undergo electroshock against his expressed wishes. My vigorous advocacy made this director ask why I was so strongly opposed to EST, a treatment he believed was effective. I told him it was because of what I had learned first hand from personal experience with electroshock. His response: "It didn't seem to hurt you . . . look at where you are now." I cringed.

The consistent results of rigorous long-term longitudinal research on recovery hold a great deal of promise. C/s/x are now able to cite research that backs up the knowledge they had to learn experientially. New research findings and their implications are receiving exposure in prestigious journals and are provoking more questions and research. Courtenay Harding, a prominent researcher and psychologist, has spoken about the almost immediate impact she has seen from her efforts. After she described her work on a national public radio program, the station was deluged with phone calls. People from all walks of life called to thank her for telling their stories – stories they said that they could not tell without great negative impact upon themselves and their families.

Harding's findings, which were consistent with similar longitudinal research around the world, demand the rethinking of basic concepts about mental illness and recovery. Beginning with recovery itself, Harding asks: What do we mean by this concept? Does recovery mean that the person is no longer symptomatic? Is it cure, or is it remission? Has the person returned to his or her initial levels of functioning? From what baseline do we make such judgments? Is it possible for such a person to be functioning better than ever before?[75]

When we shine the light of longitudinal research on this construct we call schizophrenia, we are looking at a non-linear, dynamic and complex process that defies overly simplified cause and effect models. With this perspective, one must view this "psychiatric disorder" as a process that moves through changing and inconsistent patterns that are marked by significant improvement over time, and in which recovery is maximized by an active, developing person who is permitted to freely interact with the environment.

In Harding and her colleagues' seminal Vermont Longitudinal Study,[76] the researchers, after rigorously reworking and refining the diagnostic standards for schizophrenia, defined the criteria for full recovery as: no symptoms; no psychiatric medications; working or volunteering in the community; social relationships with friends and/or family; and behaving in ways that would make people unable to tell that they were once mental patients. To be rated significantly improved, the person had to meet four of the above five criteria. In order to assess recovery, the Vermont study chose to use the Global Assessment Scale, Level of Functions Scale, Brief Psychiatric Rating Scale and twelve other scales rating twenty-one functional domains.

From her own and others' recovery research, Harding draws a thoughtful analysis of the problems of looking at a person as a "mental illness," rather than as an individual with a life course which at times may vary in the development and function of changing abilities. She suggests that the rater's epistemology strongly influences who is considered recovered. Further, Harding points to a double standard used in judging recovery. When we look at a friend's eccentric behavior, we see it as idiosyncratic and excuse it. We know where he or she is coming from and think that we know the direction and whys of the action. In research, the rater compares the person to a de-contextualized standard. Harding points us to the top rating of the commonly used Global Assessment Scale (91-100), which is defined by, "No symptoms, superior functioning in a wide range of activities, life's problems never seem to get out of hand, and is sought out by others because of his warmth and integrity." And yet despite the in-joke among colleagues, that their friends and they themselves could not meet the Global Assessment Scale score of 91 to 100, it is still used as an impossible hurdle for the "mental patient" to jump over.

Harding concludes:

> I would venture to say that to designate someone as recovered from severe psychiatric disorder is a judgment call as challenging as the decision made about when to call behavior an illness. It is trying to pin down a constantly moving target. In addition, the process encompasses cultural expectations, the state of the art, and the personality of the investigator which he or she constructs and selects the questions for the assessment, the manner in which they are

asked, and how the data are analyzed.[77]

I admire the work of Harding and other researchers for their compassionate chipping away at some of the myths and dire prognoses for schizophrenia and recovery, but they fall short of challenging the essence of a flawed disease model of madness. People cannot be understood by measuring the size and range of their levels of functioning as if time and context are irrelevant and the mind/spirit/soul is subject to the same laws as material bodies.

The mind and consciousness cannot be measured or touched – only deduced. We cannot directly see or measure love. It is only possible to evaluate actions that we say are associated with love, and when we observe such actions, we say that is love. As observers we are always outside and therefore, can only see, measure and evaluate a particular person through the lens of the most recent snapshot that we encounter. We are not able to see the unique history of that individual the way that particular person sees it and imbues meaning into that very unique and special life narrative.

The mind, the soul, self-consciousness, imagination, language, cruelty and altruism are some of what distinguishes humans from other animals. The mystery of our unique qualities also sparks our creative potential and inflames our fears. Restricting and punishing alternative experiences, interrupting an individual's search for expression and meaning, labeling those that are lost and then putting them on a path not of their own choosing, obstructs the miraculous from appearing. Not allowing the different-odd-eccentric-genius-mad winners and losers from living on the fringes dooms us to travel through mediocrity and into decay. The willingness to learn from society's least valued members enhances everyone's possibilities. Our genuine attempts to understand and clarify a person's vision of his past and projection for the future can open new possibilities in the present.

Chapter 14

Forced Treatment Versus Self-Determination

And the day came when the risk to remain tight in a bud was more painful than the risk to blossom.   (Anais Nin)

On my ride to work I heard on the radio that Art Linkletter was going to give a talk in Virginia to elderly persons, titled, "Old Age Is Not For Sissies." I immediately thought, *Recovery Is Not For Sissies*. Other titles came to mind: Childhood Is Not For Sissies, Adolescence Is Not For Sissies, Marriage Is Not For Sissies, Politics Is Not For Sissies. Yeah . . . Life Is Not For Sissies.

Today, people who are recognized leaders in the treatment and care of people with mental illness must be careful not to injure their arms from twisting into positions to pat themselves on the back. Researchers and practitioners are proud of advancements and are self-righteously shocked by the cruel treatments and inhumane conditions associated with institutions in centuries past. Yet for psychiatric survivors, there is a fundamental lack of equity. Why do we label one group of people mentally ill and deny them basic rights? A controversial medical diagnosis, based on subjective judgment, has the power to deprive people of the right to enter contracts, take care of their children, control their own money, and most egregiously, has the power to force them to live in a place where they are deprived of the right to choose when to get up in the morning and when to go to bed at night. Human rights, treatment and recovery are not independent of each other.

Persons diagnosed with a major mental illness, if they are judged to be dangerous to themselves or dangerous to others, can be legally forced to undergo objectionable treatments. In some jurisdictions, a person can also be forced to undergo treatments if he or she is determined to be at risk of becoming gravely disabled without treatment intervention.

Most people are allowed to make extremely foolish or dangerous life decisions without facing government intervention. You can choose to smoke until you die. You can eat so much that you cannot get through the doorway to leave your home. Being a member of a recognized religion allows you to make a health decision based on a tenet of your religion, even if it puts your life in danger. But if you are a mental patient there is an automatic bias to believe that you are incapable of making thoughtful, credible decisions. The court determines what is in your best interest while only minimally considering your beliefs.

The freedom to make poor choices is a privilege that is denied to the person who is labeled mentally ill. Chronicity means always having to prove that you have the capacity to make "appropriate" independent choices. To comply with the requirements of your supported group living arrangement, you may be forced to attend a day treatment program from morning until evening. Your money, and how you spend it, can be controlled by a court-appointed payee or guardian. When being a mental patient is the over-riding explanation of who you are, you must endure others' suspicion and their monitoring of your personal decisions. Substituted judgment that is deemed to be in the "best interest" of the patient is a hovering, always possible intervention for people with mental, physical, sensory and cognitive disability. Complex decisions demand more than the loose and arbitrary practices that a person faces today.

John Stuart Mill's classic essay *On Liberty*, published in 1859, confronted a question that remains unresolved to this day: In a democratic state, how can the individual be protected from the tyranny of the majority? Mill based his essay on one simple principle, which stated:

> . . . that the sole end for which mankind is warranted, individually or collectively, in interfering with the liberty of action of any of their number, is self-protection. That the only purpose for which power can be rightfully exercised over any member of a civilized community, against his will, is to prevent harm to others. His own good, either physical or moral, is not a sufficient warrant. He cannot rightfully be compelled to do or forbear because it will be better for him to do so, because it will make him happier, because, in the opinions of others, to do so would be wise, or even right. These are good reasons for remonstrating with him, or reasoning with him, or persuading him, or entreating him, but not compelling him, or visiting him with any evil in case he do otherwise. . . In the part which merely concerns himself, his independence is, of right, absolute. Over himself, over his own body and mind, the individual is sovereign.[78]

When you are diagnosed with a major mental illness, there is a corollary assumption that you are globally incompetent. The presumed incompetence extends to all decisions rather than being situation and context specific. But perhaps on some days on certain issues, you are more lucid and capable of clarity then on other days. Psychiatrist Edward Podvoll, founder of the Windhorse alternative treatment communities, describes "islands of clarity," where people have periods of clear thinking even in the midst of florid psychoses. Podvoll theorizes that at those times, a person is available to grow and change when engaged in a good therapeutic relationship.[79] However, if you are identified as incompetent – in need of confinement in a psychiatric hospital as a voluntary or involuntary patient – virtually all decisions will be made for you. When you have fallen into that status, safety is the chief concern of your caretakers.

Clinicians, lawyers and judges, administrators and policy-makers, advocates and activists take conflicting stands on the issue of who retains the right to refuse treatment and on what basis. If treatment is directed at relieving pain, should not the recipient of the treatment be the one to evaluate whether the outcome of the treatment is what he or she desires? If the government or the community determines that a person's behavior is obnoxious or stretches the limits of community tolerance, are there legitimate grounds for intervention? Are what have been called "quality of life crimes" reason enough to sweep homeless people off the streets of New York City and confine them to Rikers Island? Is there no better solution to the housing problem than *out of sight, out of mind*? It reminds me of a tongue-in-cheek word cartoon devised by sociologist Phillip Slater to explain the demise of Western culture. He said our culture began its descent into ruin when the flush toilet was invented and we no longer had to see, smell and deal with our own shit – it just magically disappeared, along with any responsibility.

Extreme and rare examples become the justification for government to formulate over-reaching mental health regulations and policies. The length to which the government is permitted and encouraged to extend its range of interventions has consequences for a person's right to maintain sovereignty over his or her own mind and body. Lessons drawn from the former Soviet Republic and other totalitarian regimes inform us that a state should not be empowered to declare its critics and dissenters insane or incompetent. When the principles and needs of treatment, rehabilitation, punishment and government are enmeshed and only separated by thin porous membranes, the loss of opportunity is the fate of many citizens.

In my work for the New York State Office of Mental Health, I had to tightrope walk the line stretching across my personal values and the dictates of a bureaucracy which operated according to a prime directive of "Never embarrass the governor." I was able to stay true to my principles as long as I was able to refuse to participate in projects that I believed were ethically challenged. Although my choices were accepted for some time, every now and then reminders of my insoluble predicament reared up.

Generally, when a person called the Office of Mental Health and self-identified as a consumer, the call was transferred to the Office of Recipient Affairs, where I worked. In one such call, the man on the other end spoke with a heavy eastern European accent. He explained that he was a Russian immigrant and was looking for information about jobs for people who had a psychiatric disability. The caller said that he was diagnosed with "sluggish schizophrenia" and had been locked up in a mental institution in Russia. He complained that he had been confined because he was out of work and was arrested at a political rally.

In 2001, at the time of his call, our office had created and been allocated funds to hire forty full-time peer specialists. I assumed that he had spoken with someone who had told him that he should call about one of the peer specialist jobs. After talking for a while, I learned that he was now living in a town close to where I was scheduled to do a self-help seminar the following week. When I explained what kind of a meeting it would be and invited him to attend, he paused and asked me who I worked for. I explained that I work for a bureau made up of former mental patients. He again asked who I worked for. Recognizing his suspicion, I explained how all of us had experiences of being psychiatric patients, and had been hired to try to improve services and protect people's rights. He would not be satisfied and insisted on knowing who I worked for, and finally asked, "Who pays you?" I told him the state. Twice he repeated the words, "You work for the state," and hung up. I never heard from him again.

Contrary to the principle articulated by John Stuart Mill, mental health services in the United States are mandated by law to prevent people who have been diagnosed as mentally ill from doing harm to themselves. I believe that the exercise of such safety requirements prevents the development of real support, guidance and help. If we are to nurture our possibilities for an awakened life and dignified death, vulnerability cannot be legislated out of existence.

People kill themselves while confined in mental hospitals and jails, regardless of how carefully they are monitored. People, whether they are diagnosed with mental illness or not, attempt suicide. People also commit suicide because they cannot face the imminent threat of being incarcerated in a mental hospital or prison. Allowing individuals to retain that ultimate choice enables each of us to exercise some control over our own destinies. Rather than increasing the suicide rate, I believe the incidence of suicide would decrease if people were free to discuss their thoughts and feelings without the threat of incarceration; they would be more likely to seek help. I believe that loved ones and professionals should do everything possible, short of forced confinement, to help change that person's stance toward life. In fact, without the faux safety net of a locked hospital room and mind-deadening drugs, family and friends might be more successful in their struggles to discover more humane, hope-inspiring ways of supporting people in crises. We can only help people extricate themselves from their encapsulated misery if they trust us enough to let us in. If we cannot tolerate and accept their right to failure, their right to end their lives, then we will not be trusted.

The prevention of those who are mad from doing harm to others is the other major control issue exercised by mental health systems. Are people in the midst of a "florid psychosis" not responsible for their actions? Or in the murky legal conception of insanity – can the person distinguish between right and wrong? To make this fuzzy criterion useful, the court must stretch its interpretation of standards and procedures, or ignore some fundamental principles underlying behavior. A person's understanding of right and wrong is more often relative than absolute, and motivation is not easily attributable to a single clear cause. "I shot him because the voices told me that the mafia sent him to kill me" – sensational and provocative, but a rarity outside of a book or movie.

How schizophrenic do you have to be in order to be excused from the legal consequences of committing a felony? Can we separate society's requirements for punishment from its needs to keep its members safe? Are we really concerned with the "rehabilitation" of the "temporarily insane" murderer?

There is a public perception that the criminal justice system grants preferential treatment to people with mental illness. Former mental patients who have been involved with law enforcement and the judicial system know from personal experience that they are treated differently from others who have been arrested, but not often in ways that they might choose. Should persons with mental illness who do not have the capacity to understand that they have violated the law be held legally responsible for their actions?

When someone does harm, the reasons for the commission of that harmful act can only be effectively factored into judicial decisions if the court refrains from using recipes that mix punishment, rehabilitation, deterrence and community safety. Many psychiatric survivors consistently express the belief that people, regardless of their emotional or mental state, should be held responsible for their actions. A violation of the law should be dealt with in the criminal justice system, not the psychiatric system. My peers have no illusion that life would be easier in a prison, and are well aware that forced drugging, humiliation, victimization and assaults on the body and spirit await them in both systems. In many states, the secure forensic hospital has the added disincentive of indeterminate commitment time. Deciding on prison or hospital offers only the choice between terrible and horrible. A civilized society has the obligation to create better alternatives.

The medicalization of moral and spiritual questions only serves to further complicate legal issues. Some mental health professionals have been elevated to the status of forensic experts and have established a lucrative market for their services. Stepping into an arena with myriad shades of grey, the doctor is asked by the courts to pass Solomon-like black and white judgments – insane or sane? And the judgment is supposed to be rendered impartially, free of influence from the source of the doctor's consultant fees. In court cases involving mental illness decisions, judges almost always decide in favor of involuntary hospital commitment, incompetence, forced medication or involuntary outpatient commitment. In real life practices involving mental illness, in which mental patients must prove to a judge that they have the capacity to understand the consequences of their choices, the patient is too often faced with an impossible task. Few people are able to receive a fair and impartial hearing when confronted with the presumed authority of mental health experts they cannot afford, and the bias of impatient judges who avoid potential criticism by being extremely cautious. By erring on the side of safety, the judge will never be faulted in the tabloid newspapers for releasing a mad killer back into society.

Anyone can develop an informed opinion on the fairness of our judicial process by attending commitment hearings. My personal best/worst story features a hearing I witnessed at Bellevue Hospital in New York City. There is a large room at Bellevue that is dedicated for use as a courtroom. While there as an observer, I saw a young African-American man escorted to his hearing in chains and dressed in hospital pajamas. As with the prior hearings, the impatient and haughty judge shortened the judicial process by repeatedly saying to the attorneys, "Enough . . . get on with it . . . we all know that." Then, waving off all objections and further testimony with a sweep of his hand and a smile that signaled his attempt to be witty, the judge said to the wide-eyed man in pajamas, "If you don't go along with treatment this time, I will sentence you to outpatient's devil's island." The judge was referring to New York's newly implemented Kendra's Law which allows the state to force a person to comply with an outpatient commitment treatment plan. The state calls it Assisted Outpatient Treatment (AOT), while c/s/x know it for what it is, Involuntary Outpatient Commitment (IOC). My peers and I wonder if living with an IOC order in a 200-bed adult home residence fulfills the promise of de-institutionalization. IOC may be the last and strongest brick in the invisible wall that keeps c/s/x segregated, and makes it impossible to integrate into the larger community.

At this writing, all but four states now have Involuntary Outpatient Commitment. People who carry a mental illness label are frightened by the further erosion of their diminishing rights – ostensibly for their own good. They can be forced to comply with a treatment plan that requires them to be injected at their homes with unwanted toxic psychiatric drugs. A mental health SWAT team is in charge of this not-free person's life.

Emotionally charged rhetoric designed to incite and frighten the public is positioned through well-funded campaign strategies to make forced treatment the dominant answer to the mental illness problem. Supporters of forced medications argue that those with serious mental illness who refuse treatments are condemned "to rot with their rights on."[80]

The Treatment Advocacy Center (TAC), a splinter group of the National Alliance for the Mentally Ill, encourages supporters to use the TAC briefing papers and database to highlight dangerousness when lobbying for laws favoring force in their respective state legislatures. Disregarding its stigmatizing impact, the TAC encourages followers to stoke the media's appetite for sensational stories by drawing their attention to acts of violence committed by persons with mental illness. Psychiatrist and leading advocate for forced treatment E. Fuller Torrey states, "It would be probably difficult to find any American psychiatrist working with the mentally ill who has not, at a minimum, exaggerated the dangerousness of a mentally ill person's behavior to obtain a judicial order for commitment."[81]

It is distressing that the promotion of Involuntary Outpatient Commitment has succeeded despite research that shows that it offers no advantages as measured by outcomes. The "Bellevue Study," the most extensive of the studies to date, demonstrated that what makes a positive difference is the addition of needed services, not the mandating of treatment.[82]

The link between mental illness and violence is a controversial red-herring that is exploited by a variety of special interest groups. Among them are mental health "experts," along with researchers from various disciplines who have carved out careers chasing a test or means to predict violence. An average "mentally ill" person will not be accosting you on the street at a higher percentage rate than the average eighteen-year-old male, and probably less often than the "normal" person who is drinking to forget about going through a divorce or bankruptcy proceedings. Psychiatric survivors bristle at the inequality of the actual practice of the law for people who have been labeled:

> Just because we believe that someone is likely to commit a crime, we cannot put that person in jail. The reasons why we believe that someone is a likely criminal often have to do with that person's membership in a class. Nearly every society has its minority group, whether they are racial, ethnic, or otherwise defined, that are often believed by the dominant culture to be dangerous and deviant. It's alright to abridge their rights, in this way of thinking, since left to their own devices, they will undoubtedly commit crimes or otherwise upset the social order. I believe this is a basic injustice.[83]

How can society create a balance between the need for public safety and the rights of people who have been diagnosed with mental illness? If a person has not committed a crime but is perceived to be threatening or dangerous, should that person's freedom be restricted? Arguments usually get polarized around extreme examples like the one a psychologist colleague had used to challenge me: Suppose your neighbor's adult son is yelling over the backyard fence that command auditory hallucinations are telling him he must kill the devil who has taken over your four-year-old son's body . . . wouldn't you want him locked up and treated in a secure institution?

Of course I would want him locked up, but I have not faced that kind of frightening situation. I don't personally know anyone who has. Yet if you are the one faced by this threat you don't care if it occurs rarely. You will do all you can to protect your loved one. However, I would know that he was being locked up for threatening to do harm to my son, not for the purpose of treatment and rehabilitation.

Does society need to define so many people as crazy and dangerous? Is locking up a whole class of people on the basis of the rare, extreme threat justified? Must our mental health laws be so broad in their authority to take away people's liberty because of the sensational, extreme exceptions?

We live in an easily alarmed society. Creating a false sense of security is not an acceptable remedy. The repressive solutions do not provide more safety or peace of mind, but rather serve to make a larger group of people lose the privileges and rights promised by a free and democratic society. We cannot legislate away the natural ambiguities inherent in living. Given our poorly proven ability to predict behavior when it is enmeshed in the complexity of real life situations, do we not create more violence by trying to prevent it with forced interventions? Isn't this like trying to teach children not to hit smaller, weaker children by spanking them so as to teach them not to hit? The model presented to the child is that it's OK for a powerful adult to hit the weaker, less powerful child. By incarcerating people who are already having significant problems, society is making it likely that they will fulfill expectations and become more hopeless, angry and violent. Most of us are not forced into hospitals because we are potential killers, but as a result of acting strangely or not meeting family or community's expectations for "proper" behavior.

C/s/x know that when they get picked up by the police for creating a public disturbance, for vagrancy or for being a public nuisance, and their past psychiatric history is revealed, chances are they will be confined for a longer period of time in a hospital or jail than the "normal" offender. Regardless of the charge, they will be scrutinized and evaluated to determine when they can be released back into the community. Often, the person with a known psychiatric history is deprived of the right to speedy trial and due process. The permeable boundaries and ill-conceived and executed strategies linking the criminal justice system to the mental health system force arbitrary decisions that only add to the confusion of those who are most affected. The Los Angeles prison system, which houses massive numbers of "mentally ill inmates," has been said to compete with the Texas prison system for the dubious distinction of being the "largest mental institution in the country."

* * *

Those of us who have been through cataclysmic, life-altering experiences are able to provide empathic understanding and serve as models to inspire hope. Yet, the capacity to offer meaningful help is not limited to c/s/x. The "examined-life" is entered into in many ways. Any form of illness or violation of what we have come to expect our minds and bodies to be has the potential to alter the way we construe our experiences and affect how we integrate them into meaningful narratives. Psychotherapy is the favored path for many. Without the risk and the devastation of existing at the bottom, psychotherapy pays for its safer method with tortuously slow, very gradual and sometimes just noticeable change. Perhaps having someone else take over and make the pain tolerable is all that the psychotherapy-seeking individual expects or wants. But what of the person who is called mad? Is there no psychotherapy that will honor and work with her? I believe such work is possible, but therapists must first relinquish their reliance on diagnoses and their illusions of precise predictability. Each person lives a personal and special life story. The relationship is diminished when the therapist squeezes an individual's evolving narrative into a rigid classification system. It is not possible to understand when we see through a prism that sorts and matches as if some sort of standard protocol can instruct us on what is right, possible and best for Schizophrenics, wrong for Multiple Personality Disorders, and never appropriate when dealing with Borderlines.

An interview with renowned psychiatrist Herbert Spiegel is illustrative of this de-humanizing stance toward people:

> If the MPD therapists knew more about hypnosis, their diagnoses would be more accurate. As it is now, they don't even know how they are molding their outcomes. They manipulate both the highly hypnotizable and the psychopath. The "grade fives" are highly gullible, and they just do what they're cued to do, quite innocently. They seem like pure multiples after they're coached. But most of the patients that the MPD experts have in the wards are not highly hypnotizable so what they are actually playing around with are borderlines and psychopaths who enter into the game for different reasons.[84]

For a well-known psychiatrist in 1997 to use words like play and games in the context of inpatient psychiatric treatment continues an appalling psychiatric history. Even more alarming is his obvious lack of awareness and sensitivity to an essential criticism – defining and seeing a person only as a function of his or her name-diagnosis. Perhaps not surprisingly, in that same interview Spiegel is proud to compare what he does to the nineteenth-century work of Pierre Janet:

> When I have people with transient dissociations where they temporarily lose their sense of identity – which is consistent with a "grade five syndrome" – I put them together. I fuse them right away, just as Pierre Janet did. The point is to help restore a sense of control as soon as possible.[85]

In contrast to Spiegel's approach, I prefer some of the later twentieth-century thinking about what occurs when "we shift our focus to recall the multiple examples of human resilience in reaction to sickness, [and] this idea of fragility disappears to be replaced by a profound respect for the power of individuals to shape their own stories, to give meaning to their illnesses, and to ameliorate their own suffering."[86]

Howard Brody described the report of an investigator doing research on the families of American soldiers missing in action in Vietnam and believed to be dead. Attracting the attention of the investigator was a twelve-year-old boy who tenaciously clung to the belief that his father was alive. The boy was generally angry, unhappy and had behavioral and emotional problems in school and with his family. During a retreat the investigator had the opportunity to go for a walk in the woods with this boy. Together they came to a large dead tree, at the base of which a sapling was growing.

> . . . the boy stopped and stared at the tree for awhile, and the investigator was very surprised when this usually sullen and uncommunicative boy said, 'That tree makes me think of my father. You know, I realize now that my father is dead. I think he's that big tree and I'm the sapling. As it dies, the big tree loses its leaves, and that lets the sunlight through so that the sapling can grow.'[87]

Brody is impressed with the ingenuity of the parable. The boy created a metaphor that allowed him to accept his father's death. He found meaning in his father's death by relating it back to his own continuing life and growth, and in so doing, he derived a therapeutic benefit for himself.

Powerful lessons are demonstrated by this anecdote:

> It would take a particularly self-confident professional to
> argue that he knows better than this boy does what counts as
> the "right time" for any therapeutic intervention, or what the
> "right" intervention is for any given time – the sort of
> professional who would declare with full assurance to
> anyone, "I know your story better than you do." Another
> reason the professional ought not to have told this story to the
> boy is that the message would be different in that case,
> compared to the boy being allowed to fashion this story on
> his own. The message in the latter instance (as actually
> occurred) is not *simply* that death must be accepted and life
> goes on but *also* that the boy was a powerful enough agent
> in control of his own destiny to divine and formulate this
> meaning for *himself*. In contrast, the investigator's telling the
> story to and for the boy would have inevitably contained a
> message of the boy's own relative powerlessness. Thus
> considerable skill in psychotherapy is needed to assist
> patients in getting ready to tell their own story without
> inappropriately completing the task for them prematurely.[88]

C/s/x learn much from each other. We also have a great deal to share
with others, but are frustrated at the lack of understanding evinced by
people working within the mental health field. Mental health professionals
believe in methods and theories that I believe are not only flawed and
ineffective, but savagely harmful to body and spirit. Slowly, c/s/x and other
advocates have made inroads, but our efforts are frustrated by the very
people who could be our closest allies and strongest supporters.

I serve on many committees, work groups and task forces which
have exposed me to people who are well-dispersed along a continuum of
understanding and compassion. The different perspectives of c/s/x are
grasped only partially and are rarely fully understood. There have been
many times when I believed that I had influenced an individual or a group
by making a convincing argument, only to learn at the next meeting that the
same issue had to be argued through again as if it was completely new. At
one committee meeting, I listened to an outrageous statement made by a
psychiatrist, who I was later told held a high ranking, politically appointed
position.

He said, "I have people coming to my outpatient clinic who are content with the medications they are taking and their station in life. What gives advocates the right to tell them they are entitled to more choice, that they should have treatment, housing and vocational training choices . . . or tell them to question their medications? If they are not aware of alternatives and are satisfied with what services they are receiving, why should you get them all stirred up and agitated?"

At first I thought he was being sardonic or joking, but he was serious. I asked him how that was different from the southern plantation owners' attitudes about the rights of slaves who knew of no other life than slavery.

A little later during the meeting, the same psychiatrist said he could not understand why he and other directors of agencies should be striving to get consumer input since most consumers were apathetic and unmotivated anyway. He claimed that his argument was supported by an example drawn from his experience at the facility he ran: "We organized and scheduled a consumer meeting and no one showed up." A few people tried to explain to him what it meant when you throw a party and no one comes.

Psychiatric survivors have found important help in numerous places. Many of us have found it centered in a person who has reached out and supported us in a special way that let us know that we continued to have value. Many have found crucial support and guidance among peers. Psychiatric survivors also have found pockets of help within the mental health profession. Those pockets have usually contained unusual individual practitioners or non-mainstream alternatives. To be in therapy with someone with whom you feel safe, where your therapist is fully present in your experience, communicating understanding and offering non-judgmental support, creates a context in which desired changes are possible.

Psychotherapy by a specially-trained, experienced clinician with an advanced degree is generally unavailable to those diagnosed with serious mental illness. Ironically, people who are experiencing what is considered the most powerful and debilitating form of mental illness usually receive services from the lowest paid, least educated and trained of the mental health professions' pecking order. Supportive counseling directed at maintenance and stabilization is the most that can be expected unless there are unusual circumstances and substantial financial resources. Even within the confines of supportive therapy, many myths surround what should and should not be part of the process. Grossly over-emphasized is the importance of accepting your "illness" before any progress can be made.

Often unchallenged is the premise that a person must be stabilized on medication before any form of therapy will be effective. Uncritically accepted is the admonition against using hypnosis, guided imagery or meditation with people with certain disorders.

The October 1996 issue of the *American Psychologist* was devoted entirely to psychotherapy outcome assessment. Chapters written by leaders in psychology examined the multiple and complex problems confronting outcome research in psychotherapy. Hans Strupp, drawing from decades of research, concluded, "The problem of evaluating outcomes from psychotherapy continues to bedevil the field as it did a century ago when modern psychotherapy came into being. . . "[89] Researchers Gottfried and Wolfe noted that psychotherapy research is currently more rigorous in its methodology, but with its reliance on clinical trials to determine how to best treat disorders, it condones the medicalization of psychotherapy. In addition, the medical model of outcome research over-emphasizes symptoms and minimizes the more difficult to evaluate relationship dynamics. Complicating matters greatly is the absence of agreement on what constitutes mental health. For Gottfried and Wolfe, the dilemma is condensed in the statement: "Our wish is that therapy interventions be based on psychotherapy research; our fear, however, is that they might."[90]

What are good therapists – do they take the place of wise uncles, grandfathers, village shamans, country doctors – those figures in the past who had taken on respect by virtue of the lives they led? I would want my therapist to have a life-long hunger for understanding and an awareness of his own ignorance. His courage and integrity would enable me to trust him. A genuine humility would be evident in his sensitivity to the delicate process of exploring the psyche. My therapist would be my guide, not my leader. He would be there to support, nurture and expand my choices, not his own. He would be able to show me through his being-in-my-world that I am not isolated, alone and unworthy. My therapist would be able to convey his caring about me as an individual. I would know he cared because I could feel that he was attentively present in the very moment in which we are relating to each other.

According to R.D. Laing, "Psychotherapy must remain an obstinate attempt of two people to recover the wholeness of being human through the relationship between them."[91]

The *personhood* of the psychotherapist and its manifestation in the interpersonal relationship builds the opportunity for positive outcome. My model psychotherapy relationship would aspire to maximize: integrity, equality, warmth, rapport, courage to risk, trust, respect, openness, genuineness, positive regard, empathy, unconditional love, authenticity and an abiding belief that the mystery of life contains the seeds of the miraculous.

* * *

I still see people in psychotherapy. I believe that it is more difficult to provide good therapy today than when I started in 1978. More people are seeking help for emotional problems. Perhaps it is reflective of how our culture has evolved and the times we live in that there is an increased demand to find help and solace from *rented strangers*.

In 1992 when I gave up my psychotherapy practice of more than fifteen years in Morristown, New Jersey, less than 1% of the people who came to see me were taking psychiatric drugs. Now, the majority of the people referred to me for therapy are already taking medication when I see them for their first session. I struggle with the conundrum of how to honor a person's choice to seek relief in this manner. Although I believe that in most circumstances psychiatric drugs should be avoided, I know that at times they can be helpful. As a non-medical practitioner, I am careful about the information that I provide to my clients. I know that some people will find relief from the drugs and during that first session, I would be foolish to think that I can judge whether the reported benefits are directly related to the biochemical action of the drug or some kind of placebo effect or "flight into health."

The person I see typically comes in to see me after complaining of various problems to their primary care physician. Physicians, like the general public, are inundated with an onslaught of sales material promoting the benefits of a particular drug in enthusiastic detail and large print. The barely heard (small print) precautions are conveyed by the drug marketers as being infrequently occurring minor nuisances.

Busy physicians, trained to be problem fixers, want to give their patients answers and too often will not provide enough information to enable their patients to make informed decisions when confronting problems of an emotional nature. The typical patient, in turn, expects to be told how to solve the problem rather than needing to consider vague and uncertain outcomes that require their active participation in the decision process.

Typically, into my office comes a person dealing with anxiety and/or depression who has been taking an anti-depressant drug, usually a Selective Serotonin Reuptake Inhibitor (SSRI) like Lexapro, and a benzodiazepine like Xanax. Quickly I need to determine what he knows about the drugs he is taking and whether he believes they are helping. I have to begin a discourse and learn what helpful information I can provide, while not undermining any positive benefits he may be deriving from the drugs. As a general principle, I operate under the assumption that a person does best when he is able to have enough information and understanding to make informed choices. If I learn that he has access to a physician whose opinion he trusts, we discuss what questions he might want to ask. With the wealth of information available on the internet, if he is motivated and capable of doing his own research, I encourage him to learn about the drugs he is taking. I might also suggest that in addition to reading the scientific research and pharmaceutical literature, he can find useful information in the posts and web logs of people who have taken similar psychiatric drugs.

Daily, in my current psychotherapy practice I adjust to the unique challenges presented by a particular individual who has a dire need for assistance. The lack of uniform and predictable responses to many of the psychiatric drugs means that I cannot pre-judge the value of a specific drug for a specific person. Acknowledging that there are situations and times when people can benefit from psychiatric drugs, I nonetheless think that people are entitled to full disclosure about the drugs, along with the right to be informed about other available alternatives with less potentially harmful side effects.

Often, after having conducted a workshop or made an educational presentation, although I have not said that drugs are of no use to anyone, and even if I explicitly say that some people find value in the psychiatric drugs that they are taking, I later am told that the message was dangerous for "our consumers" to hear – they will stop taking the drugs they need. I guess my primary message of hope, possibility and alternative routes gets lost for some.

As in my public speaking, I have found a similar principle operating in my psychotherapy practice. A young man came to see me about feeling depressed and weepy after his fiancé left him shortly before they were to be married. His physician prescribed a standard dose anti-depressant and a benzodiazepine to help him sleep while he waited the four to six weeks for the anti-depressant to become effective. During our session, he told me that he had not started taking the prescribed drugs and had strong reservations based on having seen their effects on some friends. He asked me whether I thought he could get over his depressed feelings without taking drugs. I told him that many people do very well in therapy without drugs and explained that the decision about taking drugs was his to make. After I saw him for about a month and explored what had happened with his fiancé and its impact upon him, he began feeling better. During our sixth session he reported to me that he had told his physician that he was doing better. The doctor said to him that it was good that the Lexapro had started working quickly. My client told me that when he informed the physician that he had not taken the Lexapro, he was surprised at the reaction. The fundamental objective – positive outcome – was lost in the physician's irritation that the prescribed medication had not been taken.

I admire and am inspired by the excellent therapists who have worked hard to develop their knowledge and skills. I am acutely aware of how tough it is to be a dedicated therapist providing a high quality service to diverse clients. Their therapy practices must navigate restrictive insurance company obstacles and government regulations that demand "covering your ass." Such therapists are willing to be emotionally available and do not make playing it safe their top priority. I cannot forget the obnoxious statement of a psychiatrist who was disagreeing with me on how to proceed with a patient. He believed that he closed his argument with this knockout punch, "Good medical practice means not being vulnerable to being sued." Seeing my obvious annoyance, he added with patronizing superiority, "That's what we learn in medical school."

As a therapist you are exposed to people's pain and their desperate pleas for relief. The process of psychotherapy is slow and uncertain. At times I think about the small number of sessions that are satisfying and rewarding to both therapist and client as compared to the many plodding sessions rife with emotional pain. I wonder if I need to erect barriers to keep from absorbing so much of my clients' suffering. Yet, my most important strength as a therapist is my sensitivity. Empathic understanding of another and the communication of this empathy is the platform one stands on to touch the buried strength of a hurt spirit that has burrowed into an inaccessible hiding place. A human connection is needed, a witness to validate a person's pain and expiate the shame of needing help.

I take pride in knowing that few believe in possibility more than I do. My son, when asked by a teacher to write about one thing that best described his father wrote, "He never gives up." Once a client believes in possibility, then the therapy process can scurry through a plethora of options that can facilitate a change in the dynamic interplay of emotions, actions, thinking and attitudes. But even the best therapy can result in uncertain outcomes.

I value the advice given to me by T.X. Barber when, as a novice therapist, I attended a hypnosis workshop he was conducting. During a break I asked him what he thought of the hypnotic techniques of Milton Erickson and the quick, one-session resolution of clients' problems attributed to him. Dr. Barber asked me if I had treated any clients in therapy who had successful outcomes. Following my affirmative response, he told me that if I did a credible job of writing up those encounters, I too would seem remarkable. He added, you don't see a lot of therapists writing and taking responsibility for those they did not help, which are probably the majority of most therapists' client load – unless, of course, you can be very selective about who you treat. He did not need to add what I already understood: the more famous the therapist, the greater the client's motivation and expectation for success – and thus we see the self-fulfilling prophesy.

For years I have loved listening to blues music. Why, after listening to people's real life blues, do I find enjoyment in listening to blues music? Perhaps, as I heard discussed on a blues radio program, the blues come in through your ears, go straight to the heart and end up touching the spirit. I believe I also heard some reference to the blues being the poor person's psychiatry. At a Native American powwow, I heard Grammy winner composer and singer Bill Miller say that during a low point in his life he became depressed, and was hospitalized and injected with psychiatric drugs. He then said he would have done much better if they had prescribed for him an iPod full of music.

Chapter 15

To Never Abandon the Pursuit of the Possible

Every soul has to learn the whole lesson for itself. It must go over the whole ground. What it does not see, what it does not live, it will not know.
(Ralph Waldo Emerson)

Before my initial Shiatsu massage, the therapist asked me if I wanted to focus on any particular body areas or physical concerns. With his next question he inquired about any issue in my day-to-day living that dominated my attention. Although surprised at the question, only a few seconds elapsed before I responded, "To live and work with integrity."

I survived psychiatric treatment. For more than thirty years I have not used psychiatric drugs, needed psychotherapy, or had any symptoms of mental illness – at least, those that would distinguish me from the chronically normal person. I am not, and perhaps will never become the person I strive to be, but I have doggedly sought to bring meaning and value to my journey.

How did I avoid the fate of so many, whose spirits and life courses were arrested by experiences similar to mine? "Why me" is a question I have tried to answer. *Can I really change* is a question people ask me. Who has not searched within themselves, hoping that a change is possible for that unwanted part of their being? My work with clients triggers thoughts about whether I have changed any of the core parts of me. I am no longer shy, but still a bit introverted, and I most definitely retain my ability to be suspicious. Do I still have more of the capacity to become paranoid than most people? Probably. I am not frightened of my paranoid tendencies. I regard them less as a sign of weakness than a potential ability. It would be more accurate and less emotionally charged to call it a tendency to be skeptical, questioning or cautious. When I am tired or don't feel quite healthy, as when a cold or virus is coming on, I'm more sensitive to sounds and images and I startle easily. During times when I am anxious, confused or emotional, the idiosyncratic associations increase. Even sometimes when I am driving and I let random associations flit in and out of my consciousness, logic is momentarily

239

suspended and replaced with bizarre *what if* images. In a nanosecond, I can create immediate, fantastic, unreal assessments of new people or situations. But now there is little anxiety, fear, confusion or need for grandiose explanations to satisfy a need to feel special. I am simply amused by this playful dance of my imagination. The thoughts and musings flow freely and I can choose to dismiss them quickly or expand them. Because I know that I will adjust and adapt to the demands of a situation, I do not have to be overly self-protective. Not having secrets to hide or needing to prove myself, I can trust until I am fed back information that calls for withdrawing that trust. Illogical and paradoxical as it may seem, I find it easy to trust myself and others.

When I think of the wide array of people who have struggled, who have won or lost or who have remained stuck in their struggles to become, I do not see illness. Instead, I look at the dynamic interplay of *courage, fear* and *safety*, where individual and social structure clash. Childhood nightmares inform us of the intensity of fear that the mind can create. Fear restricts the roads and landscapes available in one's journey through life, but it can also generate the motivation necessary to make powerful changes. Although some are blessed to be born with the temperament, abilities and tools that initially enable an early integration of fear-courage-safety, for many, this key triad is in an unstable flux that demands vigilance. Balancing and resolving the shifting requirements of this life-long developmental task has no immutable rules, laws or guarantees. A bolt of lightening or invading virus can cancel all prior resolutions.

What is the community standard for courage? How much fear will a peer group permit of a member before subjecting him to ridicule? What is the family standard for determining an adequate amount of safety? How much of our individual freedoms are available for sacrifice in society's quest to maintain the illusion of control, predictability and safety? Will the "mentally ill" continue to serve as the "not us" scapegoats which conveniently divert people from confronting the always possible terror that life and death present? As I watch the growing numbers of people who are diagnosed with some form of mental illness, and even more sadly, the number of children whose diagnostic labels are preparing them to become the new group of "chronic mentally ill," I worry that the price of predictability and safety is too steep.

Can we evaluate our evolutionary progress as a species by calculating the percentage of human beings who experience more joy than pain during their lifetimes? While the volume of information we are exposed to has increased exponentially, our capacity to absorb and use that information lags far behind. While the human population continues to increase, the diversity of other complex life forms appears to be decreasing. While people are being told that there are greater numbers of emotional problems and behaviors that deviate from the norm, the *norm* itself is shrinking. While the need for tolerance and compassion is increasing, competition for shrinking resources feeds our intolerance for the not-us outsiders. Identifying those that are different from us as the source of our misery enables us to avoid the pain of our existential angst, but at too great a cost – alienation from self and others. It is essential to create and multiply the number of acceptable and productive roles available to all people. With our increase in numbers and technology, our humanness needs more encouragement.

I have met and had the opportunity to share with and learn from extraordinary individuals of great courage – psychiatric survivors who are working to make positive changes so that those who come after them will experience less pain and abuse. I have also had the privilege of meeting some remarkable mental health professionals whose integrity and pursuit of truth make them outsiders relegated to work at the margins of their disciplines. Forging deep friendships with my peers, I found community in our shared experience and our passion for helping fellow travelers. We helped ourselves find meaning when we helped others.

Is it any wonder that the people who do recover are the very ones who have rejected the mental health enforcers' pronouncements and carved their own way into a new life? The people that I know who have transformed their experience are easily recognized by their passion, vitality and appreciation of life. They are winners by virtue of having engaged in the process of peering deep inside and not being destroyed by what they encountered. Victors in the fight to find meaning and identity, they are reminiscent of people who have survived *near death* experiences – their understanding and identity changes.

When you allow yourself to descend into the depths of an altered state, the need for safety moves from foreground to background. When you pass death's threshold as described in near death experiences, safety's demands are radically modified. I believe that we actively make a decision to let go when we enter a different realm of consciousness. In time-tested mystical traditions, one's decision is reinforced by a commitment to rigorous preparation. Most of us do not have the determination, clarity of vision or access to that special guide who is right for us. Instead, we accommodate to our fears and life demands. But for those who must deal with too much fear, who cannot navigate the limited number of paths presented to them, who lack the skills, self-esteem, societally approved competencies, who have been hurt repeatedly, who feel the constant pain of extreme sensitivity, who have not learned how to trust or love, or have never been loved in a way that matched their needs, who see no future and abhor themselves and hate their life story . . . when critical mass is reached, there is a choice – to forgo safety and risk all. The mental health system is not a facilitator of growth and change if it cannot permit a person to risk his life in an attempt to create a future which is not a continuation of his predictable and horrific past.

I would be foolishly presumptuous to assert that everyone who steps through the doorway into the unknown has made an active, conscious decision to do so. But would I be more or less foolish than those who proclaim that passage into madness is always preordained by one's genetic makeup? Is it not curious that the onset of "schizophrenia" coincides with an individual's need to separate from family and establish a separate identity? Why are the pursuits of spirituality and meaning such consistent themes in psychosis? Too often, the mental health profession has constructed spurious answers to these questions – answers logically derived from ever-changing favored theories. When complex individuals who share some similar elements of diverse experience are reduced to symptoms and pathological syndromes, their personal and special life stories cannot be understood. To enhance our understanding of the myriad altered states of human consciousness, we must not ignore those individuals' unique and precious stories.

Throughout our history people have been fascinated by altered states of consciousness. What is it like to live in a world stripped of others' reality rules? Too many people who work in the mental health field have learned to intellectualize, rationalize and train away their natural curiosity about what it is like to be crazy. The wonder of who we are and what we become when the self is no longer anchored to the usual and comprehensible retains its fascination. Within most of us are memories of the capacities we possessed as children. Fantasies, imaginary playmates and all-consuming intensity are learning and emotional coping tools for the developing young person. We who have lived in, out, through and beyond the experience named psychosis have developed an empathic bond born of facing dangers and fears from within and without. Yet, what we have in common with everyone is far greater than those differences that c/s/x share with each other. We all have varying levels of ability to construct inner and outer worlds and establish where the two meet.

The clinician says that child-like regression is a symptom. The madman is accused of acting like a child. The normal adult is permitted to tap into here-and-now all consuming intensity in a few time-limited, societally approved situations. You are expected to drive yourself past your physical and emotional limits while playing football, running a marathon or scaling a mountain. A soldier, in a time of war, will be required to disregard personal values, forgo his own safety and obey orders that put his life at extreme risk. We long to be madly in love; we brood over unrequited love. And it's OK to lose all of your self while having sexual relations.

Intensity accompanies change. Extreme and change are partners. Perhaps if we look at childhood and madness as states of potential development, the tidal wave of emotions they both share is more comprehensible. Joy and pain racing back and forth between fire and ice are less threatening to watch and tolerate when we can frame them as being in service of the child learning a lesson.

In the not-acceptable world models of reality drop-outs, there is no approval for an undefined mission which lacks a predictable learning plan or reasonably attainable objective. If you intuitively or subconsciously understand that the very act of living is a transitional process rather than a stable state, then it becomes clear that some of us may perceive the electric energy of too many possibilities, while some perceive themselves frozen in exhaustive despair – and yet others live in the currently defined range of "normal." When we move beyond survival into making it matter how we survive, we begin to experience the gifts of being human.

* * *

They are the "invincible kids," the survivors of horrendous abuse and neglect. They have defied their predicted fate. Unlike children whose troubled adult lives reflect the trauma of their childhoods, these children develop into "well-adjusted adults." Their ability to thrive despite the adversity of their environment and upbringing was once thought by experts to be mainly the result of being born with certain innate abilities and temperaments. The longitudinal research of child psychologist Emmy Werner[92] is helping us to understand that many children have the capacity to overcome even the most staggering odds. Her results suggested that the developmental outcome was more dependent on the quality of the environment in which the child was raised than the biological or psychosocial risk condition. Werner and Smith studied a cohort of 700 children born on the island of Kauai from 1955-1995. Due to multiple risk factors at birth, approximately one-third of these babies were considered high risk. Of these, seventy grew in healthy ways and developed no severe problems. They appeared to be invulnerable to their life-compromising risk factors. Moreover, Werner's follow-up of children at age forty suggests that a person who has faced childhood adversity and overcome it may do even better in later life than someone who had relatively smooth childhood experiences. The resilient children reported stronger marriages, better health and little sign of emotional turmoil when compared with those who enjoyed less stressful origins.[93]

I am struck by the parallels between the resilient kids and psychiatric survivors. What are the informed guesses about who will survive and who will thrive? The Kauai study shows that despite highly adverse conditions, the presence of later positive experiences with a caring adult, and circumstances like a safe place where trust can develop, can help the child to grow into a confident, caring, competent adult. I am particularly impressed by how similar buffers (protective factors) are important to both psychiatric survivors and the "invincible kids."

Just as c/s/x have recognized the devaluation of the self that occurs when you are always needing and receiving help, and the positive impact of being able to give and help others, resiliency theorists have confirmed the value children derive when they provide service to others in their community. We are empowered by having someone believe in us enough to reach out with genuine warmth and caring.

Defying the gloom-and-doom predictions of experts, the psychiatric survivor and the resilient child teach us valuable lessons. With evidence showing that children born into terrible circumstances are able to thrive, and research showing recovery from schizophrenia, we need to direct our efforts at constructing pathways to resiliency. The research indicates that the lessons learned from these nearly invincible kids can teach us how to help all kids to handle the inevitable risks and turning points of life.[94] Instead of exclusively studying children who fail, we can focus on learning from the children who survive and thrive. The same might be said for studying the stories of psychiatric survivors.

At the 2006 National Association for Rights Protection and Advocacy annual conference I met a new friend, Dorothy Dundas. In the forty years since I had those decimating insulin treatments, I have discovered only three others who have overcome similar assaults on their brain and spirit. Leonard Roy Frank, Don Weitz, Dorothy Dundas and I were among the last victims of that nonsensical, horrific treatment. Central to each of our lives has been the desire to insure the rights and improve the prospects for all of our peers.

Don Weitz is co-editor of the book *Shrink Resistant: The Struggle Against Psychiatry in Canada.* Having just celebrated his seventieth birthday a few days earlier, Don told me during a 2001 protest march in Montreal, "I live for these protest rallies." He is the consummate activist, fully committed to opposing all forms of social injustice.

And of course, my friend Leonard Roy Frank, author, researcher, historian, activist and unyielding warrior in the fight to expose the extensive harm and suffering caused by electroshock and the need to abandon its use as a psychiatric treatment. After a series of electroshock and insulin coma treatments that caused him to lose his memory, Leonard developed a paired association technique to re-educate himself. His lists of paired words were precursors to the quotations he collected and which he later expanded and published as the *Random House Webster's Quotationary.*

Later, as I corresponded with Dorothy and marveled at the instant rapport and affection we felt for each other, knowing I felt similarly about Don and Leonard, she wrote back to me:

> I think passing through the fire is definitely part of it. I shall never be the same; I know. I am a more caring and aware person because of it. A lot of it has to do with the atrocities I witnessed as well as went through myself. I think being witness to terrible injustices, without being able to stop them, can be more painful than actually living through them yourself. As I think I said to you before, I have always been left with the desire to shout about all of this with a giant megaphone from the top of the Empire State Building. The fantasy is that the sound of my voice would flow around the world into the ears of those who could make a difference.

I am grateful for these friendships. I mourn the missing casualties. I hope that this book serves as that giant megaphone.

We are all changing, possible and potential life stories. I am grateful for the genuine help and support that I received from several people in different ways. For a therapist to help those who are going through extreme emotional states there needs to be full awareness that "[h]e must stop ranking either people or talents and accept the fact that there are many roads to truth and no culture has a corner on the path or is better equipped than others to search for it. What is more, no man can tell another how to conduct that search."[95] Real help empowers you to expand your choices and supports your taking on full responsibility for the success or failure of your personal journey.

A large number of families – estimates range as high as one in every four – will struggle with decisions and questions concerning the hospitalization of a family member. Strange behaviors will be labeled as symptoms of mysterious diseases of the mind, and desperate families will turn to medically licensed healers to help their loved ones. But too many people have been deprived of their rights. Too many people have been prevented from making the false starts and stops so necessary to develop their unique potential talents. In the words of Dag Hammarskjold, United Nations Secretary General and 1961 Nobel Peace prize winner:

> At every moment you choose yourself. But do you choose your self? Body and soul contain a thousand possibilities out of which you can build many *I*'s. But in only one of them is there a congruence of the elector and the elected. Only one which you will never find until you have excluded all those superficial and fleeting possibilities of being and doing with which you toy, out of curiosity or wonder or greed, and which hinder you from casting anchor in the experience of the mystery of life, and the consciousness of the talent entrusted to you which is your *I*.[96]

After my second hospitalization, I was drawn to the theories and writings of R.D. Laing. I sensed that he had profound understanding of madness, culture and its relation to the human condition. But at the time I read his work, I found his writing too difficult for me to comprehend. Twenty years later, re-reading my tattered copies of his books, I understood and resonated with what he attempted to teach.

> Any technique concerned with the other without the self, with behavior to the exclusion of experience, with the relationship to the neglect of the persons in relation, with the individuals to the exclusion of their relationship, and most of

all, with an object-to-be-changed rather than a person-to-be accepted, simply perpetuates the disease it purports to cure.[97]

Each of us lives on an island of our own construction. Gazing out across the turbulent water that separates our islands, we try to build bridges to accommodate our need for connection. We construe the events that make up our experiences in ways that support our individual life stories. Each insists that only one narrative can be correct and if the other's construction is too different then it must be mistaken, dishonest or crazy. In the psychiatrist-patient relationship, the mainstream psychiatrist designs a bridge with toll collectors exacting too costly a price. We need to find ways to live with different constructions of reality so that all of us have the right to travel freely across safe bridges.

Changes need to be made in our thinking about mental illness and our mental health policy. We must have more than a smattering of under-the-radar alternatives to the medical model. People need and desire researched and informed options in which the strategies and goals – whether these be relief of symptoms or personal transformation and development – are chosen by the individual.

Peculiar to humans is the ability to imagine future possibilities and consciously design a course of action. We are capable of contemplating the prospect of life outside the present moment. Having the uniquely human ability to govern our instincts enables us to live in precarious balance within worlds of our own constructions. Unfortunately, the struggle to find meaning has become a privilege, rather than a birthright. Our human frailties and anxieties need not be at odds with the natural flow and dynamics of an ever-changing universe. It is time to relinquish our reverence of power, and evaluate and modify our relentless quest to dominate nature. Perhaps then we will be honoring what sets the human species apart from other forms of life and relearning that we are all parts of a *whole*.

My story along with those of fellow travelers tells us that it is possible to create mental health services that support and elevate people rather than restrict them to a life of maintenance and stabilization. My journey through recovery/transformation is not intended as a model path with road signs for others to follow, but rather it is an example of possibility. The opportunity to discover what you can do, be and understand should not be arbitrarily forbidden for specific classes of people.

The answer to "why me" still eludes me, but as long as I can search for meaning and occasionally get parts of answers, I am content to live and die without clinging to some false certainty that makes me think I know the *absolute truth*.

Epilogue

You must have chaos within you to give birth to a dancing star.
(Friedrich Nietzsche)

I first saw Ron in 1983. Impressed and drawn to this self-confident man with the clearest, most intelligent eyes I had ever seen, I was fascinated not only with the message I heard him speak, but also with the man who spoke with such passion, independence and feisty rebelliousness from the stage at the Mental Health Association symposium. I made a point of creating an opportunity to meet him. We have been together ever since.

For twenty-four years I have watched this gentle but determined man battle ignorance, stigma and opposition from inept government bureaucrats to the weighty clout of pharmaceutical lobbyists in what were at times David and Goliath situations, armed not only with the courage of his own convictions but also the life stories of hundreds of previously unheard voices. I have seen Ron work late into the night, extend himself to countless strangers, quietly do innumerable behind-the-scenes good deeds, and sacrifice career opportunities due to his steadfast refusal to subvert his truth and values to political pressure. I have also witnessed him grow as a man and become a leading voice in the fight for basic human rights and dignity to be afforded to all.

There was a time when, in those dark and hopeless days, scared, confused and ignored from behind his own locked door, he wondered if his voice would ever be heard. Today Ron's lectures and published works have touched, inspired and motivated thousands of consumers and professionals in the US and internationally. He has been asked to serve on governors' and presidential advisory committees, led state-wide task forces, and influenced the passing of precedent-setting legislation. As a clinician, advocate, teacher and consultant, his work has reached school systems, prisons, homeless persons, lawyers, legislators, social workers, law enforcement personnel, medical professionals, fellow psychologists and members of diverse disability communities. He has been chosen to serve as President of the National Association of Rights Protection and Advocacy and in 2003, he and several of his fellow activists founded INTAR, an international organization dedicated to advancing understanding and developing and promoting humane, non-coercive mental health treatment and alternatives for all.

Perhaps most meaningful to Ron are the many phone calls he receives from people all over the country who have heard of his work and, frustrated or desperate from their unsatisfying experiences in the mental health system, implore Ron to see their son, their husband, their loved one, or simply call for advice, for direction, or to tell their story to a sympathetic and understanding ear. They seek validation and to know that they are not alone. Ron's story, his message of hope and perseverance, and his call for change has resonated with the thousands of families' life stories still unfolding.

In May 2000 Ron was awarded the Ed Roberts Award for Advocacy and Humanitarianism for "his outstanding role in helping disabled citizens achieve their goals and dreams." Against all odds those many years ago, in August 2005, the American Psychological Association presented Ron the Presidential Citation for his tireless efforts as an advocate and activist to educate, empower, and eliminate stigma and discrimination and for the building of pathways and bridges with his fellow psychologists. And in April of this past year, 2006, of great meaning and significance to Ron, students of the Graduate School of Sage Colleges honored him as the Outstanding Adjunct Faculty professor. With tears in my eyes, I stood among the audience as his students gave him a standing ovation.

Ron's unrelenting efforts to reach and open young minds, educate fellow professionals and practitioners, support and encourage those afflicted with pain, fear and confusion, and his message of hope and possibility continue as a personal and professional mission. He is, quite simply, the strongest, most grounded, most compassionate and most honorable man I know. The respect of his clients and his peers is well-earned and deserving, but more, on a daily basis he is an inspiration to me and to our son as he crusades for every person's Right To Be. We love you Ron.

Lindsey Bassman

Acknowledgements

Driven by an intense need to understand myself and propelled by the conviction that my experience would benefit others, I was determined to write this book.The stops and starts of twenty-five years of writing, all of the exciting anticipation followed by the many disappointments, were valuable teachers. But it was not the acquired knowledge and wisdom that sustained my efforts but rather the love and support of family and friends – their belief in me that enabled me to bring my work to fruition.

Lindsey, my wife, my mate, my partner, how do I thank you? Your love was and is my safe place. I sought your feedback relentlessly. Your patience was inexhaustible. You read and re-read and never let me be satisfied with "good enough." Feel my gratitude and love in this public acknowledgment, an insufficient expression of how much you mean to me.

Jesse, my son, your entrance into my life opened my heart to a different way of feeling and being. My work is infused with the impact of witnessing your growth into manhood. I marvel with pride at your innate intelligence, your exquisite sensitivity, and your ability to empathize and care.Your presence keeps me clear and grounded.

I am grateful for the guidance and support of my dear friend, Darby Penney. Never shying away from speaking truth to power, you were always available to offer your direct and incisive assessment of my writing and ideas.

Thank you Leonard Roy Frank for your support, and your help in pushing me to do my best as a writer and as an activist for social justice. Your generosity in sharing with me wisdom acquired from your prodigious reading and self-directed study is greatly appreciated.

Having been very tough on the mental health system and mental health professionals, I must express my gratitude to those psychologists who have been open to my views and have supported me in my work. I have learned and benefited from our discourse and debate.

Ron Levant, your genuine listening, caring and openness about what I had to say, allowed me to shed the uncomfortable outsider role I wore at APA. Thank you for giving me the wise guidance necessary to get my views expressed most effectively. I am glad for our friendship

The work and careers of Bert Karon, Barry Duncan and Michael DeMaria reflect their passionate belief in the growth and potential for healing in all of us. Their expressed respect for my work makes me proud, grateful to them, and pushes me forward.

Pat DeLeon, I know how tirelessly you work for the causes you are committed to and that makes me all the more appreciative of the openness and respect you have shown for my work. Thank you for your support.

Thank you Stuart Miller for encouraging me to keep going and for your valuable recommendations on how to improve the articulation and presentation of A Fight to Be.

I was very lucky to have found my editor, Dania Sheldon. Thank you Dania for the care you exercised in respectfully and sensitively editing my manuscript.

And deepest gratitude to all my fellow travelers who have trusted me, opened their hearts, shared their stories and in their fights to be, taught me about perseverance and compassion.

Notes and References

Introduction
1. Walt Whitman, "Song of Myself," *Leaves of Grass* (New York: Viking Press, 1855) 51.

2. G. Harrison, K. Hopper, E. Laska, C. Siegel, J. Wanderling, et al., "Recovery from Psychotic Illness: A 15-and 25-year international follow-up study," *British Journal of Psychiatry* 178 (2001): 506-517.

Chapter 1
3. C. Jung, *Memories, Dreams and Reflections* (New York: Pantheon Books, 1963); R. D. Laing, *The Politics of Experience* (New York: Ballantine Books, 1967); J. W. Perry, *The Far Side of Madness* (New York: Prentice-Hall, 1974).

4. D. Weeks and J. James, *Eccentrics: A Study of Sanity and Strangeness* (London: Kodansha Globe International, 1996).

5. Havelock Ellis, "Impressions and Comments," *Random House Webster's Quotationary*, ed. Leonard Roy Frank (New York: Random House, 1998) 105.

6. Adam Miller, "Psycho Theory on Birth of Jazz," *New York Post*, 11 July 2001: 29.

7. E. F. Schumacher, *A Guide for the Perplexed* (New York: Harper and Row, 1977).

8. T. Merton, *The Seven Storey Mountain* (New York: Harcourt Brace, 1948).

9. *Diagnostic and Statistical Manual of Mental Disorders IV* (Washington, DC: American Psychiatric Association, 1994).

Chapter 3
10. L. Kalinowsky, "Insulin Coma Treatment," *Comprehensive Textbook of Psychiatry*, ed. Alfred M. Freedman and Harold I. Kaplan (Baltimore: Williams and Wilkins, 1967) 1288.

11. J. Friedberg, *Shock Treatment is Not Good For Your Brain* (San Francisco: Glide, 1976).

12. J. Frame, "For Your Own Good," *The History of Shock Treatment*, ed. Leonard Roy Frank (San Francisco: L. R. Frank, 1978) 71.

13. G. Blackburn, "Let Him Feel It This Time," *The History of Shock Treatment*, ed. Leonard Roy Frank (San Francisco: L. R. Frank, 1978) 78-79.

14. J. Gotkin and P. Gotkin, *Too Much Anger, Too Many Tears: A Personal Triumph Over Psychiatry* (New York: Quadrangle, 1975) 195.

Chapter 4
15. E. Hall, *Beyond Culture* (Garden City, NY: Anchor Press, 1976).

Chapter 6
16. E. F. Schumacher, *A Guide for the Perplexed* (New York: Harper and Row, 1977).

Chapter 9
17. W. Durant, *The Story of Civilization: Our Oriental Heritage* (New York: Simon and Schuster, 1954).

18. J. Campbell and R. Schraiber, *In Pursuit of Wellness: The Well-Being Project. Mental Health Clients Speak for Themselves* (Sacramento, CA: California Network of Mental Health Clients, 1989).

19. J. Greenberg, *I Never Promised You a Rose Garden* (New York: New American Library, 1964).

20. E. Stotland, *The Psychology of Hope* (San Francisco: Jossey-Bass, 1969).

21. C. Harding, *Transcript of Presentation: Roundtable Public Policy Discussion* (New York, 1995).

22. M. DeSisto, C. Harding, et al., "The Maine and Vermont Three-Decade Studies of Serious Mental Illness: I. Matched Comparison of Cross-

Sectional Outcome," *British Journal of Psychiatry* 167.3 (1995): 331-42; C. Harding et al., "The Vermont Longitudinal Study of Persons With Severe Mental Illness, II: Long-Term Outcomes of Subjects Who Retrospectively Met DSM-III Criteria for Schizophrenia," *American Journal of Psychiatry* 144.6 (1987): 727-35; G. Huber et al., "Longitudinal Studies of Schizophrenic Patients," *Schizophrenia Bulletin* 6 (1980): 592-605; L. Ciompi and C. Muller, *Lebensweg und Alter der Schizophrenia Eine Katamnestische Lonzeitstudies bis ins Senium* (Berlin: Springer Verlag, 1976); M. Bleuler, *The Schizophrenic Disorders: Long-Term Patient and Family Studies* (New Haven: Yale University Press, 1978); M. T. Tsuang et al., "Long-term Outcomes of Major Psychoses, I: Schizophrenia and Affective Disorders Compared with Psychiatrically Symptom-Free Surgical Conditions," *Archives of General Psychiatry* 36 (1979): 1295-1301.

23. C. Harding et al., "The Vermont Longitudinal Study of Persons With Severe Mental Illness, II: Long-Term Outcomes of Subjects Who Retrospectively Met DSM-III Criteria for Schizophrenia," *American Journal of Psychiatry* 144.6 (1987): 727-35.

24. W. Anthony, "Recovery From Mental Illness: The Guiding Vision of the Mental Health System in the 1990s," *An Introduction to Psychiatric Rehabilitation, ed. The Publications Committee of IAPSRS* (Boston: Boston University, 1994): 564.

Chapter 10
25. P. Breggin, *Toxic Psychiatry* (New York: St. Martin's Press, 1991).

26. P. Kramer, *Listening to Prozac* (New York: Penguin Books, 1994).

27. See any of numerous books and publications of Thomas Szasz, beginning with *The Myth of Mental Illness* (1961), a critique of the use of illness as an explanation of emotional distress and problems in living.

Chapter 11
28. D. Fisher, "A Psychiatrist's Gradual Disclosure," *OMH News* 6.9 (November 1994): 16.

29. E. Hoffman, "Disclosure," *OMH News* 6.9 (November 1994): 5.

30. F. Cardinal, "Stigma," *OMH News* 6.9 (November 1994): 3.

31. J. Campbell and R. Schraiber, *In Pursuit of Wellness: The Well-Being Project. Mental Health Clients Speak for Themselves* (Sacramento, CA: California Network of Mental Health Clients, 1989): 53.

32. J. Chamberlin, "The Ex-Patients' Movement: Where We've been and Where We're Going," *The Journal of Mind and Behavior* 77 (1990): 323-36.

33. Written by Rae Unzicker in 1984, "To Be A Mental Patient" has become anthem-like for c/s/x and is posted on many internet sites.

Chapter 12

34. J. Rappaport, "In Praise of Paradox: A Social Policy of Empowerment Over Prevention," *American Journal of Community Psychology* 9.1 (1981): 17.

35. D. Brandon, *Innovation Without Change* (New York: MacMillan, 1991).

36. N. Hervey, "Advocacy or Folly: The Alleged Lunatic's Friend Society 1845-1863," Medical History 30 (1986): 245.

37. Ibid.

38. J. Kerri, "Studying Voluntary Associations as Adaptive Mechanisms: A Review of Anthropological Perspectives," *Current Anthropology* 17.1 (1976): 23-25.

39. *AA Fact File*, Alcoholics Anonymous World Services Inc., 14 Mar. 2007 <http://www.aa.org>.

40. P. Beard, "The Consumer Movement," *American Psychiatry After World War II* (1944-1994) ed. R. W. Menniger and J. C. Nemiah (Washington, DC: *American Psychiatric Press, Inc.*, 2000); J. Chamberlin, "The Ex-Patients' Movement: Where We've Been and Where We're Going," *The Journal of Mind and Behavior* 77 (1990): 323-36.

41. J. Rappaport, "Terms of Empowerment – Exemplars of Prevention:

Toward a Theory for Community Psychology," *American Journal of Community Psychology* 15 (1987): 121.

42. S. Rose and B. Black, *Advocacy and Empowerment: Mental Health Care in the Community* (Boston: Routledge and Kegan Paul, 1985).

43. H. Brody, *Stories of Sickness* (New Haven: Yale University Press, 1987).

44. P. Stastny, "Turning the Tables: On the Relationship Between Psychiatry and the Movement of Former Psychiatric Patients," *Community Psychiatrist* 7.1 (1993): 4-7.

45. *Transforming Mental Health Care: Achieving the Promise* (Rockville, MD: President's New Freedom Commission for Mental Health, 2005).

46. J. Campbell and R. Schraiber, *In Pursuit of Wellness: The Well-Being Project. Mental Health Clients Speak for Themselves* (Sacramento, CA: California Network of Mental Health Clients, 1989).

47. L. Mosher, "Should it be Easier to Commit People Involuntarily to Treatment?" *Controversial Issues in Mental Health*, ed. S. Kirk and S. Einbinder (Boston: Allyn and Bacon, 1994).

48. R. Unzicker, "From the Inside," *Beyond Bedlam: Contemporary Women Psychiatric Survivors Speak Out*, ed. Jeanine Grobe (Chicago: Third Side Press, 1996) 15.

49. J. Rappaport, "In Praise of Paradox: A Social Policy of Empowerment Over Prevention," *American Journal of Community Psychology* 9.1 (1981): 15-26.

Chapter 13
50. E. Becker, *The Denial of Death* (New York: Free Press, 1973) 29.

51. Ibid. 30.

52. H. Harp, "The Consumer/Survivor Movement: Philosophical Models," *Reaching Across: Mental Health Clients Helping Each Other*, ed. S. Zinman, H. Harp and S. Budd (Sacramento, CA: California Network of

Mental Health Clients, 1987).

53. Ibid. 20.

54. Ibid. 22.

55. T. Colbert, *Broken Brains or Wounded Hearts: What Causes Mental Illness* (Santa Ana, CA: Kevco Publishing, 1996).

56. K. Barney, "Limitations of the Critique of the Medical Model," *Challenging the Therapeutic State, Part Two: Further Disquisitions on the Mental Health System*, ed. David Cohen, Journal of Mind Behavior 15 (1994): 19-34.

57. T. Szasz, *The Myth of Mental Illness* (New York: Hoeber-Harper, 1961).

58. J. Joseph, *The Gene Illusion: Genetic Research in Psychiatry and Psychology Under the Microscope* (New York: Algora Publishing, 2004). S. Kety et al., "Mental Illness in the Biological and Adoptive Families of Adoptive Individuals Who Have Become Schizophrenic: A Preliminary Report Based on Psychiatric Interviews," *Genetic Research in Psychiatry*, ed. R. Fieve, D. Rosenthal and H. Brill (Baltimore: Johns Hopkins University Press, 1975). R. Lewontin, S. Rose and L. Kamin, *Not In Our Genes* (New York: Pantheon, 1985). C. Ross and A. Pam, *Pseudoscience in Biological Psychiatry* (New York: Wiley & Sons, 1995). J. Leo, "The Fallacy of the 50% Concordance Rate for Schizophrenia in Identical Twins," *Human Nature Review* 3 (2003): 406-15.

59. T. Colbert, *Broken Brains or Wounded Hearts: What Causes Mental Illness* (Santa Ana, CA: Kevco Publishing, 1996) 83.

60. R. Lewontin, "Billions and Billions of Demons," *New York Review of Books* 44.1 (9 Jan. 1997): 29.

61. Ibid.

62. R. Leifer, "Introduction: The Medical Model as the Ideology of the Therapeutic State," Challenging the Therapeutic State: Critical Perspectives on Psychiatry and the Mental Health System, ed. David Cohen, *Journal of Mind Behavior* 11.3-4 (1990).

63. Ibid.

64. D. Cohen, "Preface," Challenging the Therapeutic State: Critical Perspectives on Psychiatry and the Mental Health System, ed. David Cohen, *Journal of Mind Behavior* 11.3-4 (1990).

65. P. Brown, "The Name Game: Toward a Sociology of Diagnosis," Challenging the Therapeutic State: Critical Perspectives on Psychiatry and the Mental Health System, ed. David Cohen, *Journal of Mind Behavior* 11.3-4 (1990): 385-406.

66. P. Brown, "Diagnostic Conflict and Contradiction in Psychiatry," *Journal of Health and Social Behavior* 28 (1987): 37-50; M. Dumont, "The Nonspecificity of Mental Illness," *The American Journal of Orthopsychiatry* 54 (1984): 326-34; S. Kirk and H. Kutchins, *The Selling of DSM-III: The Rhetoric of Science in Psychiatry* (Chicago: Aldine de Gruyter, 1992); J. Kovel, "A Critique of DSM-III," *Research in Law, Deviance and Social Control* 9 (1988): 127-46; J. Mirowski and C. Ross, "Psychiatric Diagnosis and Reified Measurement," *Journal of Health and Social Behavior* 30 (1989): 11-25; T. Sarbin, "Toward the Obsolescence of the Schizophrenia Hypothesis," Challenging the Therapeutic State: Critical Perspectives on Psychiatry and the Mental Health System, ed. David Cohen, *Journal of Mind Behavior* 11.3-4 (1990).

67. K. Barney, "Limitations of the Critique of the Medical Model," Challenging the Therapeutic State, Part Two: Further Disquisitions on the Mental Health System, ed. David Cohen, *Journal of Mind Behavior* 15.1-2 (1994): 19-34.

68. American Psychiatric Association, *Task Force Report: Tardive Dyskinesia* (Washington, DC: American Psychiatric Association, 1980).

69. P. Breggin, "Brain Damage, Dementia and Persistent Cognitive Dysfunction Associated With Neuroleptic Drugs: Evidence, Etiology, Implications," Challenging the Therapeutic State: Critical Perspectives on Psychiatry and the Mental Health System, ed. David Cohen, *Journal of Mind Behavior* 11.3-4 (1990): 425-64.

70. D. Cohen, "Neuroleptic Drug Treatment of Schizophrenia: The State of

Confusion," Challenging the Therapeutic State, Part Two: Further Disquisitions on the Mental Health System, ed. David Cohen, *Journal of Mind Behavior* 15.1-2 (1994): 149.

71. P. Mitchell, "Chlorpromazine Turns Forty," *Psychopharmacology Bulletin* 29 (1993): 344.

72. D. Cohen, "Neuroleptic Drug Treatment of Schizophrenia: The State of Confusion," Challenging the Therapeutic State, Part Two: Further Disquisitions on the Mental Health System, ed. David Cohen, *Journal of Mind Behavior* 15.1-2 (1994): 14, 139-56.

73. J. Lieberman et al., for the Clinical Antipsychotic Trials of Intervention Effectiveness (CATIE) Investigators, "Effectiveness of Antipsychotic Drugs for Patients with Chronic Schizophrenia," *New England Journal of Medicine* 353.12 (2006): 1209-23.

74. S. Vedantam, "Antispychotics, Newer Isn't Better Find Shocks Researchers," *Washington Post* 3 Oct. 2006: A01.

75. C. Harding, *Transcript of Presentation: Roundtable Public Policy Discussion* (New York, 1995).

76. C. Harding et al., "The Vermont Longitudinal Study of Persons With Severe Mental Illness, II: Long-Term Outcomes of Subjects Who Retrospectively Met DSM-III Criteria for Schizophrenia," *American Journal of Psychiatry* 144.6 (1987): 727-35.

77. C. Harding, *Transcript of Presentation: Roundtable Public Policy Discussion* (New York, 1995).

Chapter 14
78. J. S. Mill, *On Liberty*, ed. D. Spitz (New York: Norton, 1975) 10.

79. E. Podvoll, *Recovering Sanity: A Compassionate Approach to Understanding and Treating Psychosis* (Boston: Shambhala, 2003).

80. P. Applebaum and T. Guthell, "The Boston State Hospital Case: Involuntary Mind Control, the Constitution and the 'Right to Rot,'"

American Journal of Psychiatry 137 (1980): 720-23.

81. E. F. Torrey, *Out of the Shadows: Confronting America's Mental Illness Crisis* (New York: Wiley and Sons, 1997).

82. H. Steadman et al., "Assessing the New York City Involuntary Outpatient Commitment Pilot Program," *Psychiatric Services* 52.3 (2001): 330-36.

83. J. Chamberlin, "Citizenship Rights and Psychiatric Disability," *Psychiatric Rehabilitation Journal* 2.4 (Spring 1998): 406.

84. M. Borch-Jacobsen, "Sybil – The Making of a Disease: An Interview with Psychiatrist Herbert Spiegal," *The New York Review of Books* 24 Apr. 1997: 64.

85. Ibid.

86. H. Brody, *Stories of Sickness* (New Haven: Yale University Press, 1987) 188.

87. Ibid. 189.

88. Ibid. 190.

89. H. Strupp, "The Tripartite Model and the Consumer Reports Study," *American Psychologist* Oct. 1996: 1017.

90. M. Gottfried and B. Wolfe, "Psychotherapy Practice and Research: Repairing a Strained Alliance," *American Psychologist* Oct. 1996: 1007.

91. R. D. Laing, *The Politics of Experience* (New York: Ballantine Books, 1967) 53.

Chapter 15
92. E. E. Werner, "Overcoming the Odds," *Developmental and Behavioral Pediatrics* 15.2 (1994): 131-36.

93. E. Werner and R. Smith, *Vulnerable, but Invincible: a Longitudinal*

Study of Resilient Children and Youth (New York: McGraw-Hill, 1982).

94. J. Shapiro, D. Friedman, and M. Meyer, "Invincible Kids: Why Do Some Children Survive Traumatic Childhoods Unscathed?" *US News and World Report* 11 Nov. 1996: 64.

95. E. Hall, *Beyond Culture* (Garden City, NY: Anchor Press, 1976) 6.

96. D. Hammarskjold, *Markings* (New York: Knopf, 1971) 19.

97. R. D. Laing, *The Politics of Experience* (New York: Ballantine Books, 1967) 53.

Index

Ron Bassman lives in upstate New York with his wife Lindsey, a holistic practitioner, and their son Jesse. He teaches in the Graduate Psychology Department of Sage Colleges, maintains a private psychotherapy practice, and as a volunteer with various national and local groups, continues to advocate for change in the understanding and treatment of mental illness. Always striving to keep his heart and mind open so that he may continue to learn and grow, Ron balances the serious with his practice of Tai Chi Ch'uan and life-long love of sports — especially, for some unfathomable reason, the Detroit Tigers, his favorite baseball team.

For contact information
http://www.ronaldbassman.com